The Trilogy has two joint sub-goals as well. First, clearly disclose the processes that drive us every second of every day. Second, (based on this **How-We-Truly-Work** foundation) provide powerful **Tactics** or methodologies that explain how to: create productive or **pro-habits**, which will automatically and relentlessly strive (as this is their nature) to get you what you **TRULY** want; and simultaneously **disarm chaos-habits** (like addictions, negative self-talk, compulsive behaviours, and the like) that are keeping you from becoming all you can be.

Excitingly, once the **23 secret keys** are grasped, you will be fully enabled to consciously choose and design your own pro-habits that will automatically and relentlessly strive to *Way Better* Your L.I.F.E$^2$. by getting you what you **TRULY** want.

What could be better … really?

---

Although free to read or listen to the books in any order, I suggest an additional strategy to sequential.

Begin with book-three, *Way Better* Your L.I.F.E$^2$. ~ **Tactic**s as it contains great summaries of the first two books anyway. Then, as topics are mentioned in **Tactics**, use the first two books as resources to reference much deeper How-We-Work understandings and corresponding research driven proofs.

**Mind-Self Overview**

*Way Better* Your L.I.F.E$^2$.: **Mind-Self** or just **Mind** (book-two) picks-up where *Way Better* Your L.I.F.E$^2$.: Body-Self (or just **Body**) left-off: at **Cognitive-Alert** or the assistance-request Mind-Self in-box for **problematic** (i.e., UN-recognized and/or higher-intensity) Bombardment events.

> Recall, *Way Better* Your L.I.F.E$^2$.: Body-Self journeys initiated from the **Out-There** universe of incessant **Bombardment** or **Deluge** on event-horizons, then onward to sensory-acceptance. Post-acceptance one was travelled through multiple data-morphing mechanisms, which culminated in **Soma-Actions** and when the Deluge event was **problematic**, to Cognitive-Alert as well, whose formulation spirits **Mind-Self** resolution assistance.

Post Cognitive-Alert acceptance, **Mind** tours the reader through the many and varied Mind-Self mechanisms, constructs and processes, which drive awareness, thought, emotion, ingenuity and one's incredible capacity to **Solution**: i.e., **Figure-It-Out** and find **The-Ways**.

*Way Better* Your L.I.F.E$^2$.: **Mind-Self** explains how emotion or **excitement-gradient** plays **THE** vital role in not only data-storage and recall but also the creation of beliefs, personality, behaviour, **Cognitive-Habits** or **Experience-Senses** and so much more.

Five fascinating **Cognitive-Pathway** journeys detail how **Figure-It-Out** is able to expedite **Solutioning**: even for sensory-events that quickly escalate from **Nominal** to extremely intense Survival threatening. See diagrams near book end for additional detail.

*Way Better* Your L.I.F.E$^2$.: **Mind-Self** details how **Figure-It-Out** operates to proactively find **The-Ways** (answers) for both the short and extended-term **questions** or **Puzzles** it creates either from **Body-Sensor** and/or **Visual-Sensor** Deluge and/or from cognitive positing by **Devise-Mulling's** intuitive processes accessing data-archives (memory).

>Powerfully then, **Figure-It-Out** utilizes not only **current-new** Body-Self and Mind-Self data-streams but also **significantly-similar fodder** retrieved from data-archives (i.e., **archived-old**) to **answer** or **Solution** its **Puzzles**.

As **Solution** is being approached, regardless of **Puzzle** origin, **Parameter-Processor** and possibly **Cognition-Complex** collaboratively tailor multiple appropriate-to-puzzle (i.e., appropriate-to-Deluge frequency) outbound action-packet recommendations or **Test-Its**, which are designed to gather additional compatible sensory information.

Specifically, action-packets or Test-Its, purposed to spirit physical or Body-Self actions, promote cyclical sensory-feedback from the **Out-There**. Thus, Test-Its play a vital role in instigating the gathering of additional sensory-information critical for incrementally **Solutioning** or provisioning **answers** to **Puzzles**.

Incredibly however, to engage appropriate physical-responders, which in turn **fodder** the sensory **Feedback-Loop**, Test-Its are first sent to **Template-Component**.

>Template-Component exclusively provides the transition between the **In-Here** cognitive-world and the **Out-There** world of perpetual Deluge.

If interested in finding out about not only what makes you "**DO** what you **DO**", *so that you can take control of YOU back* and *Way Better* Your L.I.F.E$^2$. but also how we fit into and are essential in this Universe, read on.

To date, three *Way Better* Your L.I.F.E$^2$. books comprise the series: **Body-Self**, **Mind-Self** and **Tactics**. Note **L.I.F.E$^2$.** in the title is an acronym for **Living in Full Experience and Excitement**.

The Trilogies primary mandate is to explain, clearly and comprehensively, how to *Way Better* Your L.I.F.E$^2$. Purposed to empower everyone through knowledge of **How-We-Truly-Work**, the series provides **23 secret Keys** that will enable you to **unlock** your genetically provisioned range of capabilities, and thus, get anything you **TRULY** want.

**Unlocking** is accomplished by not only clarifying the differing **How-We-Work** processes of **Body** and **Mind** (or Soma and Cognitive) - books one and two - but also providing deployment methodologies or **Tactics** (book-three) that will vastly improve your **living-experiences** and thus *Way Better* Your L.I.F.E$^2$.

> In other words, the Trilogy exposes what drives us and makes us do what we do, and then offers *Tactics* that will hugely enhance one's **living-experiences** - FOREVER.

Undeniably, when unaware how 'something' works and/or its purpose – be it the 'quick' check-in Kiosk at the airport, the cellphone application on your hand-held computer or the Universe – resulting speculations about its utility will be grossly deficient.

> Conclusively, guessing **How-We-Work** as people is clearly no way to run one's life.

Thus, as it is evident haphazard assumptions result in mostly inaccurate and minimally useful conclusions, one should strive to improve decisions by fully understanding not only how 'things' but also especially **How-We-Work**: Based not on conjecture but instead on in depth, yet easy to use and understand irrefutable evidences.

The profound benefit derived by learning **How-We-Truly-Work** through reading the *Way Better* Your L.I.F.E$^2$. series is that choices and decisions will no longer be based on 'random guessing' about our functional drivers.

Congruent to the above, I believe that a competent self-help series - prior to either explaining **How-We-Work** habitually, cognitively and psychologically or offering strategies for enhancing one's life should first thoroughly explain the responsible front-line bio-mechanical and physiological mechanisms that actually facilitate experiencing all the wonders, which arrive at one's sensory-receptors from the vast **Out-There**.

In other words, to *Way Better* Your L.I.F.E$^2$., one requires some understanding of how our physiology or living-systems - such as sensory-receptors, brain-mass neural mechanisms, hormonal drivers, etc. - work and interact to produce action-outcomes or the physical movements that define one's collaborations with the unpredictable **Out-There**.

> Undeniable is that understanding **How-We-Truly-Work** (in lieu of guessing) is the vastly superior route to *Way Better* Your L.I.F.E$^2$.

The series mandates are accomplished by systematically disclosing **23 secret keys** unlocking **How-We-Truly-Work**, so you can maximize **Habit-Power** and fully enable **conscious choosing**. Within this framework, *Way Better* Your L.I.F.E$^2$. Book-two exposes how we **Solution** (i.e., **Figure-It-Out** and find **The-Ways**) and then provides easily useable **Tactics** in Book-three, which (based on understood **How-We-Work** principles) WILL ensure you *Way Better* Your L.I.F.E$^2$.

Progressively, the *Way Better* Your L.I.F.E$^2$. books resolve many, many **How-We-Work** confusions. For instance, they clarify issues such as, how habits form (there are two types, not just one); why the **Habit-Duo** is so pervasive; how to engage **Habit-Power** to easily create new and much more beneficial **pro-habits**; how to stop destructive **chaos-habits** from continuing to create you; how to inspire one's massive **Mind** or Cognitive arsenal at will and so much, much more.

> In a condensed summary then, the meticulously compiled series, by revealing the **23 secret keys** that will FOREVER *Way Better* Your L.I.F.E$^2$., definitively explain: one's neuro-physiological action impellers (Book-one); the underlying foundations for people's vast array of behavioral expressions (Book-two); and how to get what you TRULY want (Book-three).

More specifically, Template-Component first morphs the Test-It data-packet to align with current-new and then sends its formulated template-packet to **Response-Component** for final outbound configuration.

Whether designing or utilizing an existing **Response-Pattern**, outbound action-packets synchronistically activate physical **Body-Self** structures (muscles, etc.), which successively realign position within one's **Bombardment-Sphere** and therefore dually propel one away from harm and gather additional sensory-information.

>**Cognitive-Habits** compose the second-half of **Habit-Power** that is dedicated to maximizing survival.

Thus, as will be illuminated, Cognitive-Habits not only significantly manage one's Bombardment-Sphere **broader-scope** living-condition enhancements but also moderate how one's ongoing 'reality', called the **Movie-of-Your-Life**, is formulated, delivered and animated.

## A Tad Deeper

The first two books, *Way Better* Your L.I.F.E$^2$.: Body-Self and *Way Better* Your L.I.F.E$^2$.: Mind-Self were created to provide an unassailable foundation for the comprehensive, yet clear and easy to grasp, **living-condition enhancement** discussions contained in book three, *Way Better* Your L.I.F.E$^2$.: **Tactic**s.

Books one and two unambiguously expose, realign, clarify and detail the **How-We-Work** integrated wonders of **Body** and **Mind**.

Specifically, the two initial books - by the use of narrative, diagrams and graphics - illuminate not only the many fascinating neurological and physiological facilities, activities and mechanisms of Body-Self and Mind-Self (coined the **Self-Duo**) but also among many other new and exciting revelations, the extraordinary and steadfast interactions between **Body** and **Mind** that make you, **YOU**.

> In other words, another **Key** to **How-We-Work** is one's astonishing array of sensory-systems as they are the initiation-points for all we know and all we can ever know. They relentlessly gather fodder 24/7, so **Self-Duo's** cerebral mechanisms can differently provide continuity to what is going on **Out-There**.

Engagingly, the first two books carefully detail conditions necessary for raw-data from **Out-There** to be accepted, then selectively assembled, morphed, processed then data-storehoused as **action-potentials** in **Body-Self** neural real-estate and, if conditions are right, differently populate the many **Tiers** or data-archive layers of **Mind-Self**.

> Most importantly, they unambiguously explain the numerous functions and processes of the many **Inbound** and **Outbound** mechanisms, which enable survival, drive behaviours, formulate personality, enable awareness, facilitate conscious intervention and so much, much more.

Expansively, the first two books illuminate the foundational symmetry between the underlying Laws and functionality of our **Universe-H** (coined as such in *Way Better* Your L.I.F.E$^2$.: Body-Self) and the **simple-complexity** of **How-We-Work** as deployed by **Body** and **Mind** mechanisms.

*Way Better* Your L.I.F.E$^2$. ~ **Tactics** (Book-three) however takes a different approach. It not only details what is critically important to improve one's **living-conditions** but also builds extensively upon **How-We-Work** principles to provide many clear-cut immutable strategies that will absolutely result in immediate and dramatic enhancements to everyone's **living-experiences**.

> **Tactics** will show you how to not only engage **Self-Duo** to mine **Habit-Power's** massive renewable resource but also exploit both **Self-Duo** and **Cognition-Complex** to better **Figure-It-Out** and find **The-Ways** to vastly more fulfilling outcomes.

The first part of Book-three's subtitle, **Are You Creating Pro-habits to Get What You TRULY Want** is intended to suggest that once **Habit-Power** is ramped-up, it will become your continuously vigilant and automated friend (as this is the nature of Habits) entirely focused on **fulfilling your wishes** and **your dreams**: Once you fully understand how Habit-Power functions, of course.

Without question, as Habits drive one's actions more than 95% of the time, they actually define your personality.

> If it wasn't for my **chaos-habits** relentlessly limiting my options 24/7
> and negatively skewing my perceptions …
>
> I would already have everything I truly want!

Significantly, two habit-types are at work, not just one. Called the **Habit-Duo**, they spirit and are responsible for not only **Outbound** actions or movements that extensively define ones second-by-second physical existence but also thinking, speaking, perceptions and so forth.

> I bet that if I knew how **chaos-habits** form and how to disarm their detrimental agendas, I could bypass them and instead create new beneficial **pro-habits** that would automatically (as this is their inherent design) fulfill all my wishes and dreams.

Definitely true, however, to both create **pro**ductive or **pro-habits** that will absolutely get you what you **TRULY** want every time and simultaneously disengage **chaos-habits** – such as addictions, compulsive actions, negative self-talk and the like - that are detrimental to your becoming all you can be, you will need to understand **How-We-Work** as people.


**Interaction Opportunity**:

The *Way Better* Your L.I.F.E$^2$. Trilogy is intended to inspire ongoing feedback: pros, cons, suggestions, additional detail, enhancements, etc.

> In this regard, DavidHastingsTheAuthor@gmail.com is available for all to contribute what they will: For prompt response please type **Mind-Self** (only please) in the subject line.

> Additionally, watch for postings on social media sites where additional opportunities to provide your thoughts are available.

# *23 secret Keys*

## Unlocking how to *forever*

# *Way Better* Your L.I.F.E$^2$.:

## Mind-Self
### (Book-two)

## Figure-It-Out

### and find

## The-Ways

Copyright © 2017 by David J. Hastings

First Edition September 2017

**ISBN**
978-1-7750661-1-8 (Paperback)
978-1-7750661-4-9 (eBook)
978-1-7750661-8-7 (Audio)

All rights reserved.

No part of this publication may be reproduced in any form, or by any means, electronic or mechanical, including photocopying, recording, or any information browsing, storage or retrieval system, without the express permission in writing from the publisher.

Produced by:

**Living Perspectives Publishing**

www.LivingPerspectivesPublishing.com

email: DavidHastingsTheAuthor@gmail.com

# David J. Hastings PhD
*'Doctor-Dave'*

## 23 secret Keys

Unlocking how to *forever*

# Way Better Your L.I.F.E$^2$.:

## Mind-Self
*(Book-two)*

## Figure-It-Out
and find
## The-Ways

**ALSO BY** Dr. David J. Hastings PhD

**ReIgnite Your *ZEST***

*Way Better* Your L.I.F.E$^2$.: Body-Self
*Way Better* Your L.I.F.E$^2$.: Tactics

***The Beautiful Golden Butterfly***

And to keep Figure-It-Out Puzzle solving processes sharp:

Become a **SUDOKU** Master
Become a **SUDOKU** Master Workbook

**Habitology University Publications**:

Habitology Practitioner Course Book
Habitology Practitioner Questions Book
Habitology Masters (MHa) Fulfilment Manual
Habitology Doctorate (PhD) Research Guidebook

**Other Resources**:

YouTube Channel: 23 Keys to WayBetter your LIFE
www.HabitologyUniversity.com/Blogs

For my Son Brandon,

Who consistently

Figures-It-Out

and finds

The-Ways

# Contents

### Forward
Body-Self details
Mind-Self teaser
Body-Self: book-one recap

### Introduction
Body-Self details
Self-Duo

### Cognitive-Pathways Model
Transition to Mind-Self
Transition to Cognitive-Pathways Model
Universe Interaction

### Mind-Self: Inbound
Cognitive-Alert
Cognitive-Sensors
Multiple Fields-of-Vision

### Cognitive-Filter: Inbound
Cluster-Works
Visual-Works
Cross-Sensory-Bundling

### Figure-It-Out
Cognitive-Pathways Introduction
Ingenuity
Cognitive-Pathway 5
Cognitive-Pathway 4
Cognitive-Pathway 3
Cognitive-Pathway 2
Cognitive-Pathway 1

### Movie-of-Your-Life
### Layer-Intelligence Theory
### Index

# Forward

The illustration below not only depicts the *Way Better* Your L.I.F.E$^2$.: Body-Self journey to date but also hints at the next adventure: *Way Better* Your L.I.F.E$^2$.: **Mind-Self** (denoted on the diagram as Soma-Self and Cognitive-Self respectively).

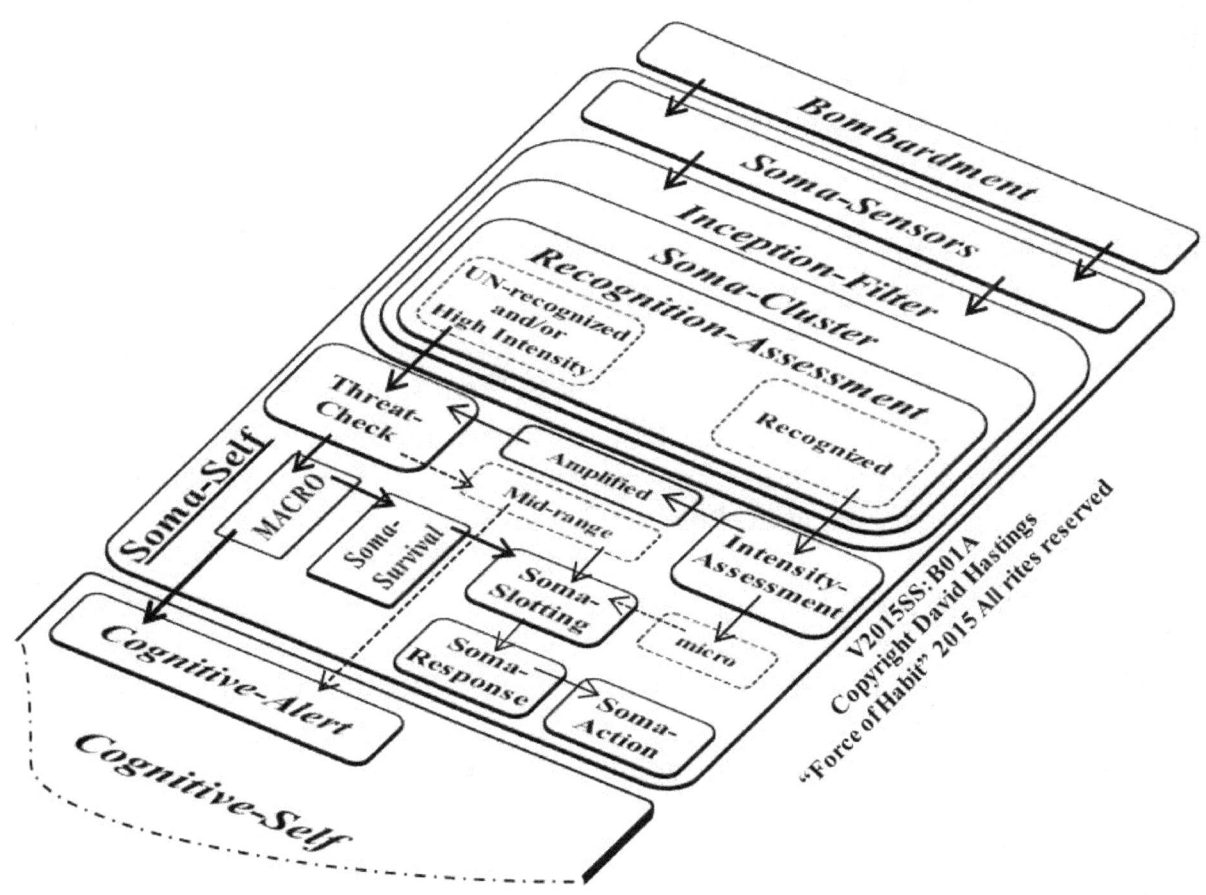

Recall, of the four Soma-Self (or Body-Self) sojourns, three of them engaged Cognitive-Self via deployment of **Cognitive-Alerts**.

Resultantly, *Way Better* Your L.I.F.E$^2$.: Mind-Self (book-two) picks-up where *Way Better* Your L.I.F.E$^2$.: Body-Self left-off: at the Cognitive-Alert transition-point between the Self-Duo's.

> Importantly, a Cognitive-Alert data-package exists as the ONLY connection between Soma-Self and Cognitive-Self (aka Body-Self and Mind-Self).

In other words, when Body-Self encounters a '**problematic**' issue (i.e., an **UN**-recognized and/or Higher-intensity sensory-accepted event), it tailors one of two types of Cognitive-Alert data-packages to inspire assistance from its Mind-Self collaborator.

To effectively 'pass-the-baton' to Mind-Self these outbound (from Body-Self) Cognitive-Alert communications are inserted into the Mind-Self **Custer-Works** 'in-box'. Thus, Mind-Self essentially performs as a high-tech **Solutioning** (i.e., Figure-It-Out and find The-Ways) extension of Body-Self, which thereby significantly enhances survival-potential by shedding a 'proactive' light on Deluge goings-on.

---

As an alternative title was mentioned for *Way Better* Your L.I.F.E$^2$.: **BodySelf**, so too is one provided below for *Way Better* Your L.I.F.E$^2$.: **Mind-Self**.

25 steps to make your basic Body-Self android robot become self-aware<br>
by actualizing artificial-intelligence<br>
through deployment of not only a dedicated superlative sensor-array<br>
but also extensive Mind-Self functionalities!

Being a little long for a book title, I offer it up for two main reasons. First, so one might, after digesting the series of three books, consider the instigation of consciousness as possible for other species as well: under certain circumstances, as it is for us.

Second, because following the principles of **How-We-Work** in books one and two can be employed to create an actual sentient android robot. Please take this statement as a fun challenge to make it happen.

In our current world of technology exploration, plans to emmulate Human functioning are being devised and evaluated: albeit for servitude within selfish parameters.

Regardless of motivation, truly interactive artificial-intelligence mobile devices require incorporation of the following requisites to work effectively and efficiently.

**Body-Self**: Requirements Recap
- Primary Sensor Platform: Physical Bombardment Impact Receptors
    - Specification for all components used for construction should be of highest quality and allow for near speed-of-light reception, transmission and processing
- Impact reception
    - Grouped within thousands of variously sized tiny impact or **landing-zones**, many tens-of-thousands of sensors, defined by specific acceptance capabilities, should completely cover external-facing surfaces
        - each sensory-accepted event must be 'Tagged' with an immutable location frequency-code or SLID, which uniquely identifies it as originating at the event-horizon of a particular sensor-group
        - to accommodate for slight variances, frequency-codes must allow for attenuation within a narrow predefined range-of-acceptance at the Soma 'landing-zone'
- Transmission and data-stabilization
    - between event-horizon SLIDs and destination processors, common transmission conduits can be utilized: however they should be supple and allow for movement without signal disruption
    - additionally, an in-line or pre-destination processor platform is required to not only amalgamate the individual "Tag" sensor-signals of a SLID, within short time-snippet 'bands' (3 milliseconds is recommended), into larger common groupings or "Tag-Clusters" but also regulate and thus smooth-out outbound signal groups or 'bands' for...
- Destination processors
    - Ranking 'band' contents ('Tag-Clusters') by greatest quantity of impacts, action-potential or intensity is mandatory to maintain focus on handling highest impact events first
    - Intensity will be determined by comparing inbound action-potential against range-of-acceptance parameters stored in each SLID compatible destination data-archive

- When unacceptably high: 'Bracket' and send data-clone to channel-two (see below); otherwise, access frequency specific data-archive to assess event familiarity: i.e., is it new or recurrence
- dichotomous Recognition-Assessment: YES (recognized) - 'Bracket' and send data-clone to channel-one (see below); Intensity-Assessment: NO (unrecognized) - 'Bracket' and send data-clone to channel-two; Threat-Check
- 'handling' requires 'simultaneous' saving, data-archiving or 'Bracketing' by frequency index of sensory-information bits or Tag-Clusters for both channel-one and channel-two

---------

- **Channel-One**: Intensity-Assessment for recognized Tag-Clusters
  - Necessary in case the event has not only occurred before but also carries intensity elevated above acceptable 'nominal' limits
    - Intensity will also be determined by comparing inbound action-potential against range-of-acceptance parameters stored in each SLID compatible data-archive
    - 'Elevated-intensity' should be forwarded to processors tuned for 'problematic' assessment: specifically to assess system threat
      - 'Normal-Intensity' should be sent to 'nominal-channel' for not only 'pattern' creation, which suggests actions for 'Bombardment-Sphere' realignments based on receptor information but also pattern data-archiving
      - Alert secondary support-system of changing status so response mechanisms can be initiated and appropriately, based on imperative for each response location, sustained and/or tapered-off for smooth operation and transition
      - 
- **Channel-Two**: Threat-Check for 'problematic' events
  - forward to processors tuned for 'problematic' assessment: specifically to assess system "threat-potential" as well:
    - Intensity-Check to ascertain threat potential from both conduits: Recognition-Assessment high-intensity and Intensity-Assessment 'flags'
    - Trend-Analysis to assess if event combinations are indicating threat-potential
    - Issue Cognitive-Alert 'type-one' for survival-critical: 'type-two' if not
    - Regardless

- send upgraded data-packets to 'Soma-Slotting' channel for not only 'pattern' creation, which suggests actions for 'Bombardment-Sphere' realignments based on receptor information but also pattern data-archiving
- also for smooth operation and transition, alert secondary support-system of changing status so response mechanisms can be initiated and appropriately, based on imperative for each response location, sustained and/or tapered-off

---------

**Mind-Self:** (book-two 'sentience' requirements, teaser and brief outline)
- Interface System: Cognitive-Alert to Mind-Self collaborator
  - Translate 'Alerts' into upgraded format
- Secondary Sensor Platform: Visible Spectrum Bombardment receptors
  - utilize high-tech Cognitive-Sensors (vision) to coordinate and augment Soma-Sensory data-flow
  - where applicable to provision broader event perspective, combine Soma-Sensor and Cognitive-Sensor data into a more representative Cross-Sensory data-pool
    - determine intensity as 'NORM' or 'PRIORITY'
  - If NORM 'Tepid' or PRIORITY 'Warm' or 'Hot', engage Figure-It-Out Cognitive-Pathways
  - Otherwise deploy on 'Cool' Cognitive-Filter pathway

- Engage Figure-It-Out
  - Bring resources on-line as applicable: such as, Equivalency, Resolution, Initialization and Parameter processors to find 'The-Ways'
  - Update 'Data-Matrix' data-archives
  - Create 'Puzzles' and evaluate against data-archives utilizing Cognition-Complex's Delving-Trio and Devise-Mulling
  - Create Test-It outbounds to prompt 'Out-There' feedback

- Engage 'Template' to create patterns alerting Body-Self of required 'Out-There' positional 'DO' adjustments or outbound actions
- Continually produce and present, without pause or break, the 'Movie-of-Your-Life' from sensory-and archive data-streams

Sound familiar…?

---

For those who have not had the opportunity to read ***Way Better*** Your L.I.F.E$^2$.: Body-Self, a brief synopsis of Book-one follows.

**Body-Self Recap**

Soma-Sensor varieties are many. They provide uniquely delineated zones of contact purposed to 'inform' what is going on 'Out-There'. As 'Out-There' is considered to be all pre-sensory events, internal-sensors are also included.

Our biology is laced with tiny Bombardment impact collectors or 'event-horizons' called SLIDs or Soma-Location-IDs: from which the abbreviated name is contrived. Each SLID receptor-neuron array is not only an ever diligent recipient of raw 'mechanical' Deluge impact-data when not in 'refresh-state' but also discretely identifiable by a unique frequency, which remains immutable throughout processing, data-archiving and recall.

Additionally, although common transmission conduits are utilized by all SLIDs (Soma-Location-IDs) to transfer sensory-receptor information to brain-mass, each ends at its own dedicated neuron-array, which only accepts its specific SLID frequency marker.

> More specifically Neuro-physiological sensory-receptor design provides SLIDs with their own exacting bent on a sensory occurrence. In other words, SLIDs possess their own specific and immutable frequency-ranged recognition signatures, which forever identify the acceptance location and content. 'Marking' thereby ensures identification of both sensory-type and the specific sensory impact point, which is essential for both 'recognition' and recall.

This strategy also ensures a sound is not confused with touch, smell or taste: neither during data-archiving nor data-recall.

Additionally critical to measure is 'event-intensity'. It is highly variable due to not only the types and quantity of SLID locations involved as a consequence of highly variable Bombardment but also the quantity of accepted events as a factor of short-to-longer

Deluge duration, neuron firing patterns, neuron activity-duration and neuron recovery time.

> Even so, event-intensity is not determined at time-of-impact but further up the processing chain at Recognition-Assessment. Here, the quantity of neurons fired at each SLID within a 3 millisecond "time-snippet" or "data-band" are evaluated to determine 'intensity' and therefore next disposition: to either 'nominal' or 'problematic' conduit.

After "sensory-acceptance", the Body-Self cycle initiates with "Inception-Filter", which "Filters-and-Slots" all accepted "sensory-data". Subsequently, "Recognition-Assessment" directs the "data-stream" into one or the other of two channels: either to 'UN-recognized', which includes high-intensity or 'recognized', which does not.

Whereas 'UN-recognized' and/or high-intensity are immediately fired to "Threat-Check" as 'problematic', the 'recognized' data-stream is shunted to "Intensity-Assessment" for additional evaluation. If its verdict is 'nominal-intensity', Tag-Clusters are shuttled to "Soma-Slotting": those which are not 'nominal-intensity' are also sent to Threat-Check for 'problematic' analysis.

> Additionally, as assessments are finalized in "Soma-Action", the Endocrine System is continually apprised. As a supporting "Integration-System", it is designed to ensure response mechanisms gracefully transition through a three stage "action-cycle": thereby providing smooth operation and movement.

The Endocrine System utilizes notifications to appropriately prepare "action-sites" for activation from rest or 'nominal' state. 'Appropriate' is based on the "ranked-imperative" about to be neuro-transmitted to each response location from Soma-Action.

Secondly, it provides variable impetus to sustain action-site activity and/or "action-alertness" after neurological signals have ceased. Thirdly, the Endocrine System allows for a tapering-off period so action-sites can 'gracefully' return to 'normal' state and refresh.

Finally, Body-Self tethers to Mind-Self by creating two distinct Cognitive-Alert data-package outbounds that are differently fashioned by Threat-Check. Notwithstanding the content and imperative variances between the two data-packages, both are designed to initiate Mind-Self assistance to 'Figure-It-Out'.

By the issuance of Cognitive-Alerts, Body-Self provides the first-half of the

**Habit-Power**

which champions species sustainability.

Cognitive-Alerts provide a valuable clue to purposefully and massively enhancing ones **living-situation** by underlining THE requisite to engage Mind-Self at will!

As long as an event is either new or of higher intensity, exciting if you will, 'recognized and low-intensity' Soma-Habitual responses will be augmnented by mid-range Threat-Check processors, which will produce Cognitive-Alerts.

This outbound is critical because Cognitive-Alert is the only opportunity to initiate Mind-Self; and therefore the opportunity for awareness and conscious choice!

Book-two's mandate is to comprehensively delve into Mind-Self to expose **How-We-Work** as a cognitive species: because once Mind-Selfs many incredible capabilities are grasped, your massive potential will be unleashed.

Resultantly, once one knows **How-We-Work**, will not only day-to-day situations be more clearly and usefully understood but also **choiceful-living** be significantly energized.

# Introduction

Although, due to genetic determiners, methodologies and neural-resources differ vastly between the Self-Duo collaborators (Body-Self and Mind-Self), they have a common mandate: deploy best-case survival actions.

Survival actions for both utilize not only similar event recognition methodologies (i.e., compare **current-new** sensory-data with frequency applicable **archived-old** or previously retained or storehoused sensory-data) but also mechanisms to adjust physical position within ones **Bombardment-Sphere** (and thus keep one safe).

However, although a Body-Self sensory-accepted 'recognized' event envokes habitual Soma-Actions, '**UN**-recognized' enables a species altering compendium of Mind-Self competencies that additionally propell not only chosen interactions with the **Out-There** but also awareness.

The following Self-Duo comparisons listing will assist in understanding not only Body-Self and Mind-Self divergences and convergences but also their differing survival strategies.

> Body-Self (aka Soma-Self) mechanisms are built for response speed - not for scenario consideration: However, Mind-Self (aka Cognitive-Self) mechanisms are.

---

Body-Self Neuro-physiological design is massively different in structure and purpose from Mind-Self. Brain-mass or neural-pathway availability, fundamental for both processing and storage functions, is the discriminator: huge for Mind-Self; limited for Soma-Self.

> Body-Self design provides a **neural-matrix** with only one to a few linear neural-pathways, which parallels Body-Self's 'few-choices / fast-response' functionality. Although Body-Self methodology is very good at enhancing survival potential, it is not so useful for volition, proactive choice or enrichment.

---

The Neuro-physiological structure of Mind-Self's neural net is very different: it can have hundreds and hundreds (even thousands) of cross-over neural-pathways thus enabling vast quantities of combinations and permutations simply not available to Body-Self. Stated differently, genetically provisioned Mind-Self neural-pathway complexities form fundamental building-blocks for Human ingenuity.

---

Body-Self persists in a millisecond-by-millisecond relm
of sequential processing:
Mind-Self, in a second-by-second relm of interactive processing.

Quick Body-Self responses accommodate few alternates:
Slower Mind-Self thrives on alternatives to provide substantial opportunities for volition.

> Hey, I'm happy if, when I reach for my cup, I get it to my lips in a couple of seconds. Of course in the same timeframe Body-Self would have impatiently drummed its figurative fingers a hundred thousand times. I'm content with its speeding along; as long as I can choose when to sip my coffee!

---

Soma-Self typifies repetitive stability such as cyclic and routine responses:
Mind-Self design enables intuition, assimilation and creation to
**Figure-It-Out** and find **The-Ways**.

In other words, Body-Self is not designed to gather disperate information pieces, assimilate from several types of data-archives, choose, discern, mull, etc.:

*WayBetter* Your L.I.F.E$^2$.: **Mind-Self**

Fortunately, Mind-Self is!

Mind-Self thus symbolizes the essence of one's
Personality and character:
Also, it is the pathway to CHOSEN interaction with the universe.

---

If neural-complexity was not provided, humans would have severely diminished sustainability and adaptability as only habitually driven **Soma-Response** actions would be available.

Thereby, one would not be human but some lower species: insect, fish or reptile.

Soma-Self is aligned to the senses with rapid (millisecond-by-millisecond) Filtering-and-Slotting capability designed to either recognize and respond and/or perform exception management by engaging Mind-Self.

In other words, anything Soma-Self 'cannot handle', it ultimately hands off to Mind-Self as a Cognitive-Alert.

As Soma-Self is the physical-world event-horizon impact manager, any "real world" action implications, 'formulated' by Mind-Self, feed directly back through Soma-Self.

In other words, the return portal for Mind-Self inspired intel is via Body-Selfs sensory-receptors, thus effecting a sensory **Feedback-Loop** as follows:

Body-Self sensory acceptance; Body-Self processing; Cognitive-Alert formulation and transition; Mind-Self Cognitive-Alert acceptance; Mind-Self processing; Mind-Self sensory array engagement (vision); Body-Self / Mind-Self sensory-data interface (Cross-Sensory-Bundling); Cognitive-Pathway determinations; physical universe response recommendations (Test-Its); Body-Self positional changes; and once again Body-Self new sensory acceptance due to positional changes (feedback-loop). See illustrations following.

**So what are the events Soma-Self 'cannot handle'?**

We tend to be somewhat predictable.

In other words, we tend to do the same things mostly in the same way: personality traits if you will. These actions (responses), which interact with one's Bombardment-Sphere can be termed established behaviours or habits.

More accurately though, there are two substantially different habit generating camps:

**Body-Self Habits and Mind-Self Habits**

The first we now understand from Book-one:
The second we are on the 'pathway' to uncover in this book!

From previous discussions, understood is both 'recognized <u>AND</u> low-intensity' Bombardment (or Deluge) events are directly shunted to and 'handled' by Soma-Slotting and Soma-Response, which by default energize physical interface via Soma-Action.

This trio, when directly engaged by 'recognized-and-low-intensity' constitute repetitive responses or Soma-Habits. 'Recognized' means a Bracket exists (i.e., neural-arrays are populated with action-potential), which denotes an identical previous event occurred.

Thus, when the inbound event is checked against the Matched-Base-Frequency data-repository (or Bracket), an exact frequency equivalent action-potential exists. In other words, the current-new event is 'recognized' because an identical archived-old Matched-Base-Frequency exists.

> Consequently, all current-new sensory-accepted events other than 'recognized <u>AND</u> low-intensity', specifically UN-recognized AND/OR higher-intensity are **'problematic'** for Body-Self, which it 'cannot handle'.

> Absolutely critical to be clear about is that without exposure to physical-world Bombardment or Deluge no Bracketing or sensory-data archiving would occur: In other words, no Bracketing; no recognition.

Second-hand exposure to events, such as having someone explain again how to do something is not enough because 'recognized' is an all-or-none sensory-acceptance proposition: 100% recognized AND low intensity or onto the 'cannot-handle' or 'problematic' current-new pile it goes.

Turns out Recognition-Assessment will fire the event to Threat-Check with even a slight recognition variance.

> Resultantly, to be explained in detail later, Threat-Check will always create a **Cognitive-Alert** of one type or the other: either a survival critical **Imperative-Alert** or a non-survival but still critical **Request-Alert**.

Notably, even when the 'problematic' current-new is recognized, determination of 'MACRO' intensity will also propagate the event to Threat-Check.

This consequence is a good thing: One might recognize a red glowing stove element but proximity and Matched-Base-Frequency data-archives will quickly alert 'MACRO' intensity.
In other words, too hot is still too hot, so **stay away** is the habitual Soma-Action.

---

**Self-Duo: Cognitive-Self** (Mind-Self)

All are gifted with two extraordinary sensory-data processing systems as illustrated above, which are uniquely designed to meet the incredibly difficult challenge of maximizing survival-potential every millisecond of every day.

Depicted to the left of the vertical dotted line on **The Self-Duo** illustration is Soma-Self. This Self-Duo member, explained in book-one, *Way Better* Your L.I.F.E$^2$.: **Body-Self**, initializes evaluations of sensory-accepted events originating from body-sensors or Soma-Sensors: i.e., all sensors except visual.

However, when unrecognized and/or mid-to-extreme intensity events occur Soma-Self notifies its Mind-Self collaborator, partially diagramed to the right of the vertical dotted line, by depositing its findings into one of two Cognitive-Alert 'in-boxes'. These actions earmark the transition to Mind-Self, whose primary mandate is to 'resolve' provided notifications.

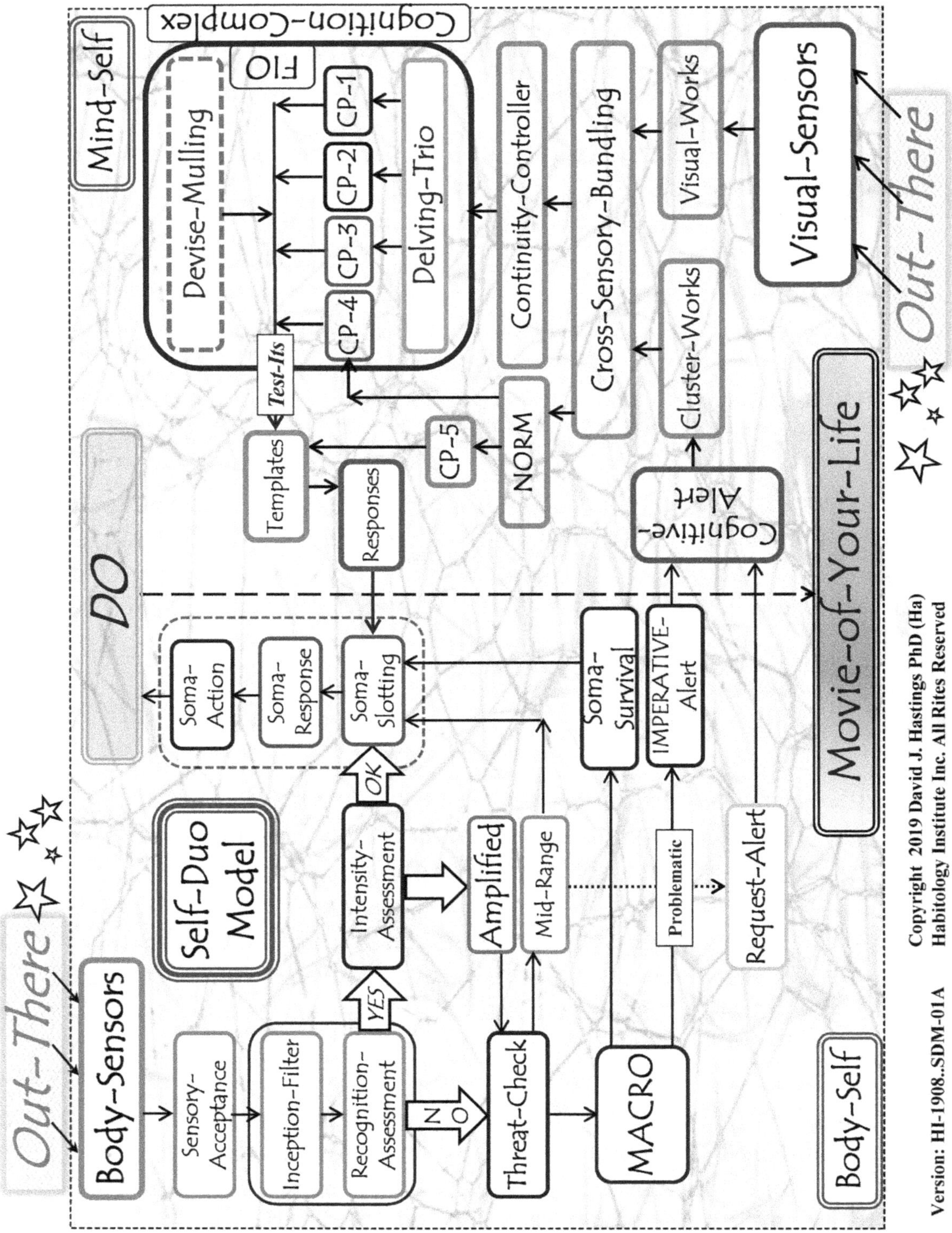




Version: HI-1908..SDM-01A

Resolution is accomplished by an array of competencies: such as, bringing its **Cognitive-Sensor** arsenal on-line; interlacing applicable visual-receptor sensory-data with Body-Self provided sensory-data; adding pertinent information from data-archives; sending action-suggestions called **Test-Its** to Body-Self; and cycling through looped-feedback until **Solutioning** is accomplished.

> By the issuance of Test-Its, Mind-Self provides the second-half of the
> **Habit-Power**
> which champions species sustainability.

The first two books of the trilogy are intended to yield a definitive explanation of how we humans roll. Fulfillment will be accomplished by explaining not only mechanism functionalities for each member of the Self-Duo but also how Body-Self's (book-one) and Mind-Self's (book-two) numerous operational wonders supportively integrate to provide actualization of **living-potential**.

**Why two control-systems with multiple independent mechanisms rather than a single mega-complex?**

> Because survival demands recognition of both 'impacting' Bombardment and 'evolving' life threatening circumstances

Presented within the above sentence are two clues for understanding why the two systems exist as a cooperative duo. Specifically, 'impacting…' is the purview of Soma-Sensors, which must receive physical Deluge 'impacts' before processing: whereas 'evolving…' is a proactive feature, which utilizes Cognitive-Sensors and "cognitive-mechanisms" to avoid or minimize obnoxious Deluge arrival at Soma-Sensors.

Event-horizons of the two systems are responsible for collecting Deluge information: notably, one-hundred percent of all we 'know' originates from here and nowhere else.

> Although both sensor groups, Body or Soma and Mind or Cognitive, have similarities there are also substantial differences.

Cross-pollination between the two systems provides the impetus for a dichotomous, yet inter-related, Body-Self / Mind-Self design.

# Cognitive-Pathways Model

## Transition to Mind-Self

Greatly outpacing its Body-Self companion, Mind-Self embodies substantially enhanced competencies and capabilities, which proportionately increases complexity.

Mind-Self is exciting to understand because its Modules, Components and processing capabilities define not only who one is as a conscious being but also who one can become.

Stated differently, Mind-Self encompasses all features, which determine possible conscious experience or awareness: i.e., it provisions and inspires thinking; speaking; beliefs; attitudes; excitement; choice; and the list goes on-and-on.

To explain how Mind-Self's various specialized Module and Component mechanisms interface, processes (Filter) and determine data-disposition (Slot) is the goal of *Way Better* Your L.I.F.E$^2$.: **Mind-Self**.

Specifically, both mechanisms and interactions will be thoroughly examined for unique enabling contributions and co-operative Self-Duo interface.

The Mind-Self journey will be illuminating, exciting, informative and beneficial.

### What conditions are necessary to enable awareness?

Encompassed within specialized groupings of intertwined Modules reside Components and their corresponding processes, which animate us. However, before meaningfully discussing the awareness 'big-picture', constituent parts first need explanation.

Therefore, the strategy to accomplish this task is to tag-along with the data-flow and discusses not only encountered processes but also pertinent alternates.

As each Module is presented three sections each with their unique discussion scope will be provided as follows: first, explanation of the Module contribution to the overall action-destination; second, the contribution a Component fulfills; and finally, the role the Module plays in relation to other Modules and Components.

## Transition to Cognitive-Pathways Model

The **Cognitive-Pathways Model** illustration below is intended to provide a fairly detailed discussion framework and visual guide for following explanations of **The-Way-We-Cognitively-Work**.

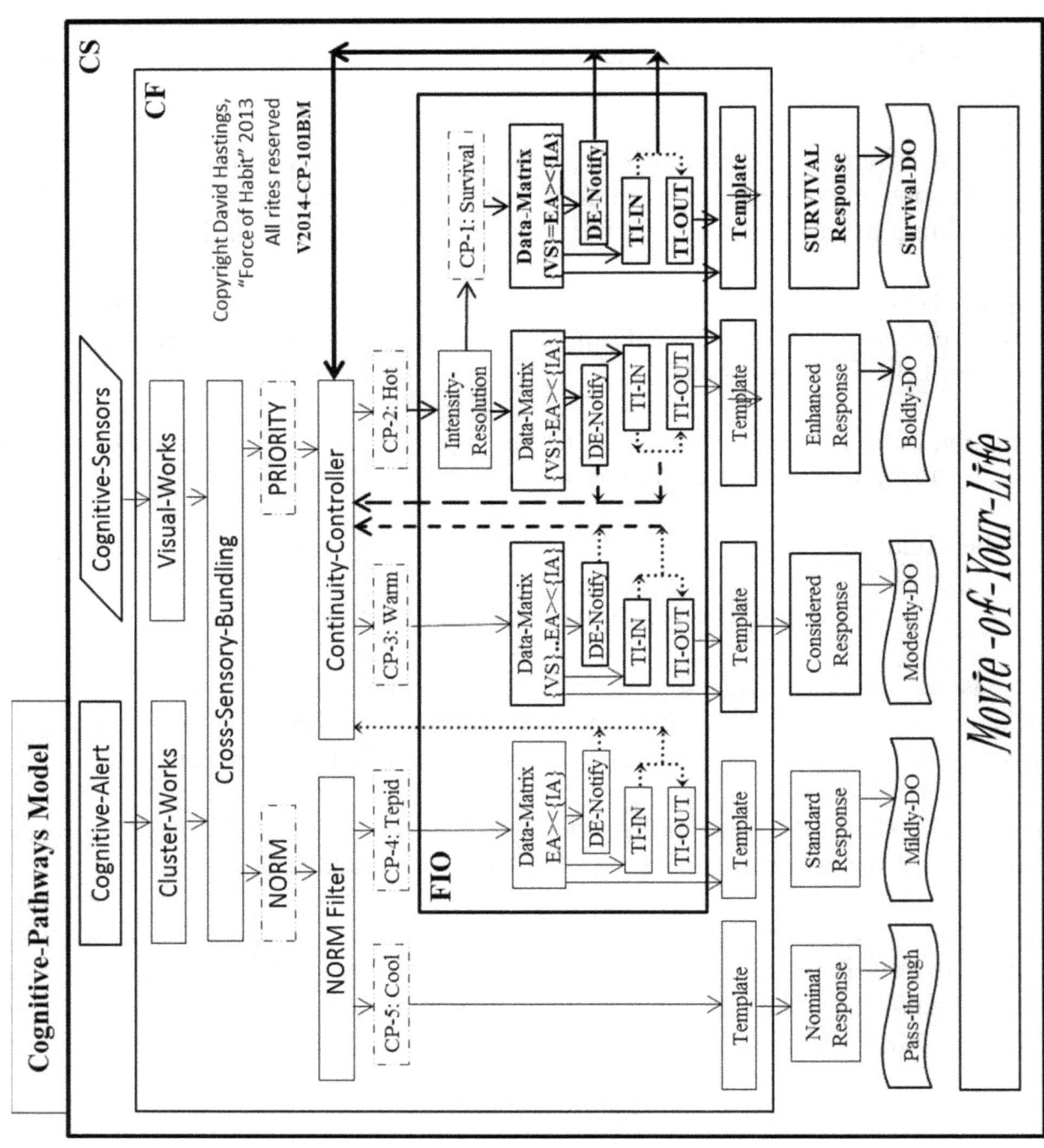

Discussions regarding Cognitive-Pathways, Figure-It-Out and outbound Mind-Self and Cognitive-Filter processes are aimed at explaining all cognitive capabilities.

Encompassed are such topics as: how individual Cognitive-Pathways variously enable ingenuity; what spawns awareness; how Figure-It-Out facilitates our incredible 'inner-universe' of possibilities; how inbound and outbound Components contribute to the overall 'Solutioning' plan; how Cognitive-Pathways play a dynamic role in the deceptively external presentation of the **Movie-of-Your-Life** reality; and so on.

**Mind-Self: Diagram Hierarchy**

The Cognitive-Pathways Model diagram above is a discussion guide. Additionally complementing the 'model' diagram is the Mind-Self Nested Structure outline provided below. It is intended to provide clarity to the Cognitive-Pathways Model illustration by listing discussion milestones from inception at Cognitive-Alert to ultimate Movie-of-Your-Life destination: please be patient while the incredible processes are unraveled.

**Mind-Self: Nested Structure:**
- **Mind-Self** Inbound Components
    - Cognitive-Alert
    - Cognitive-Sensors
        - **Cognitive-Filter** Inbound Components
            - Cluster-Works
            - Visual-Works
            - Cross-Sensory-Bundling
            - NORM-Filter; PRIORITY-Filter
            - Continuity-Controller
                - **Figure-It-Out** Pathways
                    - Inbound Components
                        - Data-Matrix
                        - DE-Notify
                        - TI-IN
                    - Outbound Component
                        - TI-OUT Test-Its
        - **Cognitive-Filter** Outbound Components
            - Template-Component
- **Mind-Self** Outbound Components

- o Nominal, Standard, Considered, Enhanced and Survival-Responses
- o The-DOs
- o Movie-of-Your-Life presentation-complex

Mind-Self (or just Mind) is the foundational platform supporting our incredible diversity. It supports not only its Components but also two intimately integrated Modules and their specialized Components. In other words, although Mind-Self forms the underpinning, progressively integrated are two additional Modules: **Cognitive-Filter** (CF), which integrates to Mind-Self; and **Figure-It-Out** (FIO), which interfaces to both.

The 'Cognitive-Pathways Model' illustration does not contain all features: To promote clarity balance was needed between diagrammatic content and detail. However, to compensate, additional illustrations will be provided as needed to enhance discussions and comprehension.

Perusing the 'Nested Structure' will make prominent Mind-Self directly supports two inbound Components, Cognitive-Alert and Cognitive-Sensors; one module, Cognitive-Filter; a response Component; **DO**; and the Movie-of-Your-Life presentation center.

Notable within Mind-Self bounds is Cognitive-Filter. It is integrated into the Cognitive-Self module and in turn encompasses three inbound Components, Cluster-Works, Visual-Works and Cross-Sensory-Bundling; one module, Figure-It-Out; and outbound Template-Components.

Furthermore, within Cognitive-Self are five **Cognitive-Pathways**: one Cognitive-Filter pathway, namely CP-5: Cool; and four Figure-It-Out pathways, namely CP-4: Tepid, CP-3: Warm, CP-2: Hot, CP-1: Survival.

Beginning at the top of either the Cognitive-Pathways Model illustration or the 'Nested-Structure' listing, Cognitive-Self provisions the only two **cognitive-initiators** of all subsequent sensory-data processing: Cognitive-Alert and Cognitive-Sensors. Each provides very different morphed-packages to dedicated follow-on Cognitive-Filter Components: Cluster-Works and Visual-Works, respectively.

Components are indicated by 'solid-outline' rectangular boxes. Generally, Components provide three broad functions: retrieve a previous components outbound **data-packet** from its 'in-box'; manipulate or **data-reconfigure** included **data-elements** according to its specific mandated requirements; send its **morphed-package** outbound to a following Component for subsequent processing.

Cluster-Works and Visual-Works in turn deliver data-reconfigurations to their dedicated Cross-Sensory-Bundling **in-box**. Consequently, Cross-Sensory-Bundling is engaged to evaluate two conditions, whose statuses will determine one of two outbound channels: either "PRIORITY" or "NORM".

More specifically, Cross-Sensory-Bundling evaluates two conditions to determine channel and thus Cognitive-Pathway. The first-stage evaluates data-element intensity. The second-stage determines whether a cross-sensory match exists between the data-packets of Cluster-Works (Body-Self Cognitive Alert) and Visual-Works (Mind-Self visual receptors): matches thus form interface between Self-Duo.

By this strategy, regardless of match-status and/or intensity-gradient, Cross-Sensory-Bundling attenuated data-flow is appropriately directed to a Cognitive-Pathway designed for the particular range of conditions each is designed to accommodate.

Notably, Figure-It-Out enfolds four of the five Cognitive-Pathways. As Figure-It-Out Components provision the primary building-blocks to comprehend everything, discussions following will illuminate the critical nature of this configuration.

At the 'center' of both the illustration and descriptive listing is located the Figure-It-Out module: note that it is integrated into both Cognitive-Filter and therefore Cognitive-Self.

Figure-It-Out also incorporates several Components: **Data-Matrix**, the inbound data-management Component; **DE-Notify**; many multi-function processors (not disclosed on diagrams but on future ones); and **TI-OUT** ('Test-It') outbound matrix.

## Universe-Interaction

Hominids have populated the planet for millions of years; Homo Sapiens for fifty-thousand plus years or so: survival was no easy feat.

Imagine being dropped naked into an unknown forest with fifty or sixty others needing food and water without a GPS, cellphone or the ability to make a fire and you can get some perspective of the challenges our ancestors overcame: as well as their bravery and perspicacity in surmounting them.

Fortunately, human **universe-interaction** had a broader mandate than can be accommodated by just Body-Self. Complexity arises due to our physical structure, which enables extreme mobility. Mobility resultantly causes changes in surrounding environmental conditions (Bombardment-Sphere) and therefore continual (millisecond-by-millisecond) variant Deluge on ones event-horizons.

> As 'mobility' will migrate a person into new situations, genetics has provisioned Body-Self with a spectacular feature, Cognitive-Alert, whose integration capabilities delineates humans from other species.

Maintaining synchronicity with ever changing external conditions to ensure survival of ones frail physical container necessitates a huge edge: more than just the capability to quickly respond to a fixed set of conditions.

To survive and also thrive our species required the ability to send Body-Self (aka Soma-Self) 'cannot handle' impacting Deluge events to an entirely different type of system: one able to evaluate Body-Self 'assistance-requests' and send proactive Mind-Self (aka Cognitive-Self) **solution-testers** (Test-Its) back through to appropriate Soma-Self physical movement activators.

By utilizing Mind-Self **Test-It** suggestions then for Body-Self feedback, one could **Figure-It-Out** to determine if 'suggestions' for physical repositioning were sufficient for event reconcilliation, escape or avoidance. If not, Figure-It-Out could continue running solution-tests or Test-Its until adequate solution was adequate.

> Soon obvious will be the extent Mind-Self features are much more wide-ranging than just a set of responder tools as many incredible mechanisms are enfolded into the Solutioning equation.

As a direct result of Mind-Self involvement, escalation from Body-Selfs response mandate to a much broader 'Figure-It-Out' scope is provisioned. Enhancement is possible in part because Mind-Self provides the capability to maintain multiple types of interactive **data-repositories**, which are actually integrated from both Body-Self and Mind-Self sensory-acceptance provisioners.

Thus, Mind-Self is able to evaluate evolving events against extensive and sophisticated data-archives.

> Mind-Self extreme elasticity is simply not provided by Body-Self.

Future discussions will underline that Mind-Self, in addition to its visual data-archives also maintains selected Soma-Self sensory occurrences.

Data-storehousing in Mind-Self neural-arrays occurs because any new event at the Body-Self level will always (on first exposure) spawn a Cognitive-Alert. Even if a specific event is never repeated, Body-Self sensory-acceptance would have resulted in population of Mind-Self data-archives. The implications of this survival strategy will be more fully detailed a little further along.

> In order for cognitive processors to successfully interact with the universe, essential is a means to influence Body-Selfs event-horizons.

Mind-Self delivers this necessary interactive momentum by employing a cyclical approach: evaluate inbound data-elements (current-new) against data-storehouses (archived-old); create and send Test-It suggestions to inspire physical motion; gather resulting Body-Self feedback via Soma-Sensors; bring Cognitive-Sensors on-line to gather extended information; source data-archives to assess current-new inbound-data from both sensory-reception systems; then evaluate again.

This feedback-cycle continues until Body-Self's Inception-Filter allocates current-data as **recognized-and-low-intensity**, which consequently results in cessation of Cognitive-Alerts.

# Mind-Self: Inbound

## Recap and Transition

At any moment without warning, the quality of sensory-data, formed from Tag-Cluster combinations and permutations originating as sensory-accepted Deluge, can shift from low-and-recognized **benign** that Body-Self handles nicely, to high-and/or **UN**-recognized **problematic**, which it does not.

Inception-Filter, the initial Body-Self interactive processor, must therefore be sufficiently flexible to accommodate rapid changes in activity. Thus, it engages **Recognition-Assessment** to manage two processes: sifting (Filtering) by assessing both intensity and recognition data-characteristics; and determination (Slotting) by allocating the current-new data-stream to either Intensity-Assessment or Threat-Check evaluation channels for further assessment.

Subsequently, depending on Bombardment conditions, Threat-Check can formulate two very different **notification-packages**, which tailor two types of Cognitive-Alerts: a **request-alert** for non-survival critical issues and an **imperative-alert** for survival critical issues.

The latter is additionally fired to the Survival-Threat Component for special handling. Although Body-Self sensory-accepted data-streams arrive at Soma-Slotting in all cases, each is handled differently.

Whether activated by either a survival critical imperative-alert or a non-survival request-alert, Body-Self has determined an imperative for extended evaluation.

Thereby, responsibility for providing enhanced assessment and appropriate 'action-suggestions' was 'handed-off' to Body-Self's interactive Cognitive-Alert assistant, which is mandated to accommodate all Threat-Check requests and imperatives. Critically, Threat-Check alerts provide the fodder for Cognitive-Alert's **Flow-Regulator** that carries out the initial Cognitive-Self Task.

---

Below is a list of Mind-Self inbound duties, which it must handle. Grouped into Levels, Stages and Tasks, they are intended to assist in keeping track of progression through the five Cognitive-Pathways.

**Mind-Self Inbound**

1. **Level 5: Stage 1 – Cognitive-Alert**
   a. Task 1: Flow-Regulator

2. **Level 5: Stage 2 – Cognitive-Sensors**
   a. Task 1: What are Cognitive-Sensors?
   b. Task 2: Visual-System Pillars
   c. Task 3: Visual Currency
   d. Task 4: Retinal Structures
   e. Task 5: Visual Support
   f. Task 6: Multiple Fields-of-Vision


**Cognitive-Alert: Level 5: Stage 1**

### Flow-Regulator: Level 5: Stage 1 > Task 1

Flow-Regulator functions as the only entry-portal or transitional buffer-zone between Body-Self, which provides 'alerts' and Mind-Self, which is purposed to re-evaluate them.

Resultantly, Flow-Regulator disposition or Filtering-and-Slotting of its two 'in-box' data-streams, 'request-alerts' and 'imperative-alerts', is pivotal to all future Cognitive-Self processing.

Although 'request-alerts' can arrive in rapid succession over an extended period, such as when focused on an exciting new venture, Flow-Regulator processing capacity is normally able to cope.

However, 'imperative-alerts', due to substantially different content and extremely elevated intensity, present another demanding set of challenges. Specifically, ongoing 'imperative-alert' can cause Flow-Regulator capacity overload and therefore serious negative consequences for follow-on Mind-Self processes.

As previously revealed, Cognitive-Alerts can potentially be 'foddered' from Intensity-Check and/or Survival-Threat. 'Potentially', because these two mechanisms only activate in specific yet diverse Deluge conditions: Intensity-Check when recognized with mid-range intensity; and Survival-Threat when highest-intensity critical events occur, whether recognized or not.

Specifically, 'alert' content is dissimilar as a consequence of intensity evaluation by Threat-Check, which thereby dictated substantively different outcomes. Intensity-Checks 'request-alerts' are comprised of a non-threatening or not-survival-threat intensity single Tag-Cluster.

> As a reminder the 'request-alert' Tag-Cluster was replicated and fired to Cognitive-Alert prior to being forwarded to Trend-Analysis: thus maintaining continuity by ensuring not only continuous uninterrupted data-flow to Soma-Slotting but also concurrent Mind-Self engagement.

Alternately, Survival-Threat was engaged because either Intensity-Check determined a Tag-Cluster demonstrated survival-critical intensity or Trend-Analysis broader-scope assessments concluded a survival-critical issue. Survival-Threat thereby differently delivers discrete 'imperative-alerts' formed from the many Tag-Clusters of a Survival-Pattern.

> Recall, Trend-Analysis broader-scope assessments are mandated to recognize involvement of not only a single SLID but also surrounding associated SLIDs. Resultantly, 'imperative-alert' "data-packages" involving larger impact areas, like

an arm too close to fire, can be effectively passed-on for further 'Mind-Self' evaluation and action-suggestions.

Interestingly, 'request-alerts' are identifiable by two Tag-Cluster characteristics, which have positive implications for enhanced living. The reason this is possible is because 'request-alerts' "rapid-sequentially" present a diverse array of SLIDs or Soma-Location-IDs encompassing a large spread of sensory event-horizon locations with elevated mid-range intensity.

As such 'request-alerts' provide the impetus via Cognitive-Alerts for slightly-to-massively altering mundane or Soma-Self habitual-responses. Consequently, the vast majority of 'request-alert' provide the foundation for enhancing ones living-conditions by contravening the 'Force-of-Habit'.

Alternately to 'request-alerts', even though SLID types are typically fewer, 'imperative-alerts' cause disruptive consequences to Cognitive-Self mechanisms. Disruptive intensity stems from 'imperative-alert' structure, which is comprised exclusively of MACRO or highest-intensity survival-threat Tag-Cluster groupings, generated by multiple SLIDs pushed to maximum sensory-reception capacity. Survival demands their priority handling: even at the exclusion of other data-flow.

Hopefully 'imperative-alerts' are scarce in one's lifetime as neither Body-Self nor Mind-Self are designed for extended survival-issue handling,.

Additionally due to Cognitive-Alert neural real-estate capacity limitations, 'imperative-alerts' will invariably quash 'request-alert' and therefore dramatically alter perception due to loss of less intense data. In other words, any data-loss will interrupt 'normal' cognitive endeavors and therefore cause cognitive-assessment inaccuracies regarding all but the imperative-event.

As Flow-Regulator has no storage capability Cognitive-Alerts are either processed on receipt or dissipate. Therefore, data-integrity endures as long as Flow-Regulator is not overloaded. It is no wonder during a survival situation little memory of less intense events exists. In Neuro-physiological terms action-potential for the less intense 'request-alerts' simply dissipated. In other words, ongoing 'imperative-alerts' simply eliminate mid-intensity sensory-events: making it 'seem' as if the mid-intensity sensory-events never occurred.

Comedy routines sometimes use a similar sketch to the following, which will work nicely as an example of how 'quashing' works. Someone opens a cupboard door, reaches for a cereal box, fumbles and it drops to floor. While picking it up, someone scares them: they startle, straighten-up and consequently bump their head on the cupboard door.

In other words, the 'imperative-alerts' produced by 'the scaring' Deluge event not only quashed 'request-alerts' to do with retrieving the cereal box but also usurped cognitive resources, which without 'the scaring' would have both retrieved the cereal box and avoided the head bump.

Without the 'request-alerts' however, the only data-flow being processed was the 'imperative-alerts': therefore cognitive-assessment was inaccurate regarding 'request-alerts', thus resulting in the unfavorable outcome. Additionally, not much can be recalled about surrounding activities during the duration of the 'scare' episode.

In summary then, Flow-Regulator in 'non-imperative-alert' situations will 'normally' process all 'request-alerts'. However, in 'imperative-alert' circumstances Flow-Regulator capacity will be maximized and due to the 'higher-intensity always overrides 'lesser-intensity' universe law discussed previously, 'request-alerts' will be minimally to not processed but instead action-potentials will dissipate.

> Important to note: Flow-Regulators capacity is genetically determined to ensure follow-on Cognitive-Self mechanisms only receive manageable "data-loads" so they remain within their tolerance and processing capacity limitations: thus this mechanism regulates the data-flow.

Before depositing its contribution into the "Cluster-Works" 'in-box', Flow-Regulator provides one more essential service. Although 'request-alerts' are independent of 'imperative-alerts', Flow-Regulator must provide a single contiguous outbound to Cluster-Works.

Its "flow-amalgamation" process is dependent on 'in-box' conditions: either both 'request-alerts' and 'imperative-alerts' are pending or only one of the two. Flow-amalgamation is designed to hierarchically arrange 'imperative-alerts' and blend-in 'request-alerts': if capacity is available.

Notably, as is consistent with sensory-reception, 'imperative-alerts' also present as a variable range-of-intensity from highest possible, as dictated by maximum SLID firing capacity to perhaps 85% of capacity: below which survival-threat will no longer be assessed. Less intense 'imperative-alerts' could thereby allow some 'request-alerts' to also be processed.

> Clearly, survival-situations present events, which ebb-and-flow in intensity. Even in catastrophic situations some rudiments of tertiary conditions can get processed: although possibly distorted by 'request-alert' flow being jaggedly interrupted due to Flow-Regulator capacity issues.

Ultimately then, the Cluster-Works 'in-box' will randomly, as dictated by Deluge conditions, receive all three combinations: only a stream of hierarchically arranged high-intensity Tag-Clusters, if 'imperative-alerts' completely floods Cognitive-Alert capacity; a stream of broad-scope Tag-Clusters of variable mid-intensity originating as 'request-alerts', if 'imperative-alert' contributions are nil; or a mix of the two 'alerts', if 'imperative-alerts' do not max-out Cognitive-Alert capacity.

---

**Cognitive-Sensors: Level 5: Stage 2**

### Recap

Body-Self accepted bombardment underwent primary evaluation by mechanisms designed to regulate disposition into one of two channels. Recognized and intensity banal events were directly funneled to Soma-Response: whereas UN-Recognized and/or high intensity events were fired to Threat-Check and Cognitive-Alert.

Cognitive-Alerts designed to engage Mind-Self for alternate perspective are comprised of two diverse alert-packets: 'request-alerts' and 'imperative-alerts'.

The latter represents a high-potential survival threats whereas the former does not. Regardless, Body-Self requires evaluative assistance for resolution of Deluge events determined extraordinary or 'problematic'. In other words, alert-packets are utilized to appropriately fodder or trigger Mind-Self into action by defining the feedback "imperative-gradient".

Cognitive-Alert represents 'hand-off' or transition from management of sensory-accepted events by Body-Self to Mind-Self purview. Cluster-Works, one of two Cognitive-Filter initializing Components, the other Visual Works, first reformats received alert-packets into cognitively acceptable format and then delivers the resulting Pooled-Assembly into Cross-Sensory-Bundling's 'in-box'.

Cross-Sensory-Bundling interacts, when applicable, originating Body-Self "soma-data" delivered as Pooled-Assemblies with Visual-Works "visual-data" supplied by Cognitive-Sensors.

However, to appreciate the 'bundling' process first requires understanding not only Cognitive-Sensor physiology and operational parameters but also how Cognitive-Sensors provide information to Visual-Works.

### What are Cognitive-Sensors: Level 5: Stage 2 > Task 1

Although not compellingly punctuated during Body-Self discussions in book-one, Visual-Sensors and therefore 'visual-data' were excluded from Soma-Self discussions.

### …Why?

There are several vindicating factors.

Most importantly, the Retina is brain tissue, which means visual-sensory-receptors are actually part of the brain and not the 'body' or 'soma' per se. Consequently, "visual-receptors" are not part of the Peripheral Nervous System, the feeder lines, as are Soma-Sensors but part of the Central Nervous System - the main trunk line, if you will. This means no transitional delivery system is necessary between sensory-acceptance and ultimate higher-processor destination.

> Resultantly, the raw capacity and speed of Retinal receptors far outpaces soma-sensor data collectors.

Secondly, Bombardment events are substantially different. Incalculable billions of reflected photons inundating the visual event-horizon each millisecond present both frequencies and intensities, which are unrecognizable by Soma-Sensors.

Thirdly, for this massive torrent to be effectively managed, efficient physical and neurological support mechanisms must be in place to not only protect the fragile brain tissue sensors but also provide extremely fast refresh and assimilation capability.

## An amazing parallel

Survival necessitates that physical body or Body-Self design provides sensors, which perform as monitors of both external and internal conditions. Its primary mandate is to deliver 'best' information to dedicated non-visual cerebral neural-arrays, whose evaluation mechanisms determine initial outbound or response action.

> However, exaggerated mobility capability requires more than passive sensors waiting for impact events to 'land': it demands proactive capability.

Enter a major biological upgrade. It provides two tough, unique, dedicated and mostly self-sufficient containers to house sensory-arrays of a different genre. In a very real way, each eye is its very own specialized 'body'. Everything about these self-contained marvels ensures not only correctly filtered 'visual-data' is delivered directly onto the Mind-Self's viewport, the Retina, but also visual-sensors are directly connected to dedicated brain-mass.

> Sight is therefore re-designated a Cognitive, rather than Soma-Sense

## Visual-System Pillars: Level 5: Stage 2 > Task 2

Clear then is the Visual-System is an amazing coalition of capabilities and competencies spanning both physiological-structural and dedicated neural-processing modalities. It provides Neurobiological components responsible not only for acceptance of non-image oriented data but also for data that will resolve into images.

What is the substance of these bombardment impacts, which specifically provide initial data for the miracle of "sight"?

> Quotations are around "sight" because, as we will see, there is more to sight than meets the eye: excuse the puns.

## Visual-Currency: Level 5: Stage 2 > Task 3

**Photons are THE "Visual-Currency"**

Photons contain one-hundred percent of the originating raw data. As straight forward as this statement seems, there is an exciting story to unfold explaining multiple fascinating processes, which seem more like science fiction than the facts they are.

Primary to the existence of the universe, Photons exhibit properties of both energy (wave) and matter (particle). This unique transitional dichotomy establishes them as THE universe building block. Photons not only encompass all frequencies within the visible light range of the Electromagnetic Spectrum (plus all other forms of Electromagnetic radiation) but are also the 'elementary particle' from which everything in the universe is 'formed'.

> Their relative motion is defined by a constant: the Speed-of-Light.

Visual-System sensory-receptors, when fully functional and operative (conscious; awake; eyes open; 'normal' event conditions) manage a much more concentrated impact flow than do Soma-Sensors under similar Bombardment conditions. The very nature of photon density, impact speed and extensive frequency range, to name a few, create an unbelievably huge concentration of "event-potentials". To accommodate and take advantage, remarkable specializations have manifested.

We exist in a dense photon soup or photon Deluge. Photons are literally bouncing in every direction possible as far as the eye can see, which really means as far as photons can bounce and still provide enough density to excite visual-receptors.

> What photons don't bounce off; one cannot see.

In any one-second time-slice, on a bright sunny day, the quantity of photons with potential to Deluge Visual-Sensors is equal to a 'one' followed by about a million zeroes. Only a small fraction of one-percent actually impact visual-sensors.

Unlike Body-Self Bombardment, all non-reflected photon presentation is consistent within a very narrow band of variance: Photons are ostensibly identical as (at least) all visible light frequencies are represented during formation. In other words, compared to the thousands of molecular variances or types responsible for smell or taste there is only one photon type, which by analogy would contain the thousands of smell or taste variations.

The Electromagnetic (frequency) Spectrum is designated as the infinite and continuous ruler on which is represented all frequencies which ever existed since the Big Bang (universe origin). In other words, it defines the fundamental Universe Law where each frequency occupies an immutable position in relation to all others.

This is why visible light wavelengths always appear in the same order, as in a rainbow. Due to the Micro range stability of 'normal' visual-receptors, these frequencies are cognitively assessed as colors (by most).

It is not, then, photon characteristics, which determine engagement parameters but instead specific receptor type acceptance frequencies. This is fascinating because it means different receptor types either "cherry-pick" their particular narrow range of frequencies from the photon or if (vast majority) reflected (possibly more than once) has had other frequencies absorbed by the atoms of the objects of reflection.

> How this occurs presents interesting parallels to frequency absorption by the original object(s) from which the photon was reflected. Both processes adhere to the same principles of particle dynamics.

## Observability

No objects are directly observable by us. The 'image' we experience is a construct. Data acceptance by visual-sensors provides the raw potential. It is reworked into its final form by extensive filtering, slotting, re-amalgamation and referencing throughout the numerous and variant Mind-Self processing evaluators.

To even be considered candidates three fundamental conditions must align: Vibration frequency must occur within collector (visual-sensor) acceptance range; 'speed' must be less than collector "refresh-rates"; and the 'observable' object must be larger than an individual receptor. Visual-Sensor design, surprisingly, enables photons to fit these criteria.

The first impeding layer, "direct-observability", occurs not at the visual acceptance event-horizon (Retina) but at the 'objects' perimeter during photon collision. Nearly massless energy/particles (Photons) strike the outer, infinitesimally small atoms of an object. Some photon energy (object/specific frequency dependent) is absorbed before bouncing off (or reflected).

> Liken this energy absorption to bouncing a ball. The ball (Photon) hits the ground, compresses slightly (spring action) then bounces off leaving some of its energy (frequency) behind (transformed to heat energy, etc.).

The result is the Photon has been changed slightly. By the very nature of this process then, right from the get-go, direct observation is not possible: it has been energy altered by its collision with a something 'Out-There'.

Visual-Works does not get a crack at the original data. This is so because, after each of many different visual-sensors selectively cherry-pick the Photon (grabbing only their individual frequency), impact energy is morphed into another form: electrical impulse.

> The exciting upcoming journeys of discovering how our Mind-Self's work is spirited by the many inventive and extraordinary manipulations established by genetics and expand upon by "Figure-It-Out".

Disclosure of responsible mechanisms and processes form the basis of discussions throughout the balance of this book.

A few teasers are offered here, which are going seem nebulous at this point, of the processing steps, through which impulses (morphed Deluge) are selectively presented: A fly-through at the local "bracket-bank" to reference previous encounters; directed disposition through one of a network of "Evaluation-Pathways"; incorporation of "assumptive-fill"; coordination of a rapid picture series (strobe or movie); short term 'picture' maintenance (comparative reference points); presentation of the 'Movie-of-Your-Life'.

### Retinal Structures: Level 5: Stage 2 > Task 4

A quick review (not a comprehensive study) of the hub of all visual-reception activity - the Retina - as well as its functional parts will assist in aligning perspectives for upcoming Visual-Works and Cross-Sensory-Bundling discussions.

The Retina is a composite structure of many layers, which provides stratified environments specialized to its functional Retinal constructs. Constructs are delineated (mostly) by three anatomically diverse groups. The Retina houses the entire variety of visual-system event-horizon receptors or sensor types, transmission conduits and collating features. Cerebral connectivity also has its origins with the Retina.

> Each visual-receptor type within the Retina uniquely contributes to the 'sight' experience.

Rods and Cones comprise two visual-receptor groups responsible for most data acquisition. They are identifiable according to specific frequency-range reception capabilities, which also provide their segregation boundaries. The third Ganglion cell group provides some data gathering and all cerebral connection.

Rods and Cones are actually specific-frequency "photon-collector" types. Each collector-type morphs their defined range of photon energy. Resultant electrical 'impulses' are channeled to a dedicated Visual Cortex pre-processor by Ganglion cells, in turn connected directly to "cascade-processors" responsible for data integration, coordination, evaluation and several other manipulations within Visual brain-mass real-estate.

Cones and Ganglion cells are divisible into "sub-sets". Cone cell individual sub-sets are sensitive to smaller segments of the group frequency range whereas Ganglion cell operating diversity accommodates several functions beyond the scope of this book.

In addition, Cone sub-sets and Rods are not uniformly distributed within the Retina. Their physical arrangement though, is very specific both across the retinal 'surface' and within its girth (more on this below).

Reception by Rod and Cone groups is accomplished by Photoreceptors (pigments): so called because their individually specialized proteins absorb photons (light) then convert it to electrical action-potential (impulse).

> In other words, each is specifically triggered by a distinct frequency and photon quantity presented during photon Deluge. Their refresh rates vary as do end-to-end transmission durations, even within their own group. This diversity provides areas of hyper to moderate sensitivity.

Ganglion cells, ultimately forming the optic nerve, variably connect to a single receptor cell or to hundreds. These 'joins' form acceptance points I term "visual-landing-zones" critical for understanding interpretation of static, motion and composite events.

In order to reduce discussion complexity the terms wavelength, frequency and color will be used interchangeably as they closely correspond. As well, provision of the following information is for clarity not for precise functional detail purpose. Feel free to access ample resources on eye structures, functions and Neurophysiological aspects.

## Rods

Rod sensors are considered extremely sensitive because their cells (specifically their photoreceptive pigments) can be triggered by extremely low light conditions (interestingly measured in photons); as few as six photons have been reported to initiate stimulation.

Approximately 120 million receptor cells operate exclusively within their narrow frequency range, rejecting all other non-compliant frequencies. In addition, copious distribution at the Retinal edge coupled with high sensitivity miraculously enables peripheral vision.

> As a low light sensor, Rod contribution to survival plays a fundamental role. By enabling movement at night and within dark caves (the first protected domiciles), hunting, escape and safety were made possible. Many deep cave paintings attest to their effectiveness. Additionally, peripheral vision, by allowing an extended field of view, significantly extended the safety zone.

## Cones

The six million Cone sensors (5 percent of Rod quantity) are actually comprised of three sensor sub-sets. Each Cone sub-set is charged to respond to its own part of the divided group frequency range. Cones require much more light (a greater photon quantity) to trigger (absorption quantity reliance).

Receptor proteins for each Cone type respond to a different light wavelength or frequency (color interpretation) within the visible light range: short; medium; long. Cones are therefore re-categorized into three sub-sets: Cone-S, Cone-M and Cone-L.

> Survival was certainly aided by this trio's combined ability: Cones provide not only superior daylight vision but also consistent data presentation, thereby

enabling subtle discrimination of hue. The hue differentiation feature assists in at least two critical survival benefits: detection and evasion of "lying-in-wait" predators; and ultimate recognition of acceptable food colors from those that are toxic.

## Retinal Ganglion Cells

Retinal Ganglion cells are where the rubber-hits-the-road and are the rarest of the three Retinal groups. Their one and a half million constituents are comprised of five sub-sets. They not only gather and transmit Rod and Cone signals but also form the Optic nerve, which connects directly to several cerebral masses including the Visual Cortex.

In turn, several internal and external package support actions are managed directly by the Visual Cortex: such as, dilation control; blinking, tearing and eye movement.

Although there many subtle variations of Retinal Ganglion cells enabling many support processes, most are beyond the scope of this book. They are however responsible for several noticeable activities: brightness perception; direct control the most obvious Visual-System filter, pupil dilating or constricting; and circadian rhythm maintenance.

## Visual Support: Level 5: Stage 2 > Task 5

Visual specializations also extend beyond the Retinal container to several external support features. As an example, although mostly taken for granted, there are three seemingly simple related functions having important implications to maximizing visual capabilities: squinting, eyelid closure and blinking.

Interestingly activation is managed by cognitively controlled responders of the Visual-System not by the Body-Self System as one might expect.

It is noteworthy Body-Self sensors have no comparable capability: Body-Self sensors are continually bombarded. The only option for the reduction of bombardment is environmental or situational change; get away from the offending stimulus.

Significantly, any situation requiring physical relocation would queue many Cognitive-Alert notifications; expressly involving Mind-Self in any action, which in turn re-engages Body-Self; continuously cycling until nominal status is attained

These example competencies effectively extend Visual-System reach beyond reception into environmental and physical (body) control. Why would this be so? Are there additional cooperative reasons and ramifications for such high-level control of these "eyelid" activities?

Turns out there are immediate and far-reaching implications because mechanism design usually provisions more than a single purpose. Initially then, all three enforce data reduction: the third, external environment stability as well.

Squinting reduces the photon flow while closing the eyelids eliminates it and blinking provides needed short pauses for neural-refresh. Amazingly, the ability to pull the blackout curtains, closing your eyelids, even briefly, is significant.

Blinking on the other hand, although very short in our second-by-second world, is a much longer event in the microsecond operating environment of receptors. As such, the duration is more than sufficient to provide long receptor and neural pathway rest states.

Also, remember a 'blink' supports a viable container environment by ensuring hydration of it and surrounding tissues.

This is true even though the eyeball container is one of the toughest, most rugged biological constructs (true for most species) quietly managing its own (virtually sealed) internal environment.

The ability to turn the massive deluge off, at will, has significant survival ramifications. These and sleep provide short and long term relief for neural receptors which would otherwise burn out very quickly if continual 'catnaps' were not supported.

Visual input reduction to enhance cognitive capacity is also part of our nature. The following frequently invoked daily activity provides significant assistance to Figure-It-Out.

For instance most, "when trying to think or recall something", responsively close their eyes and/or look away at a familiar (recognized) or plain surface (wall; ceiling; etc.).

**How would this help Figure-It-Out?**

The created 'pause' reduces visual input. When visual input is reduced, so too are Visual-Sensor processors loads. Visual processing in turn is either eliminated (eyes closed) or hugely reduced (looking at a plain or familiar spot). Visual "data-breaks" resultantly reduce the burden on Figure-It-Out processors (neural pathways) which repurpose (refocus) the freed up brain mass resources for solutioning.

**Demanding Conditions**

'Inbound' demanding visual conditions encompass pre-impact, reception (on the Retinal event-horizon) and processing (Visual-Works) events: All present significant challenge.

> Rapidly repeatable methodologies enable the Visual-System to deploy its wonders

Incredible capabilities initiate even before raw data impact. One major pre-impact hurdle for example involves heat management. Eyes receive the same quantity of photon energy, which heats up the metal exterior of your car on a hot summer day.

To eliminate this external heat energy from arriving at the Retina, the eyeball provides five transparent heat dissipation (heat sink) formations: Cornea; aqueous humor (front chamber fluid); lens and capsule; vitreous humor (back chamber fluid); retinal gel. Incredibly, the heat is removed but visual frequencies remain intact. Without these features sight, as we know it, would be impossible.

> Reception of photons at the speed of light must be the most demanding hurdle to surmount (unbelievable this is even possible). The ingenious bundle of cooperative solutions supporting receptor functioning will be exposed throughout discussions.

Ongoing data stream pressure on receptors is also enormous. As a glimpse at front line support, genetics has provided "Gradient-Limiters" that variously predispose receptor groups in two critical ways: initiate only by a particular quantity of photons and accept only a designated group frequency.

Additionally, receptors are bundled into communication groups as dictated by Retinal Ganglion connection modalities: these form the front-line of transmission to higher processes. These groups form Fields of Vision where each field independently data gathers (more on this below).

Sequential and simultaneous processors are also vigorously active during Deluge conditions, as streaming data impulses must be resolved. UN-resolved (lost) data would unacceptably compromise survival prospects.

Here is a short representative list of activities Visual-Works processor must manage: broad variances in luminescence, color, strobing intervals; object sizing in relation to proximity; acuity (shape and form recognition); trends analysis (moving toward or away); motility variances (static, slow, fast moving); recognition status; implication significance; cooperative provision to follow-on cognitive mechanisms; cooperation with Body-Self Systems; etc.

**Acuity**

Visual-System acuity is incredible. We are able to perceive minor differences in form, color, hue, brightness, proximity, etc. Love of art and design is made possible by our capability and capacity to correctly process and assess miniscule variance.

Visually experiencing new environmental combinations and permutations is a strong drive. Creation of major to minor variability is the cornerstone of art and design; demonstrated by clothing styles, architecture, travel (in order to experience "the sights"), and so on.

Stated differently…

> Humans have the capability to morph the Deluge, the Chaos,
> into beauty!
>
> Someone once wisely stated
> "Form not substance is the essence of matter"?

### Multiple Fields-of-Vision: Level 5: Stage 2 > Task 6

There is not just one field of vision. Although this was (until now) the prevailing popularized wisdom, there are actually hundreds or even thousands of "Fields-of-Vision" incorporated by the nine receptor types: Quantifying technology will need to develop sufficient granularity before establishing a more exact count.

Nonetheless, within the overall Retinal receptor matrix, I coin a single Field-of-Vision point a "VisGridID" (visual grid location identifier) or VLID for short. It, by definition, contains a finite number of its particular receptor type(s).

The ramification of this statement means there is a maximum acceptance capacity (receptor cell quantity) within each VLID.

> Therefore, within each VLID exists a range or gradient of potentially active receptor cells defining our old friends MACRO and Micro capacity. Notably, the VLID model emulates the very workable Body-Self sensory event-horizon Location ID model (SLID for short). However, there is a major difference between the two.

Body-Self senses are designed for sporadic reception: for events which occur for relatively short duration then cease then perhaps reinitiate. This is not the case for vision. It must simultaneously accommodate sporadic events overlaying continuously unfolding events.

> How is it possible for vision to continuously present contiguous background events while simultaneously permitting specific object recognition?

This is possible because micro capacity accommodates 'background' saturation; typically filling the visual field: i.e., no blank spots. Neuro-phsiologically, this represents a 'normal' number of receptor firings; normal defining no extraordinary or unusual quantity of maximizing events.

> This accommodates sufficient input to allow representation of the visual experience as seamless: once "processed-fill" (detailed a little further along) is factored in.

By extrapolating from 'normal' event acceptance, it is clear that saturation (to MACRO range) of a particular VLID indicates something out of the ordinary is occurring.

> Although one, two or ten out of a thousand VLID's achieving MACRO status may remain an insignificant occurrence, ten percent or more will definitely action that something extraordinary is evolving; especially if the change occurs rapidly.

Let's investigate two ongoing visual events, created by external object motion, with potential to compromise survival: objects coming directly at you; and objects possibly heading your way.

Although both will inspire active Mind-Self engagement, the first is allocated much higher intensity as, at a very early age, one learns object impacts on our bodies are to be avoided. Keep in mind; Bracketing or recognition (learning) transpires for both Body-Self and Mind-Self.

As a rapidly moving object directly approaches for the first time, concentric VLID's will "MACRO-out" (maximum receptor involvement) initiating a processor scramble to Bracket the event and assess threat.

One typically relates to a MACRO event as focusing: one is 100% fixed on the unfolding critical event due to micro capacity (background events) being appropriated by MACRO requirements.

> Resultantly, almost nothing will be remembered of simultaneously occurring lesser events. Micro or background information will not be available as the MACRO event utilized all resources.

As the object continues its approach more and more Retinal real-estate is captured in ever widening rings. The epicenter, determined by cascade processors, is the "VLID-Ring" with the longest duration of MACRO bombardment.

> Coupled with other involved concentric VLID's progressively achieving MACRO saturation the absolute direction of event origin and trajectory are also assessed.

Additionally, the rapidity of the "Outflow" (how quickly the concentric rings outwardly fill) provides the objects relative incoming speed: this is a specialized form of Trend-Analysis at work.

In a less critical situation where VLID's are being MACRO loaded along a line or strip (across the Retina in any direction), activation yields relative motion across multiple lateral fields-of-vision.

The arrows head, so-to-speak, is pointing where new VLID's are maximally loading (MACRO state); the arrows tail is comprised of VLID's returning to Micro state. Object size is determinable by the quantity (girth) of involved VLID's whereas the speed is calculated by the "Shift-Rate" of the leading edge.

Supplementary explanations, through to response determination, are clarified in following sections.

# Cognitive-Filter: Inbound

Below are Cognitive-Filter inbound processes: Levels, Stages and Tasks are intended to assist in keeping track of progress.

**Cognitive-Filter inbound**
1. **Level 6: Stage 1 – Cluster-Works** (SD item 12)
    a. Task 1: Frames-per-Second
    b. Task 2: Frame-Assembly
    c. Task 3: Pooled-Assembly
2. **Level 6: Stage 2 – Visual-Works** (SD item 12)
    a. Task 1: What is Visual-Works?
    b. Task 2: Inbound tasks
    c. Task 3: VLID-Traveler
3. **Level 6: Stage 3 – Cross-Sensory-Bundling** (SD item 12)
    a. Task 1: What is Cross-Sensory-Bundling?
    b. Task 2: Locus-Matching
    c. Task 3: Intensity-Grading

**Cluster-Works: Level 6: Stage 1**

Cluster-Works 'in-box' is not only loaded based on Body-Self's 3-millisecond data-band rate but also the acquired data-bands are discretely maintained in sequential order: in other words, "cluster-packets" do not mix within this neural-array but are stacked like marbles in a tube. Importantly, this "hopper-resource" is not intended for permanent storage but as a transitional processor between Cognitive-Alert and Cross-Sensory-Bundling.

> Resultantly, capacity for this hopper-resource is limited: only about 3 seconds or 1000 Body-Self maximum capacity data-bands can be storehoused. If full or compromised due to pharmacological, biological or neural issues new cognitive-alerts will be rejected. Due to sensory-data loss follow-on mechanisms (to be discussed) will be required to fill-in-the-blanks from data-archives, potentially resulting in one feeling disconnected from reality.

Cluster-packets strategy, although it ensures the order of event occurrence is preserved, also means before change from one event to another is possible, previous events must be cleared or processed through all Modules. Recollection of the last few seconds of an ongoing event, albeit by 'higher' process yet to be discussed, is possible because of this originating strategy.

Fortunately, all have probably experienced this transition: the anecdote following should help to clarify. Most have experienced being interrupted. Putting while playing Golf serves as a useful example.

> You are focused on making your putt when someone starts chatting. Slightly agitated, you step back from the ball and perhaps shoot a few stern eye darts in the perpetrators direction.

In the first couple of seconds following the interruption you will actually be able to feel the stored cluster-packets 'drain' before being replaced with the more current activity of moving back into putting position.

> "It takes a little time to change tracks...to catch up to speed". Comedians often use the 'Double-Take', which takes advantage of this predisposition. It actually exaggerates the cluster-packet transition by taking you off in one direction and

switching back. The juxtaposition caused by the transition from one 'train-of-thought' to another by higher processors can be hilarious.

The reason for the transitional availability is due to retention of about 3 seconds of previous cluster-packets, which must stream through the "cognitive-system" before being replaced by current events and reside as short-term 'memory' because action-potentials also take a few seconds to fade.

Sufficient, contiguous information flow is critical. Without the ability to maintain cluster-packets for short periods, 'reality' would seem jerky, disjointed and/or vague because resulting sporadic information flow would not provide sufficient transitional continuity.

> When we turn on our home faucet, we expect the water flow to be consistent, whether throttled up to high or throttled down to a trickle. This condition is favorable and in-line with the modality with which ones "Movie-of-Your-Life" is presented.
>
> Contrast this favorable condition to a contrary one. You turn your taps back on after a plumber has incorrectly repaired your water main. Water and air incongruously sputter and spit out as pipes sporadically partially fill and then empty.
>
> Sputter-and-spit would be a terrible way to experience living!

The original link to the universe via its bombardment on each person's sensory thresholds preserves personal connection continuity. Uninterrupted contact ensures our experiences are always based on personal raw sensory Deluge impacts. Even if massively distorted by 'adjusting substances' (medications, etc.) or dreams, the origin is sensory: even if only slightly recognizable.

### Frames-per-Second: Level 6: Stage 1 > Task 1

Pressure is enormous in intense Deluge situations, where every few milliseconds another Body-Self data-band deposits tens-of-thousands of Tag-Clusters into the "Cluster-Works" 'in-box'.

As defined in book-one, Body-Self's three-millisecond 'band-pulse' rate was determined by both the rate of Deluge impact and SLID or Soma-Location-ID neuron-receptor refresh and acceptance rates. Additionally, Body-Self's limited neural-pathways, typically one to five, although excellent for rapid response, conspicuously preclude choice.

> Clearly, Mind-Self establishes the final opportunity to resolve issues not able to be handled by Body-Self. As choice, by evaluation of broader-scope is the purview of Cognitive-Self, different strategies are necessary: specifically bigger 'data-gulps' and more neural-pathways.

In other words, Mind-Self is designed to not only 'gulp' much larger data-packets but also provide vast choices by utilizing hundreds, even thousands of neural-pathways. Although broader evaluation is more comprehensive, a trade-off manifests: processing duration is increased, thereby making Mind-Self much slower. This is OK though because while Mind-Self is evaluating, Body-Self is responding: while waiting for Mind-Self to insert its honed action-suggestions.

To accommodate larger 'gulps' Mind-Self relies on "frames-per-second" regulators to fix the duration of "frame-bands" to align Body-Self three-millisecond inundation with Mind-Self's second-by-second timeframe. Specifically, Cluster-Works deploys this strategy by converting the Body-Self data-deluge into cognitive compatible frame-bands, which control the data-flow within all Cognitive-Self modules.

> Cognitive-Self's massively enhanced neural-network can not only provide a substantially higher capacity but also manage broader "time-slices". In other words, Mind-Self analysis capitalizes on its vastly expanded neural real-estate capacity to easily process broader time-slices.

**Why frames-per-second?**

Presentation of fifty-five to seventy-six 'frames-per-second' represents the human range-of-acceptability, within which events are perceived as progressing more-or-less comfortably and 'realistically'. This "frame-rate" is fairly straightforward to proof.

Not surprisingly, as movies strived to emulate perceived reality, standardized "movie-frame-rate" came to correspond to the actual human "cognitive-frame-rate" of sixty "frames-per-second". This is the 'data-gulp' of information, which can be most comfortably processed.

> Interestingly, original black and white movies, whose creators were attempting to emulate the 'real' world, seemed jerky because projection occurred between 22 and 40 frames per second. Sustaining this lower than acceptable frame-rate was budget: more frames-per-second were costlier in material and editing. Additionally, money to progress the technology was not available in this fledgling industry.

Newer technology is capable of presenting images in our upper range of 72 frames per second, which is the realm of HD TV: perceived as slightly sharper and brighter as long as 'frame-detail' is reduced.

> In other words, we see movies the way we see them because responsible brain-mass is both processing and presenting its renderings at a compatible sixty frames or "Cognitive-Packets" per second.

When information being presented matches the 'firing-and-resting-rate' of the billions of coordinated neurons, the 'Out-There' appears correct to us: who, from the strictest sense, are the neurons in the first place.

> As a consequence of frames-per-second stability, one experiences the world, ones 'reality', our "living- experience" or as I call it, the "Movie-of-Your-Life", as continuous and contiguous; not as jerky or spattered.

---

Each 3-millisecond Body-Self 'band-pulse' contributes Tags from body-wide activated Soma-Location-IDs, whose Tag quantities can rapidly swing from negligible to maximum MACRO-range (extreme Survival conditions). If you have ever fallen out of bed and been startled awake or been shaken awake on the couch, you have experienced this broad swing first-hand.

To determine the conversion from 3-millisecond Body-Self 'data-bands' to the Mind-Self compatible 60 frames-per-second is straightforward. Body-Self's three-millisecond band-pulse increments extrapolate to about 333 'frame-bands' per second, which means a single frame-band will be loaded with the contents of 6 Body-Self 'data-bands' (rounded up).

Apology: Keep in mind the millisecond is arbitrary: however neurophysiological pulses are regular and precise. Therefore, using 333 frame-bands and 6 Body-Self 'data-bands', although not exact, is both close and conceptually useful.

### Frame-Assembly: Level 6: Stage 1 > Task 2

Retrieval of six data-bands from the Cluster-Works 'in-box is the first of five steps, which will result in creation of a 'frame-band'. Once adjusted to comply with Cognitive-Filters next task requirements, the final step deposits the compiled 'frame-band' into "Cross-Sensory-Bundling's" 'in-box'.

As each data-band is removed from the 'in-box', the Tags from each Tag-Cluster are extracted into a temporary work-resource called a Flow-Packet. Amalgamation of 'same' Tags forms the next step, which thereby creates a single larger Tag-Cluster.

> Importantly, the resulting larger Tag-Clusters are critical to provide superior "time-slice" information to all future Cognitive-Self endeavors.

"Frame-amalgamation" occurs in a specialized 'neuron-mass' exhibiting a significantly enhanced elastic structure, which equates to large quantity of refreshable Axon/Dendrite Pathways. Elasticity is necessary to accomplish the demanding restructuring because many thousands of 'same' Tags will require rapid regrouping into single much larger Tag-Clusters of which there could also be thousands.

> For example: if a Bombardment event was consistent over a one-second or one-thousand millisecond interval and resulting Body-Self Tag-Clusters contained one-hundred Tags each, representing their three-millisecond neural acceptance event at a single SLID, the following would be true. Each of the sixty frame-bands, representing the same one-second interval would all contain same 'sized' Tag-Clusters: however with 600 Tags in each, which equates to a six-fold increase.

Note no increase in the number of Tags has occurred: they have only been 'packaged' differently to accommodate Mind-Self's more pensive nature.

The following anecdote is presented to provide clarification as we traverse Cluster-Works management processes. Let's assume a single sense deluge event. In this scenario hot oil has spit out of a frying pan onto a small area, a small group of SLIDs, on the back of your hand. It is not only 'immediately' painful but lasts about three or four seconds until the fat has sufficiently cooled or receptor-neurons are destroyed.

Let's re-enact the event from the constructs so far covered and give a glimpse at those still awaiting explanation.

The drop of hot fat arrives as surprise Bombardment from the universe and lands on a Soma-Location-ID on the back of your hand. The initial, as well as about three seconds of follow up events, were definitely neurologically sensory-accepted to the full extent of active neuron participation: i.e., the drops mechanical energy was translated into electrical energy creating a hundred Tags every three milliseconds.

Inception-Filtering first amalgamated then processed this ongoing barrage of "same" high intensity Tag-Clusters. 'Recognition' would not have mattered as the reality of such high-intensity shot the ongoing data-streams to Threat-Check.

> Due to extreme intensity, it deployed its escalated results to Survival-Threat, which in turn notified Soma-Slotting, which enabled complex physical flight reactions to get away from the source.

Simultaneously, Cognitive-Alert was notified by transmission of survival-pattern Tag-Clusters to initiate Mind-Self to uncover additional parameters.

Recall an ongoing stream of 'imperative-alert' Tag-Clusters is flowing into Cognitive-Alerts Flow-Regulator, along with other 'request-alert' flow. Highest intensity gets handled first though: resultantly, the Survival 'imperative-alert' therefore utilized most of the" neural real-estate".

> Total focus was on the survival-critical event because it was the only information coming through. You later try to remember surrounding events, which to your surprise you have very little memory…they were crowded out and dropped as a result of survival intensity utilizing the majority of the neural real-estate.

As the first six Body-Self data-bands get amalgamated, the resulting Flow-Packet quickly reaches its MACRO limit, as do the second, third and the next hundred or so. Discussions to come will take us through many mechanisms on the way to "Cognitive-

Survival-Response". The journey will be fascinating as all Cognitive-Self modules maximize their contribution to "Figure-It-Out" and get safe.

### Pooled-Assembly: Level 6: Stage 1 > Task 3

High intensity events are high for a reason: they have been determined substantial by Body-Self. As previously discussed a survival-critical event will typically incorporate several Body-Self senses. Indubitably, their sensory-reception will be tuned to the unfolding scenario and thus contribute greater-than-normal 'sized' or greater intensity Tag-Clusters from multiple Soma-Location-IDs or SLIDs.

Thereby, Cognitive-Alerts whether 'request-or-imperative' are not to be regarded as permitting an alternate processing imperative.

> Cluster-Works fourth step ensures focus remains on most critical SLIDs. Therefore, because Frame-Assembly Tag-Clusters are intensity disorganized, it hierarchically sorts Frame-Assembly Tag-Clusters according to intensity from highest to lowest into a "Pooled-Assembly" data-resource.

Re-organization of Tag-Clusters by intensity gradient has obvious benefits. Propagating random order to higher-level mechanisms would kindle disastrous outcomes because less critical events would either unnecessarily gobble-up processing time and/or valuable neural real-estate thereby diminishing the Cognitive-Alert imperative.

Additionally, filtering from highest-to-lowest intensity, most to least critical events, not only serves to group multi-sensory data-elements but also will enable Cross-Sensory-Bundling to effectively "event-match" Soma-Senses Soma-Location-IDs or SLIDs to applicable Cognitive-Sense contribution.

Pooled-Assembly provisions one of the two Cognitive-Filter headwater data assemblies: the other, "Visual-Works", originates with Cognitive-Sensors.

## Transition to Visual-Works

Mind-Self's complex axon/dendrite pathways (hundreds to thousands of pathway options for each) enable a broad range of universe impacting actions from Cognitive auto-response to conscious choice.

> Discussions of "Cognitive-Pathways" beginning shortly will elaborate on these and other amazing phenomenon.

As we progress, keep in mind the intention behind separately defining Modules and Components, which comprise the Cognitive-Pathways Model, is to clearly segregate one groups functional aspects from another: Neuro-phsiologically though, processes transition seamlessly.

## Visual-Works: Level 6: Stage 2

### What is Visual-Works: Level 6: Stage 2 > Task 1

Visual-Works is best regarded as processing central for the Visual-System. It provides three powerhouse groups, which engage at different stages: namely, "Inbound" (Cognitive-Sensor provided) data management; Bracketing (of visual data); and "Outbound" presentation (the ultimate 'sight' experience). This section restricts discussions to 'Inbound' mandates.

The second powerhouse group (Bracket maintenance) will be detailed during explanation of the five "Cognitive-Pathways" whereas the last will be fully disclosed after presenting all supporting evidence, when its participation will be apparent.

Accepted data delivers all the (external locus) information Visual-Works will receive. Received data forms an extensive information compendium from which processors must perform exacting evaluations, such as: object physical structure, speed, direction, relative retinal position, proximity, relative motion (approaching; static; moving away), expected destination, body movement recalibration in relation to object, when first noticed, etc.

Even in "normal" conditions, data is flowing at an express pace. Seamless handling, in standard as well as extreme conditions, demonstrates the array of multi-faceted capabilities provided by the compound levels of integrated processors with which we have been gifted. Extensive Filtering, Slotting and aligning is required in order to shake the raw-data into useful, pertinent assemblies utilizable by follow-on processors, like Cross-Sensory-Bundling.

## Inbound Environment Recap

Cognitive-Sensors, charged with receiving image and non-image producing photon information, are comprised of three (sometimes four) structurally and functionally variant types of retinal receptor cells: namely Rods, Cones and Retinal Ganglion. Each requires different quantities of photons to initiate data acceptance.

Cones and Retinal Ganglion present sub-types as well. Each gleans a different, narrow data-range from the photon, which by its inherent nature, contains all visual information. It is incredible to have sensors "selectively-harvest" only their piece of the puzzle from the group of photons causing the cascade or acceptance event in the first place.

Additionally, Retinal-receptor sub-types are not distributed homogeneously. Genetics dictates a retinal topography with large receptor density variances throughout the entire retinal gathering array. In other words, some Retinal areas exist with high concentrations of specific receptor sub-types whereas other areas contain a more-or-less similar cross-section or mix.

Collector Retinal Ganglions originate as incredibly delicate structures. Each is charged with gathering information from various quantities (single to hundreds) of same or different types of receptor cells. These reception "gathering-points" are termed Visual Grid Identifiers, visual Landing Zones or just VLID's. Ultimately, these reconfigure to fashion the optic nerve bundle, which directly connects to several brain-masses: herein defined as Visual-Works.

> **A pressing question from the above recap: Why selectively harvest in the first place?**

The answer is straightforward. The intricate masses of information provided by a photon simply cannot be handled by a single sensor type, Cognitive or otherwise. Comparatively, information provided to Body-Self sensors is far less complex. A close analogy of the difference would be like equating the complex inner workings of a mechanical watch, comprised of hundreds of precise indicate parts, to the simplicity of a sundial.

The sundial provides a close approximation for Body-Self sensor complexity: whereas the watch is suggestive of Cognitive-Sensors.

**Inbound Tasks: Level 6: Stage 2 > Task 2**

Although Visual-Sensors provide discrete fodder enabling Visual-Works processors to expedite simultaneous calculations for changes in motion, shadow, hue, speed and other parameters, ultimate information reintegration presents a huge challenge. After all, Visual-Sensor provision of granular clues would not be useful, if for instance, information from a left VLID mushed with data from an unrelated far right VLID. An error could mean the difference between surviving or not.

> "Selective-Harvesting" then has its consequences as a data gathering methodology because it generates a significant burden for reintegration processors: They must be precise and not skew the originating photon bombardment event.

Resultantly, data integrity and continuity are two keys handled by "relational-processors" within the Visual-Works purview. They are mandated, among other requirements, to "similarity-match" reconstituted data with resident Brackets. This provisions one measuring stick against which to evaluate visual familiarity and viability.

## Motion

The physical world provides objects in motion regardless of our observational alignment. This fact is supportable by multiple scientific proofs beyond the scope of this book. Regardless, from our frame-of-reference, the external environment "seems to" offer objects in one of two dichotomous states: static or dynamic (still or in motion).

Two situations encompass the visual experience: Background without "remarkable-feature" and background with remarkable-feature. Within 'remarkable-feature' parameters, one continually assesses four observable object modes in relation to ourselves, which overlay a background: object is stationary as are we; object is stationary but we are moving; we are stationary but the object is moving; both are in motion.

> Perhaps surprisingly, our experience of these 'seen' states is a created illusion

This is so mostly because objects are not 'directly' observable. Photons collide with objects on an infinitesimally small atomic level, some energy gets absorbed, they "bounce-off" and only then Deluge Visual-Sensors. Data is fractured (selectively harvested) upon acceptance and then reconstituted by an adept series of Cognitive-Filtering, Slotting and alignment processors that conspire to devise the ultimate object representation.

Due to cognitive rendering consistency though, we come to rely on object properties as fundamental truths. It is the various end-to-end processes intricately intertwined in creating constructs of higher understanding (what we consider individual de facto 'reality'), which form the substance of upcoming fascinating discussions.

> **Knowing cognitive capacity is finite, "are cognitive resources being allocated equally for these two states (still and motion)?"**

The answer is ultimately, no. However, in the earliest formative years when everything is new or newish (Brackets do not exist or exist embryonically) all input is good input. After several years though, cognitive resources are mostly utilized for assessing the implications of objects in motion.

Motion is a learned construct beginning from the moment of birth. It is comprehensible because we continually Bracket innumerable new object configurations relative to our own momentary physical position: Either an (exterior) object is moving in relation to its background and/or we are in motion relative to the object(s).

In a first encounter scenario, 'seen' is only rendered after many adjusting intermediate events. Repeat encounter scenarios additionally adjust 'seen' by variously integrating previous Bracketing (pre-existing cognitive axon/dendrite pathway data).

"Motion-focus" persists for a good reason; moving events pose a much greater survival threat. A charging bear is much more immediately threatening than a sleeping bear. Understanding how we discriminate between static and moving events has far reaching ramifications not only for assimilation of future discussions but also (perhaps more importantly) for enhancing each persons living experience.

For instance, people in one societal group tend to Bracket in a similar fashion but differently than folks in another group. Resultantly, similar Bracketed experiences (motion events) cause similar beliefs. This manifests because specific cognitive rendering of environmental object expectations are passed to us from significantly credible contacts through language and its preponderance of (object and situational) labeling.

> Close family in the younger years delivers most of the environmental experience thus setting the stage for perceptions limited to the providers' range-of-acceptance. More importantly, one's early experiences, loaded with acceptable and not acceptable enforcement, manifest as a gradient from (respectively) expansive to restrictive Figure-It-Out (see below) cognitive habits. Severely restrictive habits can be functionally debilitating by Body-Self disallowing any views or alternates to the accepted norm (domestication / brainwash): Bigotry and zealotry certainly fall into this category.

Identification of visual motion events then is such a major requirement for data acquisition that, if an object is stationary, there are two cooperative avenues to glean superior information: Body movement (Body-Self commanded by Cognitive response) and/or eye movement (by direct Cognitive-Self, Visual Cortex, instigation). In both cases, rapid changing of visual fields is the strategy to "get a better look".

In more intense situations, Cognitive-Self has an ultimate feedback responsibility: respond to Body-Self through the "universe-Body-Self sensor-interface". Body-Self is then charged with providing its own brand of rapid compensatory responses and possibly Cognitive-Alerts if resolution is not satisfactory.

> The Body-Self / Mind-Self interactive establishes a cooperative relationship empowering maximum survivability

### VLID-Traveler: Level 6: Stage 2 > Task 3

Visual-Works has significantly morphed the original photon data. Specialized receptors variously accepted their own specific photon aspects. Once accepted receptor specific photon energy was morphed into a recognizable cognitive language (electrical signal).

First level processors attached a VLID marker (visual location identifier) to the data origin as standardized by reception retinal ganglion termination in brain-mass.

> Each VLID not only forms a unique location on the Visual-Works grid but also becomes the reference index for assessing and recombining other parameters, by 'higher' processors, like proximity, speed, direction and intensity for example.

Higher-level simultaneous processors have performed Trend-Analysis and many calculations utilizing rapid changes in VLID characteristics. Multi-phased simultaneous processing has resulted in data steam condensing, which results in a compact assembly called a "VLID-Traveler".

As a high-level image, to provide clarity hopefully, think of the "VLID-Traveler" like the progression of building a snow scene. The group initially determines the higher project mandate to create a particular scene (survival and/or improved living conditions).

Each person begins, first by getting out into the snow (raw photon data): then selectively taking some of the snow (receptor selective harvesting) and gradually morphing (processor layers) it into a desired shape. As each shape completes, it is attached to the scene (VLID-Traveler) with the ultimate purpose of having onlookers enjoy the fruits of your labor (passing completed data to other cognitive functions).

When all value has been added, including a stop at the local "Bracket-Bank" to poll for familiarity and similarity (also added if located), the resulting VLID-Traveler is sent to

Cross-Sensory-Bundling. Each stage has performed its particular data enhancement to ensure "best information".

## Transition from Visual-Works

When compared to Body-Self's sensory mechanisms, previous dialogue has established Visual-Sensors, coupled with Visual-Works Filtering-and-Slotting, are unique. Body-Self's final manipulated format, Cluster-Works Pooled-Assembly, delivers a restricted data-array to Cross-Sensory-Bundling, comprised only of Cognitive-Alert data.

> Recall recognized AND low intensity data is handled by Body-Self and not sent for cognitive evaluation via Cognitive-Alert. Visual-Works, on the other hand, delivers its configured and appended VLID-Traveler composition for all visual-sensor accepted bombardment.

Although data gathering techniques and provisioning methodologies are dissimilar, both independent systems share the same ultimate mandate: to pass 'best' information to Cross-Sensory-Bundling.

## Transition from Cognitive-Sensors

Incredibly, two completely different sensory systems feed information: Soma-Sensors and Cognitive-Sensors. Depending on Deluge conditions each is variably purposed to enhance survival prospects and/or "sphere-of-influence" conditions by either acting autonomously (in recognized **AND** low intensity conditions) or interactively (in UN-recognized and/or higher intensity conditions).

Although a common mandate underlines their purpose, methodologies and capabilities are substantially different between the two. Body-Self utilizes "old brain" simple Axon/Dendrite Pathways (2 to 5 options) to exact tried and true (Bracketed) universe impacting responses autonomously from Cognitive-Self influence: Mind-Self structure is significantly enhanced.

## Cross-Sensory-Bundling: Level 6: Stage 3

### What is Cross-Sensory Bundling: Level 6: Stage 3 > Task 1

Cross-Sensory-Bundling sustains a neural-arena for cross-evaluation of Cluster-Works 'Pooled-Assembly' and Visual-Works 'VLID-Traveler'. This task is pivotal because synchronized Body-Self and Mind-Self systems will unquestionably provide greater contribution to survival by collaboratively providing two different 'takes' on an unfolding Bombardment event.

As this Component resides in Cognitive-Filter's inbound realm the global mandates are to Filter both packets to extract appropriate data-elements and Slot the results into either one or the other of two outbound channels: "NORM" or "PRIORITY".

This process fulfills in four-phases: converge Pooled-Assembly and VLID-Traveler; determine "Locus-Matched" or a non-Locus-Matched status and populate results into two work-resources; hierarchically filter both work-resources by intensity, highest to lowest; and shunt higher intensity ("Warm" and "Hot") to "PRIORITY" and lesser intensity ("Cool" and "Tepid") to "NORM".

A difficulty with this strategy might be evident: initially it is highly unlikely both systems, Body-Self and Mind-Self, will simultaneously focus on the same Bombardment event: instead their coordination must be orchestrated somehow. In other words, one system will typically alarm first then notify the other: for instance, Body-Self via Cognitive-Alert, which ultimately uploads a manipulated data-packet to Cross-Sensory-Bundling Component.

### Alert origin in Body-Self

Using a previous section "fat-spitting" example, the 'imperative-alert' was propagated to Mind-Self from Body-Self via Cognitive-Alert. This "alert-action" originated a series of processes, which initiated the survival Cognitive-Pathway (CP-1). Resulting Cognitive-Self responses initiated visual-sensors thereby concentrating this resource on the area of intrusion as well. Subsequently as data continued to roll in from both systems, Cross-Sensory-Bundling coordinated the independent feedbacks, thus resulting in resolution.

### Alert origin in Mind-Self

Visual-Works assesses a dangerous trend as a baseball rapidly approaches (filling VLID's into MACRO gradient): The impact point determined by Visual-Works - the forehead. This imperative, depending on assessed intensity level, initiates the appropriate cognitive pathway, which initiates Cognitive-Self response, which thereby engages physical action to get out of the way. Body-Self in turn feeds back through Cross-Sensory-Bundling via Cognitive-Alert until the situation reverts to nominal.

### Locus-Matching: Level 6: Stage 3 > Task 2

Before delving into processing strategy let us first recall the data structure of both contributors. Cluster-Works 'Pooled-Assembly' provides intensity ranked Soma-Location-IDs or SLIDs representing many types of sensors and hundreds or more Bombardment sites. Visual-Works information, although similarly intensity ranked, provides a "Mosaic-Grouping" containing multiple grid Visual-Location-IDs or VLID references appended with additional trend and intensity parameters as provided by several levels of visual processors.

Locus-Matching is the first phase mandated to determine whether the two systems are reporting on an identical event or independent events. It manages matching by utilizing the location identifiers of both Body-Self Sensor SLIDs and Visual-Sensor VLIDs as primary referencing criteria.

The Visual-Works VLID-Traveler is the bastion against which Pooled-Assembly Tag-Clusters are equated. This is because cross-matching not only occurs in Cognitive-Filters cerebral territory but also Visual-Works presents a much larger matrix of information significantly beyond the capacity of Body-Self.

The operative word then is matching. Matching is necessary to fulfill the overriding mandate of both systems: maximize survival potential and/or living conditions. This is extremely necessary because continual trial-and-error to align the two systems, even in non-critical moments - like picking up a pen, would not even come close to fulfilling the primary mandate.

> Can you imagine the frustration if every time you went to pick up a pen you would have to gradually hone in on it, figure out how to pick it up and hold it, etc.

Non-Bracketing would be tantamount to remaining in the baby stage your entire life.

The superior methodology would enable remembering (Bracketing) all the minutiae, so when similar action is again needed, it would be right at your fingertips (excuse the pun). The ability to Bracket in fine detail, instantly access and then deploy appropriate elements (respond) from the Bracketed compendium defines humans as more evolved.

Practicing "a something" taps into this natural capability to add additional detail (nearly endlessly) to existing Brackets, and by so doing you get better and better at it.

Two types of matching (not mutually exclusive) are desirable to provide best-case outcome. The first type, location-ID linking or "LID-Links" is designed to avoid slow trial-and-error, is necessary to link body location SLIDs to Visual grid location VLIDs: so we can quickly look at and slap the feeding mosquito, catch a baseball, use a fork or chopsticks, read a book, pick-up a pen, etc.

The second type, Brackets the intricacies of the external environment beginning just beyond the Body-Self event-horizons where the first type left off in order to rapidly comprehend holistic physical body positioning as it navigates the external landscape.

Necessary so one can proactively recognize potential danger, avoid impact with a speeding car, climb a mountain, stay erect on your feet, etc. In this way then, VLID's also are designed for 'Out-There' recognition: to direct the body away from danger. This complex matching type is addressed in upcoming Figure-It-Out discussions.

Matching of the first type, 'LID-Links' is possible because both SLIDs (Body-Self Location IDentifiers) and VLID's (Visual Location Identifiers) are biologically in fixed positions and not floating around willy-nilly.

Previous discussions emphasized the genetically created connection between Body-Self location ID's and the dedicated brain-mass for each. Likewise, Visual-Sensor connections are a known entity on the "Visual-Grid" where each VLID is specifically represented. External event movements then are a function, determined by many processing layers, of either the stability or shift-rate of "remarkable-features" across the retinal grid.

Without a doubt, when faster processors (available to create and append Brackets) are coupled with enhanced capacity (to house various Bracket types within multiple platforms) better perspectives and outcomes will result. In this regard, we are not all created equal.

So then, before any useful LID-Link cross-matching is possible a cross-referenced SLID / VLID data-repository must be Bracketed, which will tie physical Body-Self locations to Cognitive-Self visual grid locations.

Unfortunately, we are not born with a visual grid, which recognizes Body-Self body locations or type two external features for that matter. These cross-reference joins require Bracketing through exposure or experience.

The type one 'LID-Link' Bracket accumulation process starts embryonically a little after birth when the eyes open. Clearly, newborns have no idea their feet or other body parts exist, let alone have comprehension of their potential. However, as the infant continues exploration, first of its body and later its surroundings, both types of Brackets have spawned in the billions by about two or three years of age.

Anyone with children recognizes sharply defined developmental stages. Once mobility is possible, the entire external environment is targeted for exploration providing a surge in Bracketing connections we call recognition and coordination. The more exploration is permitted, the greater the Bracketing and therefore the greater the familiarity and comfort. Once Bracketed, it is off to the next explore without regard for danger as it too is Bracketed.

The accumulation process is progressive. Parents are intrinsically aware that exposure to new "stuff" will accelerate development. From the first attempt to have the baby recognize its fingers and toes, to a wide variety of moving crib toys, transitioning to greater complexity as the child matures: even into adulthood, with tools for men and shoes for women, ever more complex video-games and social-media presentations etc., variety contributes to Bracket accumulation.

Exposure and newness are keys. Exposure is self-evident (if never exposed there can be no Bracketing) whereas newness may not be so obvious. Remember when discussing "Recognition" in Body-Self the other critical factor was "Intensity" and that anything new, by its very nature would carry a higher intensity. As such, the event would therefore create a Cognitive-Alert and not immediately become a Soma-Self habit. Future discussions will expose Cognitive-Habits as quite different.

> This Recognition process then is the primary feature explaining progressive accumulation. Touch, a Body-Self Sensory experience, is as fundamental to a baby as it is throughout a lifetime. It is difficult not to reach out and touch a "something new" when it is within grasp. Our Body-Self nature almost demands we hold it, feel its textures and temperature, turn it over, etc. The desire to touch and feel is so extremely compelling that, if not allowed, the resulting feeling by most (aside from frustration) is like a loss of something precious.

In fact, a loss it is because our Cognitive-Selves, without connection to the physical world via Soma-Self Sensors, simply cannot Bracket correctly: it literally misses-out on the foundation for its assessment and must therefore resort to assumption, which feels very unsatisfying and insufficient. More on this as the adventure continues into Cognitive-Pathways.

> The infant gradually comes to realize those objects it can see being touched are its toes and excitedly gets its first sense of controlling something. Through enough exposure, opportunity and interest, SLID / VLID connections get underway: slowly at first but the explosion of Bracketing is only months away, when everything and anything becomes the target for investigation by hands and mouth. Even the toes get tasted.

It is necessary at this point to take a small step back to cover off an incredibly interesting and important point. Understood is the following: Body-Self Sensors initiate tactual environmental contact. Additionally, if the contact is not recognized an event flow initiates: a Cognitive-Alert ensures supplementary assessment will be delivered by Cognitive-Responses, which engage the body, which returns control to Body-Self.

This cycle has a few problems though because from birth to a few months old everything is Body-Self unrecognized. Additionally, Mind-Self is mostly a blank slate without any formed responses to events. As well, Visual-Sensors are not making much sense of surroundings (still in the initial stages of creating type-two Brackets).

> However, although these seem like overwhelming barriers, this arrangement is perfect because it means Mind-Self gets exposure to everything causing a

Cognitive-Alert, which in fact is everything. Remember, once Body-Self recognizes an event and it is low intensity no Cognitive-Alert is raised.

This situation establishes the Body-Self habit-base first, which is critical for basic survival. The body must be safe before the mind can ponder: that premise is true throughout life. It also means though, no matter how brief the exposure, Mind-Self Modules have rudimentary Brackets. This will be a big deal especially when Figure-It-Out works its magic.

### Intensity-Grade: Level 6: Stage 3 > Task 3

"Intensity-Grading", as touched on above, determines which Locus-Matched events or data elements (from either package) are at MACRO state. MACRO range events are fired to the 'PRIORITY' channel. All other data elements as well as Micro Locus-Matches are simultaneously shunted to the 'NORM' channel.

Recall that both "Packets" (Pooled-Assembly and VLID-Traveler) are delivered independently to this phase of Cross-Sensory-Bundling, with all elements nicely arranged from highest to lowest intensity. Notably, preparatory systems have requested attention for a particular segment of the data flow as indicated by its intensity. Even so, Cross-Sensory-Bundling has its own critical (MACRO) rating method based on the accumulation of previously linked intensities.

This phase then has three clear tasks: one - fire Locus-Matched events exhibiting sufficiently high intensity to 'PRIORITY' channel; two - determine independent events having sufficient intensity to also be launched to 'PRIORITY' handling; three - discharge all other elements and Locus-Matched events to the 'NORM' channel.

As previously stated it is unlikely both systems will come to focus on the same event simultaneously. Locus-Matching concerned itself with coordinating information from two systems. Intensity-Grading has a different mandate: to correctly allocate a channel regardless of match status. Grading design separates very-high imperatives from lower imperatives so the most critical events will be expedited with maximum due process within the 'PRIORITY' channel.

## Transition from Cross-Sensory-Bundling to Figure-It-Out

Up to this point, extraordinarily competent receptor, transfer and processing systems have honed raw data into a format compatible with the largest and most massively competent tool known to be available: Mind-Self. Specifically designed for determination of final deployment or response, Mind-Self achieves its goal by utilizing the substantial expertise of its two integrated Modules: Cognitive-Filter and Figure-It-Out.

Cross-Sensory-Bundling was the last Task in Cognitive-Filter's outbound-to-Figure-It-Out arsenal. Each of its three Inbound Components prepared data for Figure-It-Out.

It is in the Figure-It-Out arena where flourish processes exhibiting copious intricacies defining each person's slight-to-considerable uniqueness: Unique in views, experiences, perceptions, desires, dreams, goals, etc., etc. Components within Figure-It-out create, link, access and maintain significant reservoirs of "Information Assemblies" (facts), "Experiential-Accruals" (feelings) and "Visual-Harmonics" (mental images).

---

Those who are perusing or remember the 'Cognitive-Pathways Model' illustration are probably thinking: "What happened to discussions about "NORM-Filter" and "Continuity-Controller": they are between Cross-Sensory-Bundling and Figure-It-Out".

They will be discussed in conjunction with each Cognitive-Pathway, CP-5 through CP-1. As Cross-Sensory-Bundling is a fundamental interface, it is responsible for loading specific data-packages, as a consequence of Bombardment conditions, into one or the other 'in-boxes'. Therefore, as data-packets partly determine Cognitive-Pathway, these Components will be discussed along with each pathway.

# Figure-It-Out

To help accomplish incredible feats, Figure-It-Out coordinates connections (joins) and interactions between two structurally diverse "Data-Matrix" data-repositories: "Information-Assembly", which amasses "data-element" minutiae; and "Experiential-Accrual", which captures pivotal impression or emotion-harmonics.

Additionally, in specific circumstances, Data-Matrix can also establish links between Experiential-Accrual and "Visual-Scape", which are "visual-images" housed in the Visual Cortex.

Figure-It-Out enables data-retention, recall, awareness and thought

Below are global Figure-It-Out topics: indicated Levels, Stages and Tasks are intended to assist in keeping track of progress through the 'Cognitive-Pathways Model'.

**Figure-It-Out**
3. **Level 7: Stage 1 – Cognitive-Pathways 4 through 1**
    a. Task 1: Data-Matrix
    b. Task 2: DE-Notify
    c. Task 3: TI-IN
    d. Task 3: TI-OUT

## Introduction

Figure-It-Out facilitates perhaps the most incredible of human capabilities, ingenuity, which relies solely on Figure-It-Out's "puzzle-solving" competency.

Also up for explanation is how Figure-It-Out additionally deploys "Test-It" functionality to enhance puzzle-solving by building outbound conditions designed to inspire uniquely human response capabilities. Tailored "Test-Its" not only inspire granular 'real-world' response interactions and cyclical feedback but also set the groundwork for detailed data-retention and recall.

"Puzzle-Solutioning" does have an ultimate design though: the creation of myriads of "Cognitive-Habits". Archived in "Concept-Cluster", these perception controllers ultimately direct awareness, imagination, inventiveness, planning, hopes, wishes, dreams and much, much more.

Once Figure-It-Out participation is concluded, Cognitive-Pathways depart the Figure-It-Out Module and return to the purview of Cognitive-Filter Module. Here "Template-Component" provisions outbound patterns to Cognitive-Self's "Response-Component".

Tasked to inspire appropriate physical action, Response-Component utilizes and adapts Template-Component patterns. Repurposing engages not only applicable outbound neural channels but also proportioned Endocrine System (hormonal) instigators to ensure appropriate 'motor' activation.

Fulfillment of the Figure-It-Out mandate is possible because are not only diverse data-resources encapsulated within its framework, which archive core "data-elements" and their interrelationships but also several specialized mechanisms provided, which diligently, collaboratively and continuously drive to "Figure-It-Out": by resolving puzzles and deriving "Solutions".

> Figure-It-Out's precise data-management phases shape not only inward-facing ("Private-Self") beliefs, aspirations and personality but also outward-facing ("Public-Self") behaviors and responses

**Capacity**

From a biological resources point-of-view, the intricate processes essential for all Modules (Cognitive-Self; Cognitive-Filter; and Figure-It-Out) to fulfill mandates demand a structure capable of providing vast quantities of "neural real-estate".

Significant interlaced neural-resources must be continuously accessible and fully functional, to ensure coordinated event handling can perform consistently for all Cognitive-Pathways: regardless of extreme intensity range and/or Deluge variance.

> Humanity is incredibly fortunate in this regard: Mind-Self nurtures about 100 billion neurons connecting with about 100 trillion synapses
>
> > Enough neural-capacity for a long life lived with gusto!
>
> Based on one-hundred living years are you fully utilizing your "annual experience quota" of one billion neurons and one trillion synapses?
>
> > If not, no time like the present to get excited and get experiencing!

Although genetics has gifted us with vast potential, it is up to each person to fulfill this potential through exposure to as many exciting lifetime events as possible. Critically, Figure-It-Out's framework does provide the immense quantity of required neural real-estate. It is structured to provision multiple data-repositories: each designed to preserve different configurations of "sensory-information".

Discussed below is Figure-It-Out's "experience-recall" capability, which utilizes "data-archives" to enable all "living-possibilities". A basic 'Force-of-Habit' premise: when the workings of Figure-It-Out become understood, designing and 'living-the-dream' should be a no-brainer (excuse the pun).

> Potential (genetically gifted), place (Earth – possibly Outer Space for some future folks), awareness (cognitively derived) and time (Universe tenet) are all available without a hitch…
>
> > Resultantly, at any granular point one is able to choose between two modes:
> > life or living.

One can choose to let 'life' command situation:

> Just reside in the provided biological container and acquiesce to Soma and/or Cognitive habitual Dictates

OR

Choose 'living' on purpose:

> In other words, learn how Soma and Cognitive mechanisms work and then from this understanding reconsider habitual action, engage new experiences and personally choose more useful and exciting 'living' options

> Why not choose the latter: activate "flat-out-living" and see what happens?

## Figure-It-Out: Ingenuity

Ingenuity is the capability to fashion, design and/or contrive an innovative concept and/or object. Consciousness is as intrinsic to ingenuity as Figure-It-Out's Cognitive-Pathway Components are to awareness: they are inseparable. Together their power makes everything possible.

> Ingenuity is an innate (genetic) driver!

> Homo sapiens, by the fundamental nature of interactively-complex genetically determined cognitive brain mass, have always been compelled to Figure-It-Out: this is how we have survived and flourished.

Unfortunately, freely employing one's ingenuity has only recently been largely permissible. Throughout millions of years of tribal history, its manifestation was severely abridged by those holding positions of power and influence.

Even so, ingenuity endured.

The following "Ingenuity-Journey" will assist in not only appreciating this amazing feature but also understanding the core role Figure-It-Out plays in creating each individual reality.

## History of Ingenuity

During our humble beginning as mammals, three plus million years back, early (genus Hominid) ancestors departed from a single land location to populate the world. Seemingly, these early us' had little hesitation in packing-up and getting away from each other when views collided: Off they went to discover a new someplace with improved prospects. Such ingenuity, even from our earliest origins, was then like Figure-It-Out on steroids.

Notably, many other same genus mammals simultaneously co-existed: although nine are fairly well known, there were undoubtedly more. During a million plus years, this diverse range of ancestor species, in small tribal communities, had successfully entrenched themselves around the planet. Devising and adapting (ingenuity skills) were obviously well honed; as strongly evidenced by tool artifacts and population disbursement.

> It is notable none of the alternate ancestor species survived. Archeological writings graciously state we (Homo sapiens) "replaced" them between fifty and one hundred thousand years ago. My deduction is "replaced" means eradicated (a topic for a different book).

## Figure-It-Out was Alive and Well

Ongoing venturing into the 'whatever-there-is-out-there' unknown, whether by Homo sapiens or earlier close ancestors (now extinct), was quite the amazing achievement: Especially considering estimated world populations of all human-like species numbered only about one or two million and individual nomadic group populations were less than one hundred. This number was large enough to offer relative safety and small enough to feed: Similar to the structure of today's few remaining nomadic tribes.

> Nomadic drive is quite different today considering most find it a challenge just to walk to the store or around the block: "hats-off" (my respect) to the few enduring outdoor adventurers.

Extreme survival skill competency was no doubt the sought after currency of the day. Those who could Figure-It-Out and attain superior skills would be revered; especially concerning safety, fire and food preparation. Recognition of superior skills was definitely an initial factor in evolving social order.

About one and one-half million plus years ago a great progress leap occurred with the control of fire: the capability to start a fire would have to wait for nearly one and one half million years.

There were undoubtedly specialists within the tribal group (probably family of the dictator / chief / ruler) who were charged with "gathering" fire, from naturally occurring events - like lightning, and keeping it viable. Fire raining down from the sky (lightning) was most certainly considered a divine gift as it provided huge benefits: warmth, protection, etc.

Food preparation became a revered skill. Fire enabled a significant leap in food quality. Not only does cooked meat have about twice the calories of raw meat (tenderized connective tissue can be eaten) but cooking also hugely reduces killer bacteria and parasites. As food would feed twice as many and mortality declined, social order and therefore language started its evolution as tribal members sat around a warm fire eating, making noises and gestures: much like we enjoy eating and chatting around a campfire today.

Additionally, cooked meat has a substantially longer life span; dried meat even longer. This enabled longer sojourns for scouting parties. They could not only avoid dangerous or impassable landscapes but also locate and choose a superior pit stop: instead of just stumbling upon it with the entire tribe in tow. Life seemed good and under control for the first time.

## About 10,000 BC to 1750ish AD

We existed then, for a very long time with few notable advances. There is a reason this remained so until the last few centuries.

The previous two million year plus quest by our ancestors was founded on manipulating and utilizing what was at hand: matter or tangible material for day to day needs - earth, fire, water and air; the heavens, what we now know are Suns with our predictably orbiting moon, for navigation and life pace.

Let's fast forward to about twelve thousand years ago when the next revelation changed Homo sapiens existence. We Figured-Out not only how to start a fire whenever we wanted by using flint but also how to use fire to enhance living conditions: To make more tools like cutting implements; to fire pottery permitting superior food storage; to incorporate a fireplace (a place for the fire) in a shelter now possible for a single extended family.

The pace of life began its morph from large tribal behavior to smaller homogenous kinfolk groups. Figure-It-Out was again underway; but the other savage edge of the sword was about to slice.

Tribal dictators did not much like the prospect of having their power usurped by followers who might be seen as equals to the "chosen-by-the-Gods" chief. Remember, control of the tribe by descendants of a single patriarchal monarch, had been the rule for over a million and a half years.

Not likely their misplaced beliefs regarding their superiority were going to take a back seat. Rulers Figured-Out a way to ensure their false stature would remain: quash any show of ingenuity by the purposely devalued slave followers, utilizing whatever methods wanton enforcers desired.

> Recorded history, from around the planet, clearly indicates only a selected few have been permitted expression of their ingenuity. Those in power, typically self-appointed state and religious leaders, exercised absolute control over any innovative expression. Advancements were strictly contained within the narrow confines of the ruler's pocket of influence and deployed exclusively for their benefit.

The reigning zealots of the day (and there are many today) conveniently determined any uniqueness was insurrection, sacrilege or witchcraft. As enforcers of their own agendas and without any accountability, displays of expansive thinking in the general populace could thereby be "justifiably" quelled by any means necessary.

Viewing of brutal public punishment (impaling, stoning, burning, torture, etc.) was required watching for "all-the-rabble". These events were designed to discourage any attempt at future original thinking; thereby preserving servitude and control. In reality these techniques were brainwashing by extreme fear and destruction of self-value. It is no wonder progress was stalled for many, many millennia, as so much negative energy had been expended on eradicating ingenuity; the primary progress driver.

For instance, the one thousand year European Dark ages, about 400 to 1400 AD, took a huge toll on our propensity to Figure-It-Out. Church and State killed hundreds of thousands of progressive thinkers as witches and heretics in order to establish order which they defined as serving their own selfish purposes. Europe was not the only world arena rendering brutal life conditions; nor was it the only time in history where oppression was severe and pervasive.

## 1750ish A.D.

Restricted perceptions then were the enforced norm until very recently. Fewer than five hundred years ago, the majority believed the Earth was flat; the heavens were the realm of gods; emperors were the messengers of those gods; sorcerers were real; all people were not created equal; inspiration can only be "channeled" through you from a greater power; and expanded knowledge was not meant for the "commoner".

Many more of the same type of invalid beliefs were brainwashed into young minds to keep them "in their place": the "place" being determined by others who were previously brainwashed. Shockingly, some still conform to significant chunks of outdated beliefs, which spawn debilitating self-doubt.

Fire again played a pivotal progress role after 1750 A.D. Instead of the direct application of fire to produce creations (i.e. the celebrated sword maker in those days) a huge ingenuity leap enabled fire energy to be converted to electrical energy.

The changes resulting from this Figure-It-Out, set the stage for huge lifestyle, social and perceptual changes: Including continuing transformation from small tribal groups into ever expanding populations of city-folk. Ever more condensed populations required entirely new sets of Figure-It-Out innovations.

> In 2025 it will be just 400 years since Galileo Galilei presented the first method of finding "smaller stuff" (the micro world); the compound microscope - based on pioneering work by Hans Lippershey. The first telescope to get a closer look at the heavens (the macro world) celebrated its four hundredth anniversary in 2008; also Hans Lippershey. The reflector types we use today were a significant adaptation which occurred in 1932 – a scant 80 years ago!

## Last Fifty Years

Actually, ingenuity was very sparingly allowed even up until about 1950, after which its acceptance started gaining ground. Those in authority still held on tightly; mostly in an ongoing quest to preserve their own variously deranged need for power and dominance.

To this day, most broadly accepted inventions were developed under the auspices of military (protection or aggression) requirement: they include petroleum products – gas and plastics; vehicles; roadways; bridges; flight technologies; untold variances of chemicals; computers; the internet; cell phones; genetic manipulation; nuclear power; spaceflight; well you get the picture.

In fact, only in very recent history, within the last fifty years, is it becoming more and more acceptable for the general populace to fulfill its fundamental right to exercise ingenuity. Even so, communications and visual media still support many negative beliefs regarding inventiveness.

> For instance, in many types of media productions stereotyped and supported the vision of an inventor as a disheveled, old, white haired, half insane male. It was not intended as a positive role model.

Women are still not considered inventors even though their contributions in many complex fields, including being mothers, attest to their exceptional ingenuity.

---

Hopefully, the above history has assisted in enhancing the validity and power of our 'dangerous' ingenuity predisposition. Better informed, we can expect its continued emancipation will provide incredible progressive future benefits in awareness, perception, understanding, tool refinement, living conditions, and so on.

> A pivotal Force-of-Habit goal is twofold: to unfetter this dynamo and let it, and therefore us, realize untold potential; and to disclose not only how ingenuity interacts with end-to-end evaluation mechanisms but also what optimal conditions enable ingenuity to "super-engage"

## Why Now?

There is no doubt ingenuity was penned in, but why are broad innovations suddenly manifesting?

Five core reasons are evident which support why advancements in both knowledge and technology are currently developing at historically express pace: Approval of knowledge acquisition for everyone; broad acceptance of ingenuity as a right; easy access to expert information; preponderance of brain mass bio matter; proximity.

Planet population was about 750 million until the eighteen hundreds. It is now 7 billion plus. We therefore have ten times the brain mass available: two million pounds then versus twenty-one million pounds now.

> All these three pound brains are not only in close proximity (physically and/or virtually) but also have easy information access nurtured in a social structure which accepts open knowledge as the desired norm.

Today we think of innovation as a most excellent trait. Globally, rapid invention and production is evidenced by vast arrays of ingenious new perceptions enabled by three dynamic Figure-It-Out Cognitive-Pathway Components: Data-Matrix, "DE-Notify" and Test-It (Each will be fully detailed in dedicated sections below).

> In relation to current belief that innovation for all is not just accepted but celebrated, society is in its infancy. For the first time in history on this planet there are billions, who not only believe in, but also manifest their prerogative to Figure-It-Out, be noticed and be rewarded!

## Recap and Transition to Figure-It-Out Cognitive-Pathways

Force-of-Habits 'Cognitive-Pathways Model' illustration is intended to represent all cognitive processes. Within its schema beat three unique controller Modules whose many Components uniquely configure, data-transition and/or Filter-and-Slot the data-stream.

> Two of these Modules, Cognitive-Self and Cognitive-Filter, each provide Components designed to not only pre-process inbound sensory-data by aligning the data-stream for the benefit of the 'Figure-It-Out' Module but also tailor data-elements for outbound purposes as well.

"Cognitive-Pathways" (CP's), CP-4 through CP-1 (least-to-most intense) initiate within Figure-It-Out. Although each Cognitive-Pathway interacts with the same data-resources, both inbound and outbound intensities differ substantially. As these variances provision significantly diverse impacts on recall, awareness and response vigour they will inspire much future discussion.

> Cognitive-Pathway discussions are purposed to reveal 'How-We-Cognitively-Work' by uncovering the functionality and variances between each pathway.

Disclosure will be accomplished in stages, including: delving into Figure-It-Out inbound data-structure; data-handling processes; data-resource purposes and implications; ultimate outbound (from Figure-It-Out) disposition; and so on.

At the Figure-It-Out doorway, inbound data-characteristics have been unquestionably determined by previous manipulations of Cognitive-Self and Cognitive-Filter Components. Data-packets were pre-evaluated (Filtered), then aligned (Slotted) according to key parameters: such as, intensity, load, duration and bundling-status.

Cognitive-Pathways are separated (on the 'Cognitive-Pathways illustration') to indicate variances in neural real-estate utilization and in handling capabilities regarding data-intensity. In other words from initialization through disposition, they manage variable intensities and deliver specific end-to-end functionalities.

> By providing unique capabilities, Cognitive-Pathways thus enable the processing vibrancy, which hallmarks each person's individuality.

Discussions will begin with Cognitive-Pathway CP-5 (Cool) and proceed to CP-1 (Survival). Progressing discussions from least-to-most intense will permit gradual introduction of the many incredible Component and Module functionalities responsible for individual complexity.

> It is probably obvious neither bombardment nor resulting data-flow are constant. Sensor acceptance (Tag formation) increases and decreases in direct proportion to environmental interaction; whether or not planned.

For instance, data-flow for a planned event, like quickly skiing down a challenging run, is much more robust than when sleeping peacefully. The same would apply for unplanned events: A car careening out of control toward you will foster huge Tag formation, whereas accidentally overfilling your cup with tap water would result in a much smaller Tag surge.

Regardless of activity driven intensity, cookie-cutting a "data-slice" of any time duration would result in a 'cookie-chunk', which would contain 100% of the available information. Although this seemingly states the obvious, it is useful as a starting-point because unlike generic cookie dough, many very different data-parts (Tags) are represented within the data-slice.

> Additionally, these variably intense Tag data-elements or data-parts could very well involve all Cognitive-Pathways: though at substantially different intensities and/or volumes.

For instance, extract any short duration "Normal" event-stream: for instance, a 30 second snippet while walking down a very familiar street having a "chatter" conversation (no radically unfamiliar content) with a good friend. In this simplified portion the two "NORM" Cognitive-Pathway (CP-5 and CP-4), differently handle about 95% (or more) of this data-slices minimally notable, lowest intensity data-stream activity: repetitive-familiar (CP-5); and minimally-eventful (CP-4).

By referencing the Cognitive-Pathways diagram once again, it is clear CP-5 performs as a conduit without any Figure-It-Out manipulation: whereas Figure-It-Out engages CP-4, which presents extended features (Components) to be discussed further along. Combined though, normal data-flow is fairly constant as background noise persists the day.

> Previous discussions, including the above, have referenced a "Normal" day where we are awake to unfolding, relatively safe, standardized or routine events. However, to fully disclose all Cognitive-Pathway and associated processes, plus similarities and variances, a critical event will better serve. Modifying the previously utilized 'fat-spitting' scenario will work nicely.

The strategy is to track this designed critical event (described below) from pre-occurrence through escalation through return to normalcy: In other words, from "Cool" through Survival and return to 'Cool'. Sequencing as such will reveal the controlling methodologies of all not only Cognitive-Pathways but also inbound and outbound Components.

The intense data-flow aspects of the scenario (below) would not therefore be construed as "Normal" by the above definition.

### Hot-Fat Scenario: Updated

You are standing next to the stove peacefully contemplating life, when you feel a sharp burning sensation. Hot oil just spit from the frying pan onto the back of your hand. You involuntarily snatch your hand out of range, turn your head to look at the incursion area and move quickly away from the stove.

> After two or three seconds of torment, the pain subsides somewhat. You cautiously return to the danger zone, note the burner was incorrectly placed on the highest setting, put a lid on the pan and reduce the heat. Gradually, after taking care of the burn, all returns to 'Normal'.

The Hot-Fat scenario has been dissected into eleven escalating levels, which will be presented (1 through 11) within a discussion framework as follows.
> First will be an introduction section entitled "Characteristics Summary". It will present a synopsis of the data-flow impact upon Component's: i.e., a pre-emptive point-by-point current status summary.

Second, a "State-of-Affairs" section will more fully detail the 'Characteristics Summary' in order to disclose both context and Component transitions. In other words, this section will describe existing conditions of not only the variously intermingling Module processes but also Component tasks.

> Lastly, an "Implications Section" will specify the impact of not only the end-to-end Cognitive-Pathway process on the data-stream but also the many processes affecting cognition.

---

**Characteristics Summary: Level One / Cognitive-Pathway 5**

### Tranquil

**Mind-Self** inbound
    Cognitive-Alerts: 1 out of 9; 'Cool' mid-range intensity
    Cognitive-Sensors: background

    ---------
    **Cognitive-Filter** inbound
        Cluster-Works: lowest intensity Pooled-Assemblies
        Visual-Works: no VLID alerts
        Cross-Sensory-Bundling connections: None
        Channel: NORM
        Continuity-Controller: None
        Pathway: CP-5 'Cool'

    **Cognitive-Filter** outbound
        CP-5 Template-Component
    ---------

**Mind-Self** outbound
    Nominal-Response: Pass-through
    Movie-of-Your-Life presentation centre: no remarkable

**CP-5 State-of-Affairs**

All is well with the world. The data-stream is tranquil, as Body-Self (via Cognitive-Alert) and Cognitive-Sensors (visual sensors) are only producing nominal contribution. Also, Cross-Sensory-Bundling can neither establish pertinent Cluster-Works / Visual-Works cross-references nor locate any high intensity occurrences from their individual flows: i.e., both flows are unremarkable and unmatchable.

In other words, the resulting Cross-Sensory-Bundling outbound data-stream may have amalgamated some lowest intensity Soma originating Tag-Clusters (most of the Deluge was shunted to Soma Auto-Response) and/or Cognitive-Sensor background data-flow.

**Cognitive-Pathways Model**

```
                Cognitive-Alert      Cognitive-Sensors            CS
                      ↓                     ↓
                 Cluster-Works         Visual-Works               CF
                      ↓                     ↓
                    Cross-Sensory-Bundling           Copyright David Hastings,
                              ↓                       "Force of Habit" 2013
                           NORM                         All rites reserved
                              ↓                        V2014-CP-101BL
                         NORM Filter
                              ↓
                         CP-5: Cool

                         Template
                              ↓
                         Nominal
                         Response
                              ↓
                         Pass-through

                      Movie-of-Your-Life
```

However, as a result of the above noted 'tranquil' conditions, Cross-Sensory-Bundling shunts its outbound data-stream to NORM filter. There, NORM assessment (Filtering) establishes (Slots) the data-flow to "Cool" range and thrusts it onto the CP-5 Cognitive-Pathway as illustrated on the graphic below.

Important to underline Mind-Self is not bubbling with activity at this point because Body-Self is keeping our physical selves on the straight-and-narrow by executing Soma-Actions for the onslaught of recognized data events.

Key to remember for "How-We-Cognitively-Work" discussions, Mind-Self is mandated to handle "Alerts" or exceptions; not the repetitive or mundane (from Mind-Self perspective).

CP-5 Template-Component appropriately matches the event data-flow to one of its genetically provided baseline templates or "T-Patt's". The selected T-Patt is then passed to CP-5 "Nominal-Response". Nominal-Response in turn assesses the delivered Template against its tried-and-true genetically provided 'motor' links and then deploys.

**CP-5 Implications**

In Level One, unremarkable visual information is simply flowing through to Nominal-Response. Even though Nominal, Response-Component is still adept at impacting the physical world by "Response-Directives" designed to not only send level appropriate outbound "Neural-Packages" to muscles and organs but also appropriately solicit the Endocrine System for supporting instigators.

Additionally, even though visual information lacks any specific alerting content or "Remarkable-Feature", it still silently provides positional and associated sensor information, which Nominal-Response utilizes to ensure granular physical orientation and other necessities are not being eroded.

All information is integrally integrated to the Mind-Self presentation center which innocuously morphs and fills blank pockets so no breaks are perceptible in our seemingly external and continuous visual reality experience I call the "Movie-of-Your-Life" (more on this later).

**Transition to CP-4**

> Although Deluge waxes-and-wanes due to both external and internal condition variances; and receptor acceptance fluctuations; data-flow never stops. In reality therefore, isolating a synchronous-event "data-packet" would be impossible. However, to permit step-by-step analysis of Component methodologies to clarify working principles, a 'data-packet' is assumed identified and observable: Thereby, permitting documentation of its journey as it is utilized and morphed.

Torrential bombardment continuously impacts sensory-receptors: although only a portion is accepted and coalesced into "data-packets". Each 'data-packet' is destined to potentially activate any-and-all Cognitive-Pathways: hopefully, CP-1 (survival) only sparingly. Even in CP-1 conditions though, lower intensity 'data-packets' are being directed to other Cognitive-Pathways, thus providing one an ongoing ebb-and-flow of congruous experience.

> Notably, CP-5 is always on; accepting "Cool". Even in high intensity situations 'Cool' background bits-and-pieces persist ones day.

## Transition to Cognitive-Pathway Four

CP-4 is activated when the data-stream is escalated by 'NORM', from 'Cool' to "Tepid". Accordingly, as this engages Figure-It-Out, exploration of the four Cognitive-Pathways commences with CP-4 (Tepid). The first Component encountered on CP-4 is Data-Matrix (see illustration). It is utilized by Figure-It-Out to populate its reference data-repositories with CP-4 base-plate or building-block data-elements.

> Ones expanded recall, learning and survival capabilities initiate on CP-4

Many Figure-It-Out Components, processes, functions and interactions are being encountered for the first time on CP-4. Each is essential to understand in detail because they not only are utilized (although in augmented fashion) by other Cognitive-Pathways but also engender far-reaching implications. Although the needed thorough explanations will result in the CP-4 section being long: it will be worth it.

> Cognitive-Pathway repercussions are huge. However, we would not be the species we are, not by a long shot, without all these capabilities

**Characteristics Summary: Level Two / Cognitive-Pathway 4**

**Contemplating Life…but something is imperceptibly scratching for attention**

**Mind-Self** inbound
    Cognitive-Alerts: 2 or 3 out of 9; 'Tepid' mid-range intensity
    Cognitive-Sensors: background still
    ---------

    **Cognitive-Filter** inbound
        Cluster-Works: slightly escalated Pooled-Assemblies
        Visual-Works: Nominal; no VLID alerts
        Cross-Sensory-Bundling: None
        Channel: NORM
        Continuity-Controller: Yes

        ---------
    **Figure-It-Out**
        Pathway: CP-4 'Tepid', slightly elevated
        Experiential-Accrual: Bracket and Links
        Information-Assembly: Brackets
        DE-Notify: Yes; to Continuity-Controller
        TI-IN
          Parameter-Processor: Yes
          Delving-Trio: No
          Devise-Mulling: not directly
        TI-OUT
          Test-It: rudimentary
    ---------

    **Cognitive-Filter** outbound
        CP-4 Template-Component: normal activity
---------

**Mind-Self** outbound
    Standard-Response: Mildly DO
    Movie-of-Your-Life Presentation center: unremarkable

## CP-4 State-of-Affairs

Although all still seems 'well with the world', something is nibbling at the fringe of awareness causing a mild apprehension: something illusive, which you can't quite "put-your-finger-on".

> Post-event, it was clear. Exploration of the situation revealed an imperceptible Soma Sensory event was initiating. The source of the initial sensory information of course was the 'too-hot fat in the frying pan'. It was just beginning to emit a very faint smoky smell coupled with a muted low-frequency rumbling.

Body-Self, not recognizing certain smells and sounds began germinating non-survival Cognitive-Alerts. In other words, Threat-Check was nudging Mind-Self to use its competencies (accessing stored information and/or initializing its sensor array - vision) to "Figure-It-Out".

> The slight uneasiness was actually being caused by Parameter-Processor deriving Test-Its.

Initially, unrecognized SLID stimuli (Sensory-Location-IDentifier) were too sparse to alarm Threat-Check into MACRO status. Threat-Check therefore did what it is designed to do: create a Cognitive-Alert.

> Specifically, substantial enough intensity was occurring for Threat-Check to create a mid-range "request-alert" to inspire Mind-Self to give an assist.

As will soon be clear, Cognitive-Alert thus initiated the first in a series of Cognitive-Module activations (escalation level 2 of 11) as a direct result of escalating intensity, which will correspondingly escalate response complexity.

> Received by Cross-Sensory-Bundling the low intensity alert was not able to be matched to any Cognitive-Sensor data (which remained nominal because the event as yet had not inspired visual connections): it was therefore passed onward to NORM-Filter.

Cluster-Works data, recognized as greater than "Cool" by NORM evaluation filters (due to the existence of a slightly intensified Pooled-Assembly), was shunted onto Cognitive-

Pathway 4 (Tepid). Although not sufficiently potent to cause Cognitive alarm, intensity was sufficiently escalated to engage CP-4, graphic below, rather than CP-5.

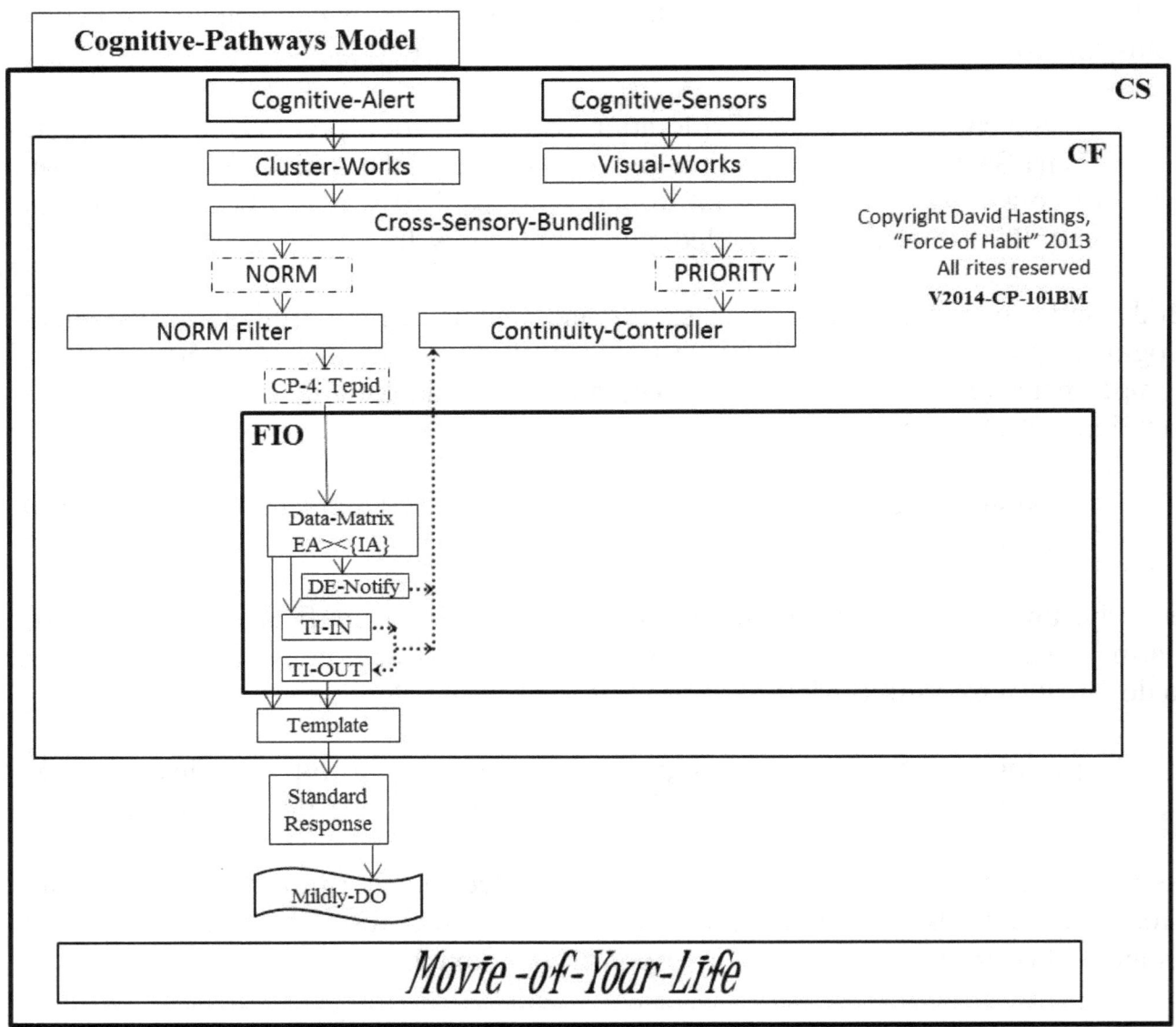

Figure-It-Out employs Cognitive-Pathway (CP-4) Components in the sequence shown in the illustration above.

As Cognitive-Pathway Four (CP-4) engages several Components for the first time, they will be discussed first. Consequently before continuing with CP-4 'State-of-Affairs', Component players and their inter-relationships need explaining: namely, Data-Matrix;

Experiential-Accrual; Information-Assembly; Joins; Links; symbolic notations; Test-It and DE-Notify.

## CP-4 Introduction

By examining the four Figure-It-Out pathways on the complete Cognitive-Pathways Model diagram, variances in graphic presentation are evident: such as, shading; typeface bolding; and Data-Matrix Component box content, whose symbolic notations vary from CP-4 through CP-1.

Pathway differences are intended to indicate not only greater demands on processors but also an increase in data-stream intensity and/or complexity. Even though each Cognitive-Pathway seems like it houses different Components with the same name, they do not. For example, only a single Data-Matrix data-repository exists for all Cognitive-Pathways.

> Separately illustrating Cognitive-Pathways serves to provide not only a clear view of specific functionality variances between them but also a forum for discussing each pathway individually.

As Data-Matrix on Cognitive-Pathway Four (CP-4) is the first Component to be encountered, discussions will begin with it.

## Data-Matrix

CP-4 'Data-Matrix', which exists within Figure-It-Out neural-assets, is graphically reproduced on the right. Although it is least complex of the four illustrated on the complete Cognitive-Pathways Model depiction, it is not quite accurate due to space restrictions on that diagram.

| Data-Matrix |
| --- |
| EA><{IA} |

To truly represent Data-Matrix, it is necessary to update its graphic: first by including one additional data-resource; and second by pointing out the graphic characters, which account for its two join-resources.

| Data-Matrix |
| --- |
| EA><{IA{DE}} |

The updated model presented to the left will be used for discussions. Also, notice the white background and the non-bolded standard typeface: they are used to discriminate CP-4 Data-Matrix from the others, hint at its specific functionality and indicate CP-4 as handling 'Tepid' intensity.

Three independent Data-Matrix data-resources are evident in the above graphic: Experiential-Accrual, Information-Assembly and "Distinct-Episodes". Each contributes data-members (or data-elements): namely, "EA-Harmonics"; "IA-Facets"; and "DE-Events" respectively. Convenient contraction of their names provides their graphic abbreviations: 'EA'; 'IA'; and 'DE'.

Additionally, two "join-resources" exist, which are not self-evident: "EI-Join" and "IE-Join". Indicated by the facing arrow-heads (><), they provide quintessential connection between an 'EA-Harmonic' and its many associated 'IA-Facets'.

> The importance of these join-resources will become clearer when data-retrieval and Test-It Component are discussed in sections following.

Notably, EA-Harmonics (EA's), IA-Facets (IA's) and DE-Events (DE's) vary in form, function and characteristics. Although these data-resources will be discussed in separate sections, an introductory overview will serve to initiate discussions and align their interrelationships.

More specifically then (see '101BM' illustration below), one EA-Harmonic (dotted lines) is always forever 'joined' with many IA-Facets by 'EI-Join' (EA and IA first letter), which enables retrieval of all IA-Facets when the EA-Harmonic is known.

Differently yet symmetrically, each Information-Assembly 'IA-Facet' (solid lines) is also permanently 'joined' to its EA-Harmonic within 'IE-Join' (IA and EA first letter).

This arrangement facilitates retrieval of one or more EA-Harmonics, when the IA-Facet is known. Distinct-Episode 'DE-Events' will be discussed a little further along.

> Graphically speaking, the braces around {IA} indicate multiple IA-Facets are joined to a single EA-Harmonic and the braces around {DE} indicate multiple DE-Events are linked to a single IA-Facet.

The Data-Matrix depiction, EA><{IA{DE}}, should be 'read' as follows: EI-Join and IE-Join preserve countless "one-EA-Harmonic-to-many-IA-Facets-to-many-Distinct-Episodes" relationships.

> The following restates the EA /// EI-Join ~ IE-Join /// {IA{DE}} relationship:

One…to…Many…to…Many

EA $_{<\text{join}>}$ {IA} $_{<\text{link}>}$ {DE}

  One EA-Harmonic…to…many IA-Facets…to…many Distinct-Episodes

As the '101BM' graphic below is fairly complex, it will be rendered and discussed in sections. Additionally, other simpler supporting graphics will be provided to aid understanding.

  Notice for now EA-Harmonic joins are indicated by dashed lines; whereas IA-Facet connections are indicated by solid lines.

We will soon come to appreciate how this comprehensive structure establishes us as a premier proactive species.

  The importance of these connections cannot be overstated as data-member joining provides the underpinnings for human cognition and behavior.

As mentioned above, Experiential-Accrual, Information-Assembly and Distinct-Episodes house data-members purposely created with markedly different natures.

Therefore, examining their individual features will uncover not only individual uniqueness but also pertinence to Cognitive-Pathways and thus cognition.

  Although each data-resource requires clarification, EA-Harmonics provides the 'driving-force' and will thus be discussed first.

# WayBetter Your L.I.F.E$^2$.: Mind-Self

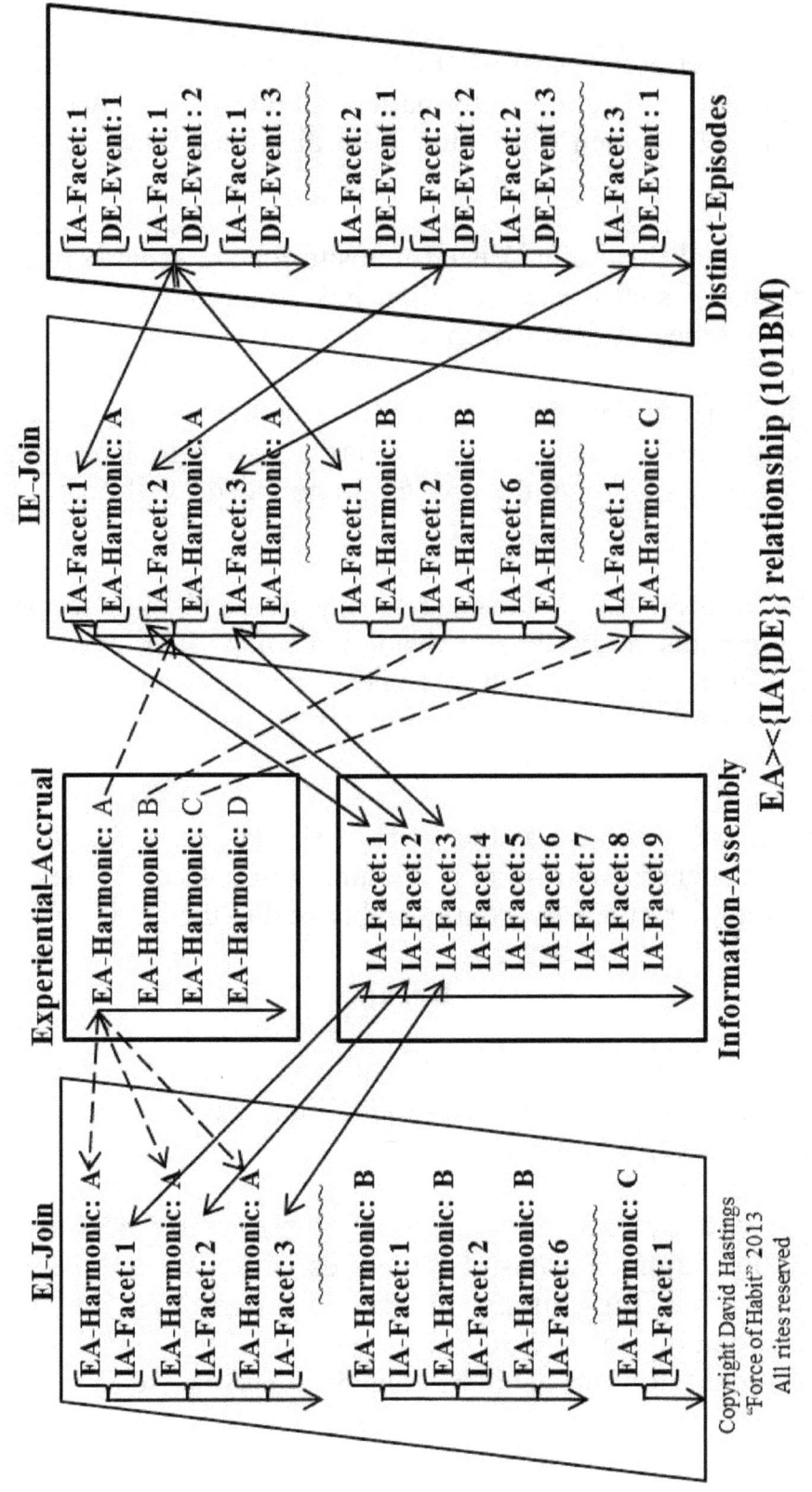

## Experiential-Accrual

Stated differently, Experiential-Accrual 'EA-Harmonics' are the backbone to which not only its direct constant companion, Information-Assembly 'IA-Facets' but also Visual-Scape (VS) "VS-Facets" attach (the latter to be discussed when applicable conditions present in CP-3).

> Worthy of note at this point, Visual-repositories are separately maintained in the matrices of the Visual Cortex: it is the link to the Visual-Scape data-repository, which is maintained by Data-Matrix.

We are emotionally driven creatures: It is the core nature of one's genetically purposed cognitive neurophysiology. Easily evident in any situation first manifests a feeling, an interest or an emotional spark, subtle through pronounced; well before one grapples for facts or details.

> Energizing Figure-It-Out to engage in any inbound or outbound activity is an originating impetus, a gripping motivation, a compelling 'event-sense', a cathartic reason, if you prefer. Archived in Experiential-Accrual are EA-Harmonic data-elements, whose feeling/emotion/impression "driver-cores" are indispensable and pivotal to all cognitive activity.

Not only is this the case but also as the swirl of similar event details begin to emerge, another remarkable phenomenon occurs: 'Pictures-in-our-head'. These image splashes, diffuse to sharp, singly or in pulses are inexorably tied to the eliciting emotion.

## Recap

The 'Hot-Fat scenario' will once again be utilized to clarify presented concepts by paralleling its stages to explanations. Also, to facilitate a convenient starting-point, data- and-join resources are decreed empty or null.

Frequency-transitioned by 'accepting-neurons', representing only a few millisecond pulse of sensory bombardment, tens-of-thousands of Tags were assembled with their 'frequency-matches' into Tag-Clusters of various intensities. Tag-Clusters assembled within a Pooled-Assembly thus represent a 'sensory-event': for explanation purposes the first landed drop of 'Hot-Fat' could be considered as one 'sensory-event'

An EA-Harmonic is unique when compared to Data-Matrix 'IA-Facets'. Recall, an EA-Harmonic was coalesced into a single harmonic by blending all Tag-Cluster contents of a Pooled-Assembly: thus forming a single "harmonic-signature".

IA-Facets on the other hand were transitioned from the frequency-signatures of each Tag-Cluster of a Pooled-Assembly. In other words, in contrast to the potentially thousands of Information-Assembly 'IA-Facets' created from the Tag-Clusters of a Pooled-Assembly, Figure-It-Out forms but a single EA-Harmonic by harmonizing the same Pooled-Assembly.

> The first drop of 'Hot-Fat' would not involve many heat sensitive SLIDs but would excite most 'ready-state' neurons. Therefore the EA-Harmonic, although escalated, would singly not cause excessive alarm. Additionally, individual IA-Facets would not be significantly intense either, as they were just created and therefore remain within 'normal' range

Storehoused in Experiential-Accrual, an EA-Harmonic is a specific purpose aggregate of a 'sensory-event'. Comparatively, Tag-Cluster frequency-signatures are utilized to differently populate Information-Assembly and Distinct-Episode data-resources: indicated by the {IA{DE}} representation in the Data-Matrix illustration previously.

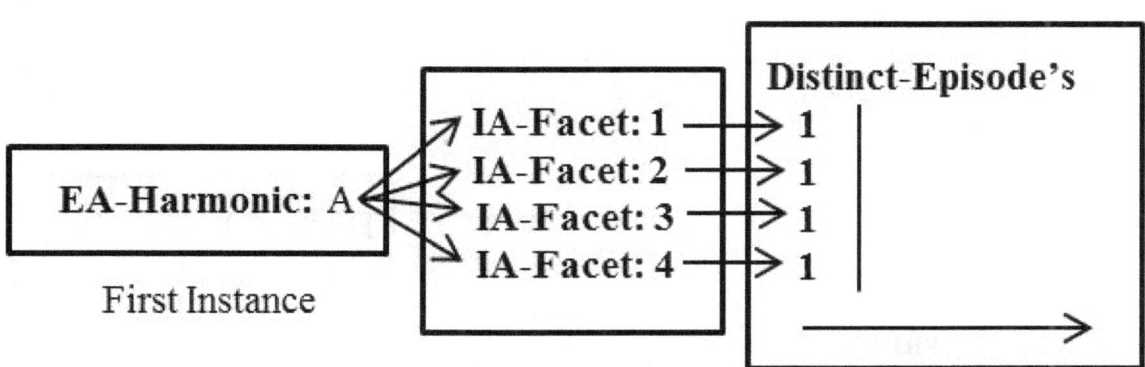

First Instance

Specifically, when a Tag-Cluster is encountered for the first time (i.e., the scenarios empty data-resources or when very young) both an Information-Assembly 'IA-Facet' and a Distinct-Episode 'DE-Event' are created in their respective data-resources as in the simplified depiction to the left.

Arrows from the EA-Harmonic to the four IA-Facets (for clarity only four are shown of potentially thousands) are intended to indicate the one EA-Harmonic-to-many-IA-Facets relationship.

Arrows from the four IA-Facets to Distinct-Episode ONE (1) are intended to indicate the replication and population of the four representative IA-Facets with a 'Time-Stamp' thereby creating a DE-Event (see the 101BM illustration Distinct-Episode data-resource depiction above as well).

However, subsequent occurrences both increments the intensity of an existing IA-Facet (by instilling Tags) and creates a new Distinct-Episode 'DE-Event'. For instance, as the 'fat-drops' keep landing are not only additional 'significantly-similar' EA-Harmonics created and 'same' IA-Facet intensities incremented but also additional Distinct-Episodes created.

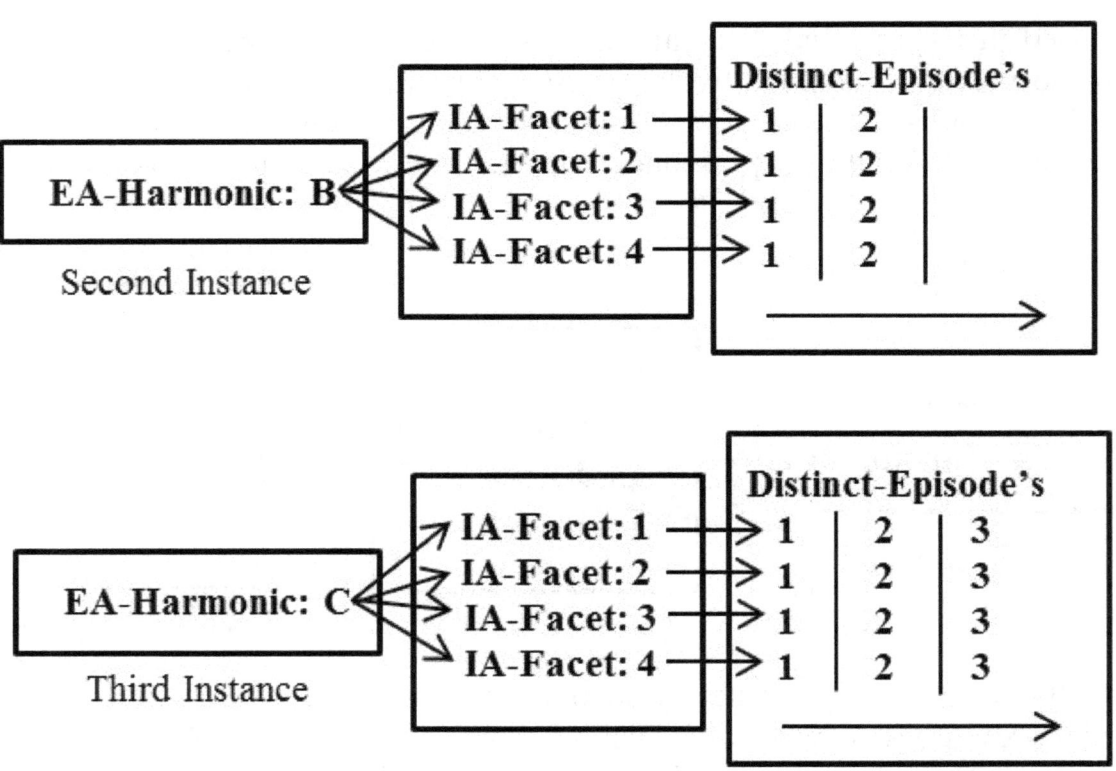

Each of these events as will be explained form part of the escalation process. The two illustrations above 'Second Instance' and 'Third Instance' represent the next two drops, which create two new EA-Harmonics (EA-Harmonic: B and EA-Harmonic: C). For explanatory purposes it is established the same four IA-Facets are involved: i.e., the next two fat drops landed on the same spot.

## EA-Harmonic Structure

Although harmonics were encountered in Body-Self, designed for one time communication of Tag Cluster configuration to Soma-Response, their formation was only temporary: After the harmonic message was conveyed, its potential dissipated. Although EA-Harmonics share a similar creation process, they are instead persistent.

Two variable Tag Cluster characteristics ultimately determine an EA-Harmonic's distinctive harmonic-signature: type and size. Recall 'type' relates to SLID (originating sensory impact location identifier) whereas 'size' relates to SLID intensity: the quantity of neurons simultaneously accepting bombardment at each SLID; therefore Tag-Cluster size due to the quantity of Tags.

> Stated differently, a Pooled-Assembly provides the fodder for the creation of a singular-frequency harmonic-signature.

When Pooled-Assembly is harmonized, the resulting EA-Harmonic not only represents a specific impression of the original Deluge event (its harmonic-signature) but also exhibits an energy potential, which mimics the intensity of all Pooled-Assembly Tag-Cluster participants.

## Harmonic Nature

It is useful to liken an EA-Harmonic to the 'impression' you get when you look at someone's hair.

In this explanation scenario, let's assume that you have a close friend who has never changed their hair style. As it is always the same their style is recognized and therefore is never talked about.

However, one day you meet up and there is a part on one side; the next day the sides are sheared short; the next day a blue streak runs conspicuously down the middle.

As these hair styles were **UN**-recognized, Cognitive-Alerts ensured Mind-Self is aware of the change. One can be sure that part of Figure-It-Out's Test-It outbounds included visual scrutiny and a few choice comments as well.

Point is that the hair style was accepted as a whole or harmonic. Even so, it is notable that the individual hairs, which are analogous to IA-Facets are still able to be independently assessed.

As with hair, which can have almost unlimited recognizable styles, so it is with EA-Harmonics, which capture very small incremental differences: thereby allowing for extremely granular current-event assessments against archived-old.

Figure-It-Out then diligently Brackets every compiled EA-Harmonic. This is similar to Body-Self Bracketing except the possible combinations and permutations of EA-Harmonics borders on the infinite: whereas Body-Self possibilities are limited by SLID quantity; merely tens of thousands.

Consequently, years of experience yield not only vastly diverse EA-Harmonics resulting from divergent activities (like sky-diving and spelunking) but also very harmonically similar ones due to similar activities (like writing with a pen or pencil): all however are joined to SLID granularity.

> EA-Harmonic similarity (and consequently difference) is identifiable by harmonic-frequency comparison

This variance provides a definitive cognitive leap from Body-Self's dichotomous (Yes/No) evaluation methodology because a third possibility is born: **significant-similarity**.

When a noxious something occurs, thus inspiring a Cognitive-Alert, Figure-It-Out is enabled to evaluate the inbound information (TEA-Dats) against Experiential-Accrual data-archives (Data-Matrix) to establish a 'familiarity-range' from 'vaguely-similar' to 'very-similar', then decide on its outbound action based on "close-enough": instead of on exact match.

EA-Harmonic's subtle frequency slicing allows for recognition of something "feeling almost the same…but not quite". Rapid identification of something not feeling 'quite-right' thereby could impel life-saving caution or avoidance.

Additionally, significantly-similar EA-Harmonic groups can have a comparative size (intensity), which can directly impact the intensity of outbound responses (there are other mitigating factors discussed below): generally then a large-potential will result in large-response (even knee-jerk reactions); whereas small, will not.

For instance, a second occurrence of a similar 'Hot-Fat' event would result in a much faster response as 'sensory-event' recognition (multiple 'significantly-similar' EA-Harmonics) coupled with intensified IA-Facets and an additional Distinct-Episode would enable response creation from archival resources without the need to go through the entire event again.

In other words, the next time the 'hot-fat' burning smell occurs it will be recognized from data-archives in its initial stages, which integrate new TEA-Dats with established Data-Matrix experiences therefore providing more honed and faster responses: such as, immediately turning down the heat. Thus experience thus plays a vital role in proactive cognitive processing.

> Harmonic inter-relationships are fundamental in this universe. They allow for discrimination of subtle 'wave' and 'particle' properties, which we rely on for physical world consistency 24/7.

For instance, the most basic elementary particles have discrete vibrational frequencies until joined with another, then another. An atom vibrates differently as a whole than its individual parts (electrons different than Protons), and so forth.

> Stated differently, fundamental parts 'coming together' form a new vibrational harmony. As changes in combined structure occur and complexity increases, so too do resulting amalgamations vibrate differently.

In other words, when smaller particles, Hydrogen and Oxygen atoms, become coalesced into an even more complex compound, water, the harmony of the whole morphs: thereby providing a new and unique harmonic-signature. Even mosquitoes rely on the unique harmonic vibration of expelled carbon-dioxide (a simple compound) to discover their human prey.

> Due to an EA-Harmonic being groomed from a Pooled-Assembly, which was assembled from myriads of variably intense Bombardment SLID's, the EA-Harmonic thus provides a direct physiological tie to the originating event.

Most have been exposed to a challenging or traumatic experience typically earmarked by high intensity and/or prolonged exposure. In these situations, a variety of substantially intense EA-Harmonics will result when processed by mechanisms yet to be introduced.

At some future time, if re-exposure to a same-or-similar traumatic event occurs, whether milder or not, it may evoke "feelings" as strong as an originating occurrence: this "linked-cascade" is directly tied to Experiential-Accruals ability to 'lash' EA-Harmonic events to real-world occurrences.

'Lashing' also serves to enable proactive recognition of recurring conditions well before they escalate to disastrous proportions. In other words, the created EA-Harmonic Brackets save us from having to relive the same trauma over-and-over: we get to Figure-It-Out or devise avoidance or escape strategies by evaluating experience significance and/or variance ranges.

## Recall Process

Interrelationships between EA-Harmonics and IA-Facets are being perpetuated by EI-Join and IE-Join (see 101BM illustration), which thus become crucial go-to join-resources for event recall or event-reconstitution.

> Indubitably one recalls event details:
> sometimes vaguely; sometimes in vivid detail

> Clearly recall capability is not a pinpoint competency but instead presents as a broadly variable gradient from rapid-and-easy through slow-and-arduous.

Also clear is recall speed, ease, vividness, detail quantity, etc. correlate to many interrelated factors: target-topic familiarity; allotted access time-frame; elapsed time from last access attempt; original and current target-topic interest; original and current Deluge intensity; Circadian rhythms (i.e., sleep/awake, etc.); and so on.

> Specifically, recall-capability dependencies align as a consequence of internal or external conditions: both when archived and retrieved. The importance of these factors will become clear as discussions proceed.

Additionally, the target-topic never perks into awareness alone but is instead accompanied by many loosely to tightly related tag-along variably intense feelings, details and cognitive-images. Notably as well, tag-alongs do not necessarily all present in one go but can phase-in gradually.

Foundationally, the very nature of discussing recall assumes the following: there is something to recall; this 'something' got there somehow; one has the desire or an impetus for recalling; and a mechanism is available to coordinate not only all the mined bits-and-pieces but also present findings from an ongoing parade of data-significance, which link to same and/or similar impression and/or cognitive images.

The main point being, whether vague, vivid or somewhere in-between, recall of the sensory-detail previously established in Distinct-Episodes, is always inspired by EA-Harmonics to which it is inseparably 'joined' via IA-Facets.

> Undeniably, a large contributor to our success as a species relies on our ability to recall and then proactively recognize (associate) and quickly compare complex events both transparently and consciously.

Certainly, if the same or closely similar event-group reoccurs one instantly recognizes the 'situation' (EA-Harmonics) and/or at least some closely similar aspects (Distinct-Episodes).

> What is strange for beginners is old-hat to veterans. This is because many cross-reference (EA //{IA{DE}}) Brackets established by Figure-It-Out, are being continuously recalled and assessed against new Bombardment. Incredibly, these continue to be enhanced by repetitive exposure, contributing to not only ever more precise recall but also better responses: that's why practice works.

Actually, only activities engaging CP-3, CP-2 and CP-1 can incite recall: CP-4 is relegated to collection only. Much discussion will elaborate why this is so: especially when CP-3 is discussed.

In those Cognitive-Pathways, recall additionally utilizes a Link to Visual-Scape, whose associated image or images will be perceived as spontaneously 'coming-to-mind'. CP-4 has no such Link as its data-strategies are designed for initialization of Data-Matrix 'EA-Harmonics', 'IA-Facets' and Distinct-Episode 'DE-Events' only.

---

> Substantial individual differences in spontaneous recall capability are obvious

Why is such dramatic recall variance the case? Why do some seem to have extremely good detailed recall, whereas others not so much? Why are event aspects reported so differently between people? Why is it that all recall is not consistent for all people regardless of situation?

> Globally speaking, data-archives and therefore recall rely on neural capacities and experiential opportunities. Ultimately though in restrictive environments, a whole set of limiting beliefs become the controllers, which deny Figure-It-Out full reign to fulfill its calling: thereby coming full circle to limit passion and therefore EA-Harmonic access

Following CP-4 discussions will begin to illuminate implications of diminishing any of the fundamental data-retrieval provisioners.

> I have a friend whose recall capability is quite different than mine. He can instantly retrieve copious granular detail. He can recite date, time, weather and numerous minutiae attached to an event, for which I have no immediate recollection.

Interestingly though, there are times, if enough particulars are presented, my recall will spontaneously spark into existence. There have been many occasions when someone's event descriptions not only enabled my factual recall but also simultaneously evoked some impression or feeling coupled with a visual memory, all which were somehow tethered to the recall.

Such occurrences normally result in my exclaiming "Oh Yah" or "I remember now", at which point I begin verbalizing my excited factual recollection while referencing the changing pictures and tumbling emotions and facts in my head. This type of prompted recall is common for most, if not all, people. How does this work?

I also notice when a person queries some aspect of a story I have shared, more-often-than-not, their questions provide memory prods stimulating my own dramatic to diffuse additional recall.

What mechanism is at work allowing recall of a personal experience to be stimulated? As well, some aspects of the information I retrieve are only vaguely similar to the focal query and contain a broad spread of likenesses.

Why is this so? Why and how does such a variant capability exist between people in the first place?

## Information-Assembly

Recall assumes two fundamental pre-requisites: a mechanism must be functioning, which is capable of discretely instilling (Bracketing) sensory-information into data-resources; and non-volatile neural-facilities must be available permitting long-term granular storage.

Notably, if data-events (Tag-Clusters) were not either able to be suitably Bracketed and/or could not be effectively archived, recall would be compromised or simply not possible. Stated more succinctly: storage first; retrieval second.

*Variances in 'pre-requisite' effectiveness thus raise diverse proficiencies between people*

When compared to Body-Self, Mind-Self has substantially broader requirements. Critically, mechanisms must be available to actively and accurately data-archive not only a massive array of Deluge combination possibilities but also individual sensory-events.

Only by so doing is Mind-Self enabled to effectively Figure-It-Out: especially when it comes to maximizing safety and survival by comparative-recognition assessment.

*Multi-linking capability is unique to humans:
It profoundly sets us apart from other mammals*

Notably, to accomplish the expanded cognitive data-archive mandate requires substantial enhancements. Generally, a shift must occur from Body-Self uni-dimensional Brackets to Mind-Self inter-relational data-matrixes.

Specifically, data-elements must be recorded in such a way to facilitate multi-comparative analyses, such as: how often the event has occurred (frequency); does it occur sporadically or regularly (rate); how many incidents (quantity); when did individual event(s) occur – recently or long ago (temporal); what are key companion events - significant to permit avoidance of potentially dangerous situations (Figure-It-Out); likelihood of reoccurrence (evaluation); and many etcetera's.

**Mind-Self's paramount proactive is to avoid trouble in the first place**

Information-Assembly is comprised of IA-Facet data-elements, which perform as not only pivotal SLID placeholders but also an activity-to-date monitor or usage gauges. It is Distinct-Episode 'DE-Events', which are responsible for storehousing the individual SLID characteristics (IA-Facets) of individual Bombardment-events though.

> This strategy propels significant ramifications. Critically, IA-Facets are both created and their intensity incremented only by SLID event-horizon activity.

In other words, only accepted sensory events can initialize and/or augment an IA-Event. Resultantly, there can be no IA-Facets for missing SLID locations: such as, when born deaf or without a limb. Consequently, DE-Events will also not be created. In such a situation 'experience' archives will remain null and therefore one would remain unaware of their possible contribution.

> Even though EA-Harmonics remain "intensity-stable", IA-Facets do not as their intensity is continually incremented by bombardment, which impacts their SLID and therefore Tag-Cluster counterparts.

In this way IA-Facets provide an accurate gauge of specific event-horizon activity-to-date. This is critically important for experientially-driven proactive capability: Most used means most experience and therefore greater reliability; whereas minimally utilized means the opposite.

IA-Facets instantaneously provide a great usage guide, without which most event recall would be without variance and therefore a not useful bland. Complimentary to IA-Facet indicators, event specifics, housed within the IA-Facet joined Distinct-Episode data-archive, take proactive capability to a much improved level.

**Distinct-Episode 'DE-Events'**

> To exactly fulfill Body-Self Cognitive-Alert 'assistance' demands, requires Figure-It-Out to provide both upgraded data-archives and broader-scope processes, than needed for Body-Self recognition endeavours.

Specifically, Data-Matrix must permit deeper event granularity by configuring Distinct-Episodes to additionally not only storehouse DE-Events but also tie them to appropriate IA-Facets. Also, to fulfill enhanced cognitive significantly-similar recall requirements, retrieval and analysis processing capabilities must be substantially augmented.

Inseparably linked to a corresponding IA-Facet and EA-Harmonic via IE-Join, DE-Events discretely preserve each Tag-Cluster occurrence within the Distinct-Episode data-repository. As IA-Facets are also integrally joined to appropriate EA-Harmonics this makes possible not only reconstitution of an originating event but also the cascading to other events when so required by Figure-It-Out.

The DE-Event strategy is very different than for Body-Self Brackets, which much more basically only expand a Brackets information base without regard to retention of individual occurrences. Figure-It-Outs expanded purpose maintains one same-frequency Tag-Cluster event from another.

> In other words, DE-Event creation enables subtle discrimination of one Tag-Cluster occurrence (stored as a Distinct-Episode 'DE-Event') from another. This is a major proactive enhancement as will be evidenced throughout discussions.

Distinct-Episode methodology is pivotal in assisting recapture of individual events. DE-Events are fundamental for selective comparative recall of global events, such as: reading a familiar poem for the fourth time; watching a favorite movie for the fifth time; going for a walk and being aware the route is familiar. To create Distinct-Episode DE-Events from Tag-Clusters resultantly requires a temporal ingredient as the discriminator.

---

## Temporal-Clustering

Incredibly, data preservation complexity has taken a giant leap from Body-Self's requirements, where Bracketing was necessary for much less demanding dichotomous recognition purposes: either yes, recognized; or no, not recognized.

The primary Bracketing / Tag-Cluster accrual requisite, based on discussions above, proposed a dual thrust: Join an individual Tag-Cluster event to its homogeneous IA-Facet Bracket; and discretely maintain each occurrence as a DE-Event within a discrete data-resource.

How is this achievable?

Biological time-clocks or Circadian rhythms are a fascinating area of study. Although beyond the scope of this book, the pervasiveness of these rhythms across species is remarkable.

Endogenous oscillations have not only been observed and documented in "higher" species but also in fungi and cyanobacteria; the bacteria considered responsible for converting the planet's atmosphere to Oxygen sufficient, thereby promoting life as we know it. A definite THANK YOU to them!

Additionally, there are particular external events, coined Zeitgebers, which are responsible for modulating organism biological rhythms: such as, night/day, lunar and seasonal cycles, etc.

"Temporal-Clustering" is fulfilled then by maintaining Tag-Cluster's with an additional physiologically provided endogenous key or harmonic augmentation I call "Time-Stamp". The key requisite for this capability is not only identifiable but also unshakable; it functions regardless of awake-state or environmental conditions.

Every Tag-Cluster gets associated to its frequency-matched Information Assembly 'IA-Facet' Bracket. However, Figure-It-Out upgrades basic Bracketing for selected Tag-Clusters by instilling a Time-Stamp, which maps to the relative (biological) time of occurrence. This process thereby uniquely redefines a Tag-Cluster as a DE-Event within the Distinct-Episode data-resource.

Time-Stamp provides one necessary foundation for cognitive complexity because Distinct-Episodes provide two simultaneous properties: they are both a member of their frequency-matched IA-Facet and individually identifiable or sovereign. This duality feature is unique when compared to Body-Self Bracketed Tag-Clusters, in that Pooled-Assembly Tag-Clusters (now Distinct-Episodes) don't necessarily get mixed or blended into one large, combined, homogenous group.

Visualize the Temporal-Clustering Bracket structure by considering the following.

In front of you there is a huge tile mosaic (Information-Assembly). Its bulk is composed of closely positioned colored tiles of various sizes (IA-Facet Brackets), which do not overlap other tiles (frequency specific).

> Upon closer inspection however, evident is each IA-Facet tile has either one or many smaller tiles (DE-Events) of the same color, whose sizes and shapes vary subtly to dramatically one from the next, forming a second layer covering its surface. Additionally, the quantity of DE-Events layered on different IA-Facet tiles varies dramatically.

This model is workable as it provides several useful constructs supporting retrieval. The size of an IA-Facet tile (an IA-Facet Bracket) within the overall mosaic (all Information-Assembly Brackets) indicates its relative usage or experience-gradient.

The quantity of differently shaped member-tiles (representing Distinct-Episodes) layering a single IA-Facet indicates not only the quantity of occurrences but also relative event frequency. Additionally, DE-Event size (indicating originating Tag quantity) defines a single DE-Events relative activity-gradient in relation to its IA-Facet.

Additionally, the ability to dig for not only similar but temporally different events or Distinct-Episodes (i.e., this is what happened the time before last) but also divergent event associated detail (here's what else happened at the same time) is available when EA-Harmonic activation inspires Distinct-Episode retrieval via IA-Facet ferreting.

Temporal-Clustering methodology then ensures one Tag-Cluster data-set is not mushed-in with a previous Tag-Cluster occurrence when deemed significantly different by the appropriate evaluating mechanism.

If variances were ignored, it would make for very vanilla or non-specific recall. Notably, excluding granular variances could mask trouble. After all, granular, not general, assessment and evaluation was the purpose of the Cognitive-Alert request for Mind-Self assistance in the first place.

## Questioning

Most have either witnessed an accident or been requested to recant some vacation adventure. Regardless, there are always easily recalled and articulated memories, which actually turn out to be the higher intensity ones. Invariably though, there are also memories only retrievable or accessible by questioning: i.e., the lower intensity ones.

> In both cases questioning engages Figure-It-Out to access Information-Assembly IA-Facet Distinct-Episodes by utilizing EA-Harmonics as a guide. Under questioning, one remembers surprising details because, as will be revealed, questioning provides a sensory impetus and EA-Harmonic impetus.

Spontaneous retrieval of one or more "lost" nuggets can even be inspirational. This is an incredibly excellent feature because data-resource access not only provides immediate answers but also can sustain long term access if a located EA-Harmonic is sufficiently intense: these are the "Ah-ha" moments. More on this and associated processes when Cognitive-Pathway Three is discussed.

## Hypnosis

Accessing "unconscious-shards" as this author prefers to think of them is a purview of the Hypnotherapist inducing a state of relaxation called Hypnosis.

This professional deploys a methodology utilizing specialized questioning techniques. These actually prompt EA-Harmonics to retrieve and potentially accumulate vague 'shards' (Distinct-Episodes) into larger bundles. (This will be discussed in detail during CP-3 explanations).

> By directed suggestions many thousands of disparate Distinct-Episodes can be amalgamated so at least temporary recall is affected.

Session recall is normally disjointed though because retrieved fragments are not being processed from the "normal" Cognitive-Pathway channels but are being prompted into awareness relatively randomly.

> In other words, they "surfaced" without connection to a sensory originating emotional source (EA-Harmonic) and therefore present only fragmented, low intensity bits (Distinct-Episodes) of an experience.

## Dreaming

Figure-It-Out is hard at work while in the deep rest / recovery sleep state. Its reconciliation function attempts to re-align, Filter and Slot, the daily plethora of Information-Assembly, Experiential-Accrual and/or visually linked Brackets by associating related or similar attributes.

> During its maintenance processing, it stirs up huge quantities of data-elements, which Figure-It-Out tries to reconcile within its virtual processing neural-arena.

Dreams are also not easily remembered as they do not spawn from inter-related sensory origins but rather from the attempt to parse Bracketed data-elements. This process though can touch on some fairly poignant opposites, which can result in spectacular "dream-visions".

---

## CP-4: Data-Matrix

This section investigates Cognitive-Pathway Four (CP-4) methodologies and functions. The extended neural-resources mentioned above not only fulfill current and future data-repository 'storage-space' requirements but also provision the processing muscle needed to manage progressively complex 'data-acquisition' and 'data-retrieval' tasks.

> As stated earlier CP-4 serves as a front-line initiator responsible for installing first encounter data-elements into Data-Matrix data-resources. As this 'priming' step is crucial for future discussions, let's start at birth, assume blank data-resource slates and investigate methodologies and considerations behind data-archive creation and population.

Notably, Bombardment sensory-events, Soma or Cognitive, are negligibly recognized by a new-born: Additionally, physical response capabilities are also lacking.

> Importantly, these competencies are not missing but simply wanting enabling 'fodder': i.e., archived referenceable data-elements needed for recognition and response are simply not yet available in 'sufficient' quantities.

In other words, sensory gatherers are working fine as are processing methodologies: however, without retrievable archived data-elements against which to evaluate and compare current input, recognition is simply not possible.

> Not available by genetic implantation, data-element accumulation is instead a gradual process of amassing or data-archiving Deluge sensory-unknowns from both Soma and Visual-Sensors.

Only by utilizing genetically provisioned end-to-end sensory mechanisms however (acceptance/processing/data-resources) can Brackets become populated and expand to usable proportions: significantly notable though, (double underlined and bold) only to magnitudes correlated with exposure or experience.

Critical to remember is "experiential-magnitude" determines ones "familiarity-range": from novice-to-expert. Consequently, Force-of-Habit updates its "recognition-principle" to: storage first; retrieval second; comparison third; recognition fourth; response fifth. Notably recognition is a complex process: It will be elaborated upon throughout discussions.

> Remember… Mind-Self is only apprised (via Cognitive-Alert) of Bombardment, which is not able to be reconciled by Body-Self

This being stated, ostensibly all bombardment events are new at birth and thus unrecognized by Body-Self. Consequently, Cognitive-Alerts were absolutely raised for countless numbers (if not all) new Body-Self sensory-accepted Bombardment during formative years.

Although Cognitive-Alert generation continues throughout life as one engages in new activities, one's first few years of life are the most active due to creating and/or populating myriads of empty Soma and Cognitive data-resources.

> Interestingly, even Body-Self issued Survival Alerts by Threat-Check would absolutely be cognitively assessed as low intensity because minimal Data-Matrix Brackets existed for Figure-It-Out to cross-evaluate and thereby potentially escalate status.

Stated differently, to emphasise and extend understanding of the critical cooperation between Body-Self and Mind-Self data-resource population, if a Body-Self Deluge event is new for it; it would also be new (via Cognitive-Alert) for Cognitive-Self as well. This is important because it means both 'selves' capture every new Bombardment event on an ongoing basis throughout life: albeit in different forms (to be discussed at length).

Notably, myriads of sensory-events arrive either once (like a stranger admiring ones baby) on the cognitive neural-scape or perhaps a few times; whereas others reoccur (like being held, fed, etc.). Event occurrence frequency is significant because new sensory inspiration is necessary for Cognitive-Alert issuance; otherwise it will be recognized and handled by Body-Self, which will never again issue another Cognitive-Alert for this type of incidence.

> Therefore, in the case of a minimal occurrence, only a single Cognitive-Alert, providing very few Tag-Clusters to cognitive-resources, would have been issued, which would have been shunted to CP-5 due to its nominal intensity.

Significantly in more intense cases, except when "Cool" or CP-5 was allocated, CP-4 would have been initiated. Resultantly, CP-4 mechanisms would fulfill Data-Matrix Component mandate by creating embryonic Experiential-Accrual, Information-Assembly and Distinct-Episode Brackets as well as EI-and-IE joins.

> Consequently, in almost any new-event situation, CP-4 is the Cognitive-Pathway chosen to initialize data-resources.

'Tepid' situations are inherently low intensity because escalation to higher intensity also requires recognition, which is unavailable with 'new': at least when new originates with Body-Self.

> However as will be soon revealed, this is not necessarily the situation for other Cognitive processes to come.

Even though these minimal CP-4 Bracket fragments could in no way be construed as involving consciousness, their archiving is absolutely necessary to evolve higher cognitive recall processes.

Figure-It-Out is designed to fetch the smallest same and/or "significantly-similar" data-elements during a time of Body-Self need (Cognitive-Alert). This expanded mode of cognitive-retrieval is critical to ensure a driving EA-Harmonic "familiarity-sense" remains synchronised to related Distinct-Episodes.

> CP-4 then embeds the sensory data-substrate or data building-blocks for passion, greater knowledge and deeper understanding: this is where it starts

CP-4 contribution pervades our lifetime whether Cognitive-Alerts are provided by random Deluge or by Figure-It-Out seeking resolutions by using Test-Its to tailor sensory-feedback requests (discussed below). All storage activity is for one purpose: to be able to use data-archives as a reference to evaluate 'new' or inbound data to better survive. Recall effectiveness is therefore life critical.

**Recall-Cascading**

The arrangement of one EA-Harmonic (EA) to many IA-Facets (IAs) to many Distinct-Episodes (DEs) provides for another amazing, uniquely human capability I call "Recall-Cascading".

This ability is enabled because of three convergent conditions. Firstly, a single EA-Harmonic is not globally joined willy-nilly to all Information-Assembly Distinct-Episodes but only to those Distinct-Episodes (Tag-Clusters) which were captured within the original Pooled Assembly, which was utilized to create it.

> Secondly, a single Distinct-Episode can be joined via IE-Join to IA-Facets of other EA-Harmonics.

Thirdly, due to a finite number of sensory locations (SLIDs), different Pooled-Assemblies invariably contain many same Tag-Clusters. This extrapolates into multitudes of different EA-Harmonics being joined to the same Information-Assembly IA-Facets; albeit to different Distinct-Episodes.

## Retrieval-Bundle

This 'single-EA-to-many-IAs-to-many-DEs' condition (EA><{IA{DE}}) means many different EA's are attached to Distinct-Episodes within same as well as different Information-Assembly IA-Facet Brackets. This arrangement results in one EA-Harmonic having the potential to cascade to other EA-Harmonics when both are joined to the same IA-Facet: although to different Distinct-Episodes. This provisions a vast interlaced network.

> Important to also keep in mind is retrieval methodologies look for significantly-similar as well as same.

In other words, EA-Harmonic inspired recapture mechanisms are able to retrieve a range of closely similar EA's and IA's not just the identical harmonic or frequency, respectively. Similar EA's can additionally cascade across their associated IA's thereby providing a large "Retrieval-Bundle". In this way an enhanced range can be made available from which Figure-It-Out can appraise what is applicable to a situation (Filter and Slot) and what is not.

> In order to Figure-It-Out then, we are enabled to select from a 'scoop' of similar data, which provides superior depth and/or range to a new 'significantly-similar' initiating event. This is vastly more comprehensive than Body-Self simpler dichotomous 'recognition'

Incredibly, because some Distinct-Episodes are attached via IE-Join to the same IA-Facet but to different EA's which are additionally attached to closely similar Distinct-Episodes these thereby also cascade or drag-along additional emotional (EA) textures.

> One repercussion, when the cascading is too great is feeling overwhelmed. This equates to an oversized and poorly defined frequency pool of feelings (EA's) and IA details (DE's), which cannot be fully reconciled.

## Cognitive-Impetus

When one truly wants to do something, why is it easier and performance better than if not inspired? The abbreviated answer: because not only does passion/engagement/interest 'turn-on' substantially more EA-Harmonics but also associated access to IA-Facets and therefore Distinct-Episodes is tremendously expanded thereby providing more cross-referenceable data-elements for Solutioning.

Digging deeper into causality reveals IA-Facet 'tremendously expanded' (above) is directly enabled when passionate because larger quantities of EA-Harmonics are engaged: now known to be the pivotal drivers to access Information-Assembly and Distinct-Episodes.

> Resultantly, more EA-Harmonics inspire retrieval of larger quantities of Distinct-Episodes and thus amass a substantially larger Retrieval-Bundle than 'Ho-Hum' endeavors. Resultantly, "passion-quests" are not only easier-to-do but also result in improved task performance.

Alternately, when you don't want to do something, access to Distinct-Episodes is much less effective because one is attempting to drive access using ingenuine or contrived 'feelings'. A non-specific EA-Harmonic driver, rather than being a bright focussed spotlight is instead like a dim diffused glow: thereby resulting in vague or minimal IA-Facet retrieval at best.

> In other words, sparse and/or non-specific EA-Harmonic // IA-Facet connections result in minimal Distinct-Episode retrieval: thus the non-preferred task is hard-to-do.

A Pooled Assembly is formed from sensory reception, from which Cognitive Manipulation creates one EA-Harmonic plus many IA-Facets plus many Distinct-Episodes.

> Inexorably then, EA-Harmonics are sensory experience amalgams, sensory impressions or 'feelings', which provide pivotal recall impetus for not only details (Distinct-Episodes) but also 'images' (Visual-Scape)

The pre-emptive instigator, when intent on Figuring-It-Out, is always a want, a desire, a sense, a need or a similar nudging spark. In other words, 'feelings' are the spearhead for recall: a feeling first; particulars second.

> Only after the 'driver' starts the process does Figure-It-Out proceed to source Information-Assembly and/or access Visual-Scape links.

It is no wonder a well prepared 'Pep-Talk' tied to common team goals can 'psych' members into action. It taps into conglomerates of feelings or EA-Harmonics, which cascade to not only direct specific detail (Distinct-Episodes) recall but also access related EA-Harmonics, which elicit associated feelings: sometimes to a fever-pitch.

Notably then, Information-Assembly event details do not articulate independently. Inseparably 'Joined' is an EA-Harmonic feeling, ranging from mild to intense, which thus provides the context for Distinct-Episode event specific recall.

## Why would this be so?

The answer will incorporate multiple concepts to be discussed throughout explanations of Cognitive-Pathways. Although the 'Join' relationship between Experiential-Accrual and Information-Assembly as well as Visual-Scape "Linking" (addressed in CP-3 when it first manifests) will continue to be foundational, many other exciting ingredients will be introduced.

---

## DE-Notify

DE-Notify is the next CP-4 Component on the 'Cognitive Pathways Model' depiction. Although shown separately for illustration purposes, it is really a Data-Matrix outbound function charged with apprising Continuity-Controller of Distinct-Episode creation.

> Additionally, it may appear separate DE-Notify processes are available for each Cognitive-Pathway on the illustration: however, only one exists

Comparative evaluation of inbound Tag-Clusters to just previous Tag-Clusters (now archived as Distinct-Episodes), for either repetition or significantly-similar event resemblance is vital as a 'match' could very well indicate a treat is brewing.

If a 'match' is assessed, the replicated Tag-Clusters are inserted into Continuity-Controller's "CC-Match" hopper-resource, thereby providing additional fodder, which can be evaluated by Continuity-Controller to regulate intensity and thus Cognitive-Pathway determination.

Notably, greater intensity requires not only greater processing-resources for resolution but also engagement of methodologies to achieve escalation. When Continuity-Controller determines escalation is necessary, it directs the intensified data-flow to a Cognitive-Pathway with a "threshold-range" capable of managing demands.

Without the ability to recognize a noxious Bombardment as repeating, survival would be compromised as everything would 'seem' a first-time occurrence to Continuity-Controller: i.e., one would simply stand in front of the hot-fat-spitting frying pan and become severely burned.

Fortunately, this is not the case as Continuity-Controller has the capability to progressively evaluate and thereby not only recognize repetition but also escalate and de-escalate relevance before engaging an appropriate Cognitive-Pathway.

Notification is accomplished in two steps. First, each Tag-Cluster (employed to create an IA-Facet) is duplicated: this is necessary to ensure uninterrupted data-flow to both TI-IN and Template-Component (future discussions). Second, replicants are deposited into Continuity-Controller's CC-Match data-resource.

Think of CC-Match as a "conveyor-resource" with regularly partitioned compartments. Its loading-point 'hopper' receives Tag-Cluster replicant deposits from DE-Notify. Continuity-Controller cross-evaluates the entire length of CC-Match conveyor contents to a current Bombardment Tag-Cluster. When a match occurs it is snatched from the target conveyor section and processed: unmatched data-elements simply dissipate.

You may have correctly assumed a Tag-Cluster imbedded SLID frequency is the basis for comparison. Recall SLIDs are the genetic foundation upon which Body-Self Deluge recognition and therefore similarity is based: i.e., close frequencies are potential matches; whereas disparate frequencies are not.

As CC-Match is adapted for managing a 'normal' flow of occurrences, its neural reserves are limited: i.e., accommodating for a baseline quantity of 'matches' only.

Due to restricted neural space as well as continual deposit pressure by DE-Notify (especially in high-bombardment conditions), Tag-Clusters, which either result in overflow or are unmatched simply drop off the 'conveyor'.

This methodology serves to keep CC-Match comparatives within a narrow few second time band: thereby ensuring escalation will not happen for similar events occurring days apart.

## Figure-It-Out Solutioning Introduction

> Persistently striving to uncover 'What-it's-all-about' by resolutely stirring Bombardment-Sphere objects and events to instigate sensory feedback, characterizes Figure-It-Out Test-It to a 'T'

Each person exists inside their very own continually shifting "Bombardment-Sphere". Every millisecond Deluge presents chaos to our event-horizon, whose front-line sensors muster a series of incredible capabilities designed to handle immense quantities of impacts.

> Although one has little direct control over bombardment, one is enabled to purposefully design circumstances, which can amend Deluge arrival at the sensors.

For instance, by choosing either physical location within our Bombardment-Sphere (getting out of the sun) or pre-filtering modifiers (sunglasses / sunscreen) one can intercede: thereby altering bombardment influence. Such 'choosing' epitomises Figure-It-Out's relentless self-stated mandate.

> Several following sections will present new and exciting building-blocks and concepts in order to define 'The-Way-We-Work' as a cognitive species: hang-in-there as the lengthened journey will be well rewarded by greatly expanded understanding, which will in turn inspire more useful personal choices

Whether inspired by potentially damaging bombardment or by discerning cognitive processes, Figure-It-Out continually quests for 'The-Ways' to resolve incongruities.

> In this paradigm, 'The-Ways' are represented by the 'It' in Figure-It-Out. Whether operating transparently or overtly (in the background or with consciousness), Figure-It-Out ceaselessly strives to fulfill its mandate - to do what it is designed to do - Figure-It-Out by solving Puzzles.

Prior to detailing Figure-It-Out structures and processes a review and expansion of previously established foundational concepts or 'underpinnings' will provide a launching platform for the many disclosures still to come.

## Underpinnings

Soma and Visual sensor accepted data is the initial provisioner for all data-archive content. Sensors specifically exist to monitor and report: i.e., each monitor its own unique Bombardment frequency range and reports on event-horizon accepted Deluge conditions. Literally, without sensors there would be no "living-experiences": only nothingness.

Excellent detection systems though would have no use without "data-resolution" also being possible. In other words, when sensors accept noxious bombardment, methodologies need to be available to 'DO' something about them: i.e., avoid, mollify and/or rectify.

> Although not previously referred to as such, a 'noxious Soma-Sensory event' (about a three millisecond snippet) propagates a substantial 'informant' data-stream.

It is formed of recognized and/or unrecognized high-intensity bombardment "data-elements" from hundreds if not thousands of diverse Soma-Sensor locations. Within each data-element is imbedded not only a discrete location identifier (SLID) but also a specific measure of sensory activity or intensity: these distinguish or characterize each in relation to a single event.

> Sensory capture and precise delivery methodologies ensure higher processes are kept apprised of not only bombardment locations but also bombardment intensities

Ultimately, Event-horizon informant notifications dump into the common neural transmission channel to arrive at various Body-Self Component processors. Processors in turn utilize specialized methodologies to determine those within and those outside their acceptable parameters.

As a survival-level threat might be brewing, rapid assessment is always critical. When potential danger is detected, appropriate data-elements get earmarked for special treatment (i.e. dispatched to Cognitive-Alert): if not, they get handled by Soma-Self.

Sensors do not then function just as passive observers. Instead they operate as informants to "up-line" mechanisms, whose protocols can take action to 'normalize' impacting Deluge-conditions.

> When referring to sensors however, there is a complication - two vastly different types exist: Soma-Sensors and Cognitive-Sensors (or Visual-Sensors).

Although they both receive bombardment, reception media and processing protocols are worlds apart. Soma-Sensor informants must actually sustain impact and then energy convert individually accepted events before spitting their data into communication channels.

Cognitive-Sensors on the other hand (although in the strictest sense they too must receive photon impacts), enable pro-activity: due to enhanced Deluge acceptance natures, sensory apparatus and processing capabilities. For instance, Cognitive-Sensors are comprised of cognitive neural-mass, which significantly reduces the transmission, connection, collection and translation time.

Additionally, Cognitive-Sensors are able to contribute information before physical impact because speed-of-light is much, much faster than 'physical' object movements. This speed variance fodders cognitive processors with many sequenced snapshots or "Frame-snippets'" of an incoming something, thereby providing 'time' for "processor-teams" to evaluate and suggest 'DO' action based on approach assessments rather than on impact.

> In other words, Soma-Sensors need a baseball to actually impact before reacting; whereas Visual-Sensors provide approach information. 'Frame-snippet' capability thereby enables Figure-It-Out to strategize 'DO': i.e., pro-actively avoid, mollify and/or rectify

---

## Event-Condition

We are now aware there is a fundamental initializer of all that follows: an accepted "Deluge-Event". It is formed of a few-millisecond 'packet' of 'Soma-sensory-data'.

A 'packet' is comprised of variable quantities of data-elements (Tags) from potentially tens-of-thousands of Soma sites. Each data-element or 'Tag', within a 'packet' is uniquely identifiable by an intrinsic frequency: i.e., Sensory-Location-IDentifier or SLID. As a SLID forever defines individual 'Tag' origin, it thus establishes the first of two immutable 'Tag' characteristics.

> During Component 'Filtering-and-Slotting' manipulations, Tags get assembled into frequency identical SLID groups called Tag-Clusters. Highly variable describes not only Tag-Cluster mix (SLIDs within the 'packet') but also the quantities of Tags within each Tag-Cluster.

Responsible is the changeability in bombardment potency and focus, which results in proportionately variable quantities of not only SLID activations (which will become Tag-Clusters) but also instigated SLID neural-receptors (Tags).

In that 'Tags' are the base building-block whose quantity within a Tag-Cluster quantifies the original Deluge potency at a SLID site, it thus provides the second immutable characteristic: 'Intensity'.

> In other words, facing the early morning sun in a skimpy bathing suit on a clear summer day will not involve as many receptors as facing the sun at high noon: due to the significant difference in bombardment potency. In both cases however, ones shaded 'back' will only receive minimal impacts from reflection and therefore involve far fewer neural-receptors.

Resultantly, Tag-Clusters formed from ones 'front' SLIDs will contain not only significantly greater quantities of 'Tags' but also the 'front' will provide far more Tag-Clusters as the focus and potency far exceeded 'the back'.

> Although Tag-Clusters work well for Body-Self's limited competencies, individually they are not sufficient for Mind-Self to determine superior proactive suggestions or 'best-attempts". Fortunately, multiple methodologies are available to fulfill expanded needs.

Firstly, Mind-Self is always dealing with higher intensity Body-Self situations: i.e., those Soma-Self was unable to handle (thus a Cognitive-Alert).

Next, Mind-Self requires huge neural resources to not only provide multiple archive data-resources but also focus processing on the target event: especially for retrieving essential supporting information. Additionally, to filter, slot and incorporate appropriate aspects of Cognitive-Sensor data (VLID's) into the data-stream requires enormously sophisticated neural capacity.

Finally, Mind-Self is charged to not only Figure-It-Out by evaluating and incorporating (previously populated) data-archives but also tailor beneficial outbound action suggestions or "Test-Its".

Figure-It-Out simply cannot rely solely on segregated Tag-Clusters to perform Solutioning because they do not provide the 'big-picture'. A much more comprehensive scope is needed: one which incorporates an entire occurrence or at least a representative 'scoop' of it. Fortuitously, Figure-It-Out has its own 'currency': an "Event-Condition".

To support resolution and not sustain chaos, an Event-Condition must of necessity be derived from the same few-millisecond time-slice within which Tag-Clusters were enveloped into a Pooled-Assembly. Recall from previous discussions this coordination (Pooling) was critical in order to maintain sensory-event integrity.

> Data-Matrix executed a pivotal task when it created an EA-Harmonic from the coalescence of the frequencies of all Tag-Cluster constituents of a Pooled-Assembly. By so doing each EA-Harmonic became not only the harmonic representation of a sensory-event but also its Event-Condition.

---

Before discussing how Event-Condition's enable extreme human cognitive proficiencies though, a few more pieces of the Figure-It-Out mosaic require explanation: such as how constructs expanded in the 'The-Ways Solutioning' illustration provide fulfillment of one's remarkable capability to "Solution". As the illustration (next page) will be referred to fairly often, bookmarking the page will be advantageous.

> Spawning from the stored cognitive amalgam of experiences, Mind-Self with its Modules and Components operating in concert with Cognitive-Pathways, ultimately drive living choices: life-style, self-worth, beliefs, points-of-view, and so much more

---

**T I-Inbound Component**

Even though the **TI-Inbound** (TI-IN) and **TI-Outbound** (TI-OUT) Components may appear unremarkable on the **The-Ways: Solutioning** illustration (opposite), they are pivotal to receiving (inbound) and sending (outbound).

## *WayBetter* Your L.I.F.E$^2$.: **Mind-Self**

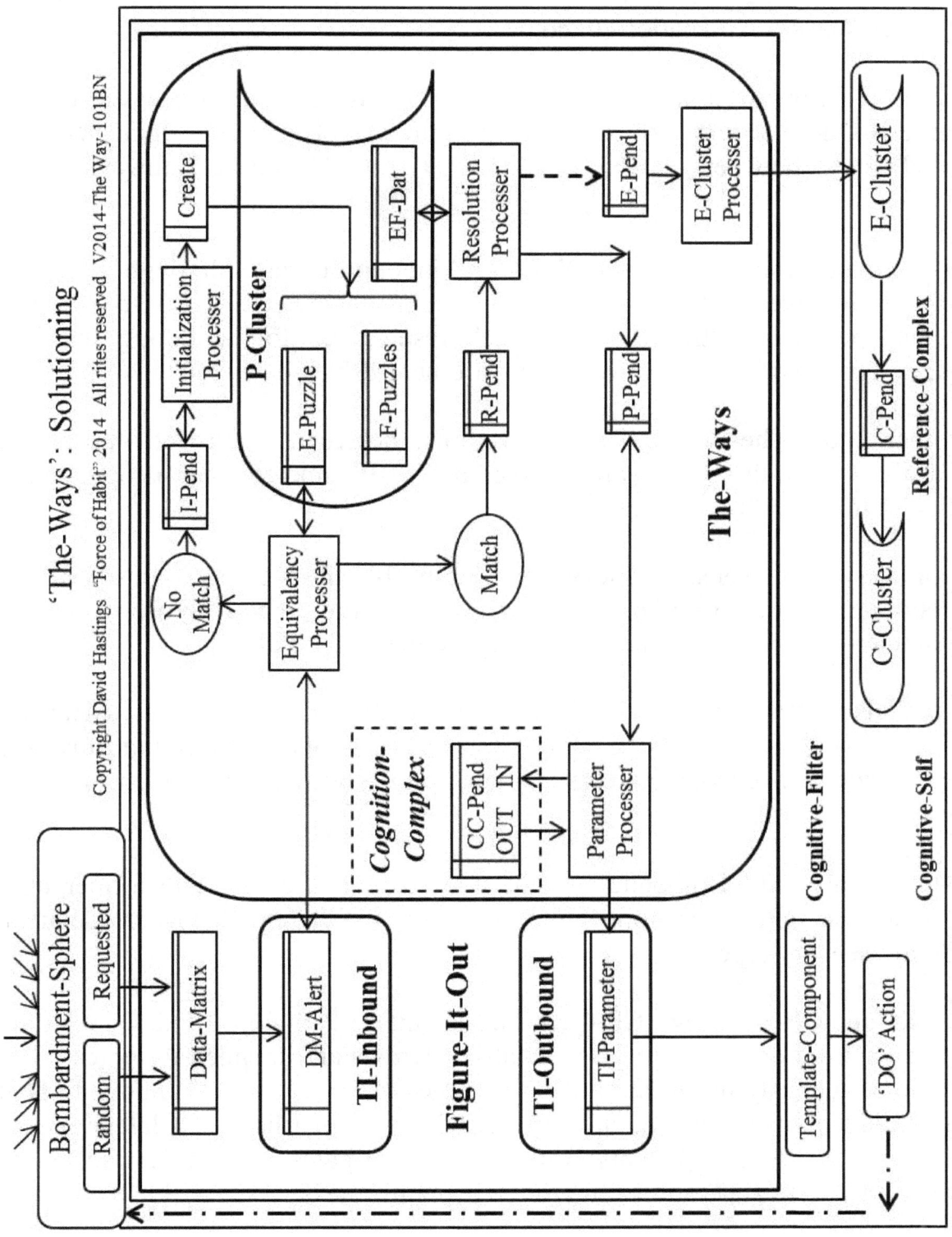

The 'TI' preface is used to reference Test-Its, as they will always be the outcome of traversing 'The-Ways': explanations to come.

> Cognitive-Pathway journeys will expose the many methodologies enabling Figure-It-Out to accomplish Solutioning or finding "The-Ways": indicated by the dotted lines between TI-IN and TI-OUT on 'Cognitive-Pathways Model' illustration.

Solutioning strategies initiate at the "DM-Alert" inbound portal. Although TI-Inbound delivers the evaluative (Filtering-and-Slotting) competencies, it is DM-Alert, which provides the specialized "transition-resource" responsible for foddering the initial "Equivalency-Processor" evaluator with bombardment-driven data-flow.

On the other end, 'The-Ways' Test-It creations, designed to proactively instigate specific feedback from the Deluge are received by "TI-Parameter" and manipulated into final outbound form by TI-Outbound.

> In a very real sense, 'The-Ways' Figure-It-Out methodologies brilliantly transition existence from being a bombardment target to actively flourishing as a proactive initiator: Sometimes cautiously; sometimes boldly

TI-Outbound also plays a vital role as the outbound platform. However, discussion of its contribution, as well as those of the remaining constructs displayed on the illustration, will have to wait until encountered, as we tag-along with the data-stream to uncover 'The-Ways' of each process.

> TI-Outbound and TI-Inbound provide a synchronous cycle: The former injects outbound "action-suggestions" into the fray; the latter accepts consequential inbound sensory repercussions

Please re-examine CP-1 through CP-4 on the 'Cognitive-Pathways Model' illustration: note the three arrows originating at Data-Matrix. Arrows are intended to indicate Data-Matrix as simultaneously propagating data-packages to DE-Notify, TI-Inbound (TI-IN) and Template-Component. Although Template-Component (discussed later) and DE-Notify receive Tag-Cluster replicants, Data-Matrix propagates a dissimilar package into TI-Inbound DM-Alert data-resource: it will be explained next.

## DM-Alert Structure

DM-Alert provides neural data-resources best characterized as hopper-like and volatile. The hopper configuration forces temporal sequencing; critical if data-events are to be reconciled one to the next.

If sequencing was not the standard, events would not contiguously flow. Instead they would randomly pop in-and-out, causing disheveled and chaotic perception. Such is the case for certain pharmaceuticals, which can cause tousled effect by intermittently jumbling data-flow, thereby interrupting contiguous feed to cognitive processors.

> Volatile is also key to ordered reconciliation: especially in high data-flow conditions such as with 'The Hot-Fat Scenario'. Any data-stream elements not able to be handled when Solutioning processors are fully occupied must be dropped.

Any attempt to retain them for more than a few seconds would back-up new critical inbound data, which could be the very data-elements needed for survival. Without their timely arrival Figure-It-Out would be forced to evaluate using outmoded information, which would certainly result in incorrect assessment and compromised responses, which could very easily cause disaster.

## DM-Alert Formation

The data-package Data-Matrix inserts into the DM-Alert data-resource is termed a "TEA-Dat". The 'T' is pulled from TI-IN; whereas the 'EA' points to the originating EA-Harmonic (EA) data-structure, which was replicated to accomplish TEA-Dat creation: thus TEA-Dat and EA-Harmonic are equivalent.

> Critically, an EA-Harmonic is not only the Event-Condition but also the picot-point enabling both detail (Distinct-Episode) and visual (Visual-Scape) recall. Therefore, the importance of EA-Harmonics and TEA-Dats cannot be overstated.

EI-Join and IE-Join relationships are of major significance. Recall EI-Join, housed in Data-Matrix, forever captured the inter-relationship between an EA-Harmonic and all its associated IA-Facets.

Later stage discussions will detail how this essential join ensures a TEA-Dat is immediately referenceable to not only its originating EA-Harmonic but also all associated IA-Facets and of course, Distinct-Episodes (via IE-Join) as well.

To recap, TEA-Dat is a replicated EA-Harmonic: both exemplify the Event-Condition. Therefore, both simultaneously represent the overall impression of a bombardment event (as originally captured in a Pooled-Assembly).

> Remember, TEA-Dat was originally a Pooled-Assembly containing thousands of location and intensity diverse Tag-Clusters, which were not only archived as Distinct-Episodes but also coalesced to form a single EA-Harmonic (EA). The EA-Harmonic was subsequently linked to each Distinct-Episode within the Information-Assembly IA-Facet (IA) data-resource, thus forming an IE-Join data-element denoted as {IA{DE}}.

TEA-Dat thus forms the perfect inbound comparative for "Equivalency-Processor" (see above illustration). The reasons will be discussed after some requisites are explained: such as, 'what is being compared to what'; and 'how the comparative construct exists in the first place'.

It is DM-Alert, which provides the initializing "element…to be…utilized by Solutioning strategies". Addressing 'Solutioning' first then, should provide a convenient segue to other discussions.

## Solutioning

As a broad perspective, Solutioning refers to collections of Figure-It-Out strategies designed to find 'The-Ways'. As a DM-Alert 'TEA-Dat' provides the 'fodder', it must in some fashion contribute to solution fulfillment by meaningful comparison and/or evaluation of new-data (TEA-Dat), against previously Bracketed data (to be explained). 'Meaningful', in this context denotes resolving-a-something, which previous Components could not.

Additionally, 'Solutioning' by its very nature implies both progressive stages and variable time-frame be available for achievement. Therefore, methodologies must be available to incrementally gather bits of pertinent data over time, as an overall solution is being pursued.

Also, as multiple solutions are always being tackled, a methodology must exist to accurately associate and identify new-data as pertinent to 'Overall-A' rather than to 'Overall-B' (or C or D, etc.).

However, before diving into detailed explanations, let's first standardize the terms to be used throughout discussions. Rather than 'solutions being tackled', the term 'Puzzle' is substituted. In other words, the updated Figure-It-Out mandate is to solve Puzzles. This is wonderfully accurate as we are often puzzled by how something works and driven to Figure-It-Out.

For instance 'Force-of-Habit' required Solutioning thousands of Puzzles in order to provide explanations of not only how cognitive puzzle-solving methodologies work but also how Figure-It-Out enables awareness, conscious choices, recall and so much more

Also, instead of 'overall resolution' spoken of above, "Event-Condition-Puzzle" or just "E-Puzzle" will be inducted. Next, 'progressive stages' will be replaced by "Facet-Puzzle" or "F-Puzzle".

Additionally, all puzzles and their associated linked files (explained below) are maintained within "P-Cluster" ('P' is for Puzzle), which in turn utilizes specific Figure-It-Out neural resources. There are also additional P-Cluster constructs, which will be introduced when appropriate.

## P-Cluster Structures Introduction

Several interdependent members will be disclosed in this segment: such as, the structure and purposes of E-Puzzle, E-Puzzle and "EF-Dat"; data-and-link resource interactivities; data-populating methodologies; and the many ways Figure-It-Out performs as "Chief-Facilitator".

To focus discussions, 'The-Ways: Solutioning' illustration will be additionally employed to provide clarity for structures, connectivity and many other inter-relationships.

Of initial focus is "Equivalency-Processor", which occupies the convergent position between DM-Alerts and P-Cluster's E-Puzzles (implied by the arrow heads on the line between them). Its general function is to evaluate for 'equivalency' by comparing a

DM-Alert to E-Puzzles in order to determine either one of two conditions: 'Match' or 'No-Match'.

> Although P-Cluster is the discussion objective, it does not show all constructs. In order to avoid clutter only three data-resources are illustrated of the total compliment of eleven data-and-link resources.

Additional items will be added and discussed as they become pertinent. Of the three, E-Puzzle and F-Puzzle independent data-resources form an inseparable foundational duo. As referencing will be frequent, the 'duo' has been designated a group name: "Core-Puzzle-Set" or just "CP-Set". To subtly indicate data inter-dependency, P-Cluster presents E-Puzzle and F-Puzzle as slightly offset, one from the other.

The CP-Set {E-Puzzle // F-Puzzle} association forms THE integral foundation for all that follows


## P-Cluster Populating

Previous CP-4 discussions established pre-birth events as having the potential to create rudimentary entries in P-Cluster data-and-link resources. However, this section's initial 'Test-It scenario' dictates P-Cluster be empty: i.e., a 'blank' P-Cluster.

As a contrived 'clean-start' will permit unambiguous data-flow activity tracking, commencing from TI-Inbound, progressing through all Figure-It-Out processes and into TI-Outbound, developing concepts should be clear and understandable.

> Current status: 'The-Ways' have already been triggered as a consequence of DM-Alert being populated with a TEA-Dat by Data-Matrix (above discussions). Consequently on one hand, TEA-Dat forms the "fodder-half" or the 'comparator'. On the other hand, the TEA-Dat's pivotal harmonic structure will be utilized by Equivalency-Processor to attempt location of a compatible E-Puzzle or 'comparatee'.

As might be expected, Figure-It-Out provides a different set of action procedures for 'No-Match', than for 'Match' conditions: note the two divergent channels on "The-Ways Solutioning' illustration.

---

**Initialization Processor: No-Match Condition**

Initially then, due to the designed empty P-Cluster scenario, the opening result upon cross-comparison, TEA-Dat /to/ E-Puzzle, is a 'No-Match' condition. Invariably in the first hours after birth a 'No-Match' condition would be the rule because external sensory experiences, which populate P-Cluster and establish the potential for comparable 'Match', have not yet occurred.

> Little-by-little you become you, by Bracketing new experiences:
> All originating as sensory accepted bombardment events

When a 'No-Match' outcome results, Equivalency-Processor transfers the TEA-Dat 'comparator' to the "I-Pend" data-resource ('I' = "Initialization-Processor"; 'Pend' = pending) on the 'No-Match' channel. This action not only substantially fulfills Equivalency-Processor's objective for this TEA-Dat 'comparator' but also effectively transfers control to another processor.

> By providing many independent, special purpose processors, Figure-It-Out is the master at 'load-sharing'. This ongoing strategy, enabling simultaneous processing, is vital for Figure-It-Out's expansive capabilities, without which…well…amoeba comes to mind

Conspicuously, even in this 'first instance scenario', load-sharing was implemented. Thereby, the hopper-like I-Pend data-resource provisions the 'fodder' for a different actioner.

> Stated differently, Equivalency-Processor shared the load by populating an intermediate data-resource (I-Pend), whose contents are destined to be picked-up (due to continuous 'in-box' polling) and evaluated by a dedicated follow-up processor.

In this case Initialization-Processor is designated to not only continually troll for the next I-Pend but also adopt responsibility for establishing **CP-Sets**. In other words, its daunting 'No-Match' mandate is to populate P-Cluster's E-Puzzle and F-Puzzle data-resources by exploiting the retrieved I-Pend TEA-Dat.

## E-Puzzle Formation

As additional data manipulation is not required due to TEA-Dat providing an "E-Har" with an identical harmonic-signature, creating an E-Puzzle 'E-Har' is relatively straight forward.

Specifically, each E-Har is equivalent to both the TEA-Dat and the Data-Matrix 'EA-Harmonic' key-identifiers from which it originated. Significant to remember: E-Har is also equivalent to the Event-Condition from which the 'E' in E-Puzzle is derived. Therefore, the I-Pend 'TEA-Dat' is simply instilled as a new E-Puzzle 'E-Har'.

The representation at the right provides a simplified depiction of the E-Puzzles data-resource showing only three E-Puzzles: 'E-Har: A'; 'E-Har: B'; 'E-Har: C'. The down-arrow is intended to indicate the E-Puzzles data-resource as containing many more E-Har members.

```
E-Puzzles
↓ E-Har: A
  E-Har: B
  E-Har: C
↓
```

> Decisively then, an 'E-Har' is a fundamental data-element. It not only harmonically represents a Bombardment event but also granularly defines CP-Set required baseline resolution-magnitude (discussed shortly).

An 'E-Har' is identical (in terms of both harmonic-frequency and intensity) to an EA-Harmonic, which was previously positioned as the pivotal impetus for detailed recall. Detailed recall is possible because many IA-Facets and subsequently Distinct-Episodes are connected to a single EA-Harmonic 'driver' via EI-Join and IE-Join.

These essential join-resources preserve the one-to-many relationship between a Pooled-Assembly harmonic-amalgam (maintained as a single EA-Harmonic) and its many Pooled-Assembly Tag-Clusters (retained within Data-Matrix as IA-Facets and Distinct-Episodes).

## F-Puzzle Formation

In a 'No-Match' situation, creating F-Puzzle members is more involved than for their associated E-Puzzle because fulfillment requires Initialization-Processor to data-mine Data-Matrix to locate all E-Har associated IA-Facets.

Important to remember IA-Facets were structured from Pooled-Assembly 'Tag-Clusters': in turn morphed from accepted event-horizon sensory 'Tag' data (SLIDs). Additionally, these same Tag-Clusters were harmonized to create their forever associated EA-Harmonic or synonymous Event-Condition, which thus provides critical synchronicity between E-Har and TEA-Dat

Recaptured for reference from the 'CP-4' Pathway of the 'Cognitive-Pathways Model' diagram and displayed to the left, is the Data-Matrix graphic depicting join relationships: between EA-Harmonic (EA) and its many (EA) related IA-Facets ({IAs}); and IAs many related Distinct-Episodes ({DEs}).

$$\boxed{\text{Data-Matrix} \\ EA><\{IA\{DE\}\}}$$

F-Puzzle creation is achievable due to the homogeneity of TEA-Dat and EA-Harmonic, which thereby allow TEA-Dat to be employed to pinpoint its identical EA-Harmonic mate in Data-Matrix (by now familiar 'harmonic-frequency' matching methodology).

The first stage locates and replicates all 'EI-Joined' IA-Facets. As encountered, each replicant is utilized to form an "F-Freq" (Facet-Frequency) data-element (indicated in the graphic below): denoted with bold typeface.

Creation continues until one F-Puzzle 'F-Freq' has been created for each IA-Facet of the target EA-Harmonic: the down arrows in the F-Puzzle illustration below are intended to suggest many more F-Puzzles. Additional F-Freq data-element creation is accomplished by instilling the replicated IA-Facet frequency-identifier of each companion EA-Harmonic as an F-Puzzle 'F-Freq'.

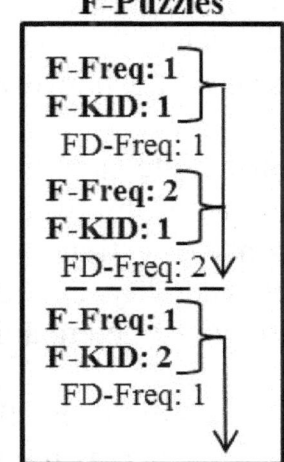

Keep in mind an F-Freq is not a harmonic but instead the base frequency-identifier equivalent to a Soma location-ID (SLID), which uniquely discriminated Tags and therefore Tag-Clusters (one-from-the-next) in the first place.

This characteristic will soon be shown to be critically important for Solutioning and Test-It 'Outbound' management.

Concurrently, two other data-elements are also created: an "F-KID" (also bold) and an FD-Freq. FD-Freq is a parallel companion created with 'null' value (discussed further along).

Regarding the F-KID strategy, two overlapping CP-Set mandates drive its necessity: ensure rapid F-Freq location within its independent data-resource; and concurrently maintain integrity of an E-Har to all its F-Puzzle 'F-Freqs'.

As SLIDs are a limited resource and F-Freqs mimic SLIDs, their repetitive involvement in Bombardment events is unavoidable (F-Freqs therefore also get reused): for instance, similar events like clapping your hands will involve most of the same SLIDs; although seemingly different events such as scratching your foot can also involve some of the same SLIDs (i.e., those on the hand).

Consequently, many same F-Freqs can reside in both similar and different CP-Sets; albeit joined to different E-Puzzles. Therefore, if a same F-Freq was not uniquely identifiable as part of one Bombardment rather than from another, events would clump together thereby making granular discrimination impossible and finely honed sensory receptors not useful.

To uniquely identify a same F-Freq then as not only 'belonging' to a specific E-Har but also still independent in its own F-Puzzle data-resource requires an integrating strategy, which in this case is F-KID (F-Puzzle Key-IDentifier), which uses (previously explained) 'Time-Stamp' as the basis for its unique encoding.

> Once distinctively allocated, it is coupled as part of a dual F-Puzzle access-key: namely, {F-Freq // F-KID}; thereby encoding one F-Freq as unique from another.

Examine the three F-Puzzle sample depiction above. It incorporates several characteristics intended to assist with understanding structure: numbering, bolding, braces, down arrows and dotted line.

First, note each F-Puzzle data-element (F-Freq; F-KID; FD-Freq) has a number placed to the right of its identifying label. Numbers are intended to not only provide a consistent framework for discussions but also indicate inherent features: such as, connectivity and data-group recognition; access-key distinctiveness; F-Freq (SLID) frequency; companion FD-Freq; etc.

> Notice the first F-Puzzle 'F-Freq' is 'numbered '1' and its F-KID is also '1'; whereas the second 'F-Freq' is '2' but its F-KID is also '1'; and finally the third 'F-Freq' is '1' again but its F-KID is '2'.

The first two F-Puzzles are intended to show different SLIDs (of course there could be thousands): i.e., SLID frequency '1' (F-Freq: 1) and SLID frequency '2' (F-Freq: 2). However, as they both have the same F-KID ('1'), they both therefore 'belong' to the same E-Har (joined via "E-Link": discussions below).

The third F-Puzzle has a repeating SLID, '1' (F-Freq: 1) but its F-KID is '2': thereby indicating it, although its F-Freq ('1') is a repeat, belongs to a different E-Har. Notice also FD-Freq numbering parallels the F-Freq numeric identifier because it is a mimic companion.

> Not to be ignored though because FD-Freq provides the basis for some incredible cognitive capabilities (discussed below).

Notice also: braces indicate the dual access key {F-Freq // F-KID}; the two down arrows indicate many more data-elements exist for each of the two F-Puzzles (again, there would be thousands); the dotted horizontal line additionally reinforces F-Puzzles 'belong' to different E-Hars as ascertained by F-KID grouping numeric identifier (F-KID: 1; F-KID: 2).

Thus the joint and several mandate is fulfilled: F-Freqs have been uniquely identified as belonging to a specific E-Har; and the F-Puzzle data-resource remains autonomous and searchable by F-Freq. E-Link and F-Link fill out the compliment of CP-Set data-and-link resources ensuring connectivity remains unbroken.

## E-Link and F-Link

CP-Set E-Puzzles and F-Puzzles, although storehoused in autonomous data-resources are associated by two independent link-resources: 'E-Link' and "F-Link" (graphic below). They are concurrently created during the above E-Har and F-Puzzle populations. Although both ensure 'E-Puzzle to F-Puzzle' integrity their functions are distinctive.

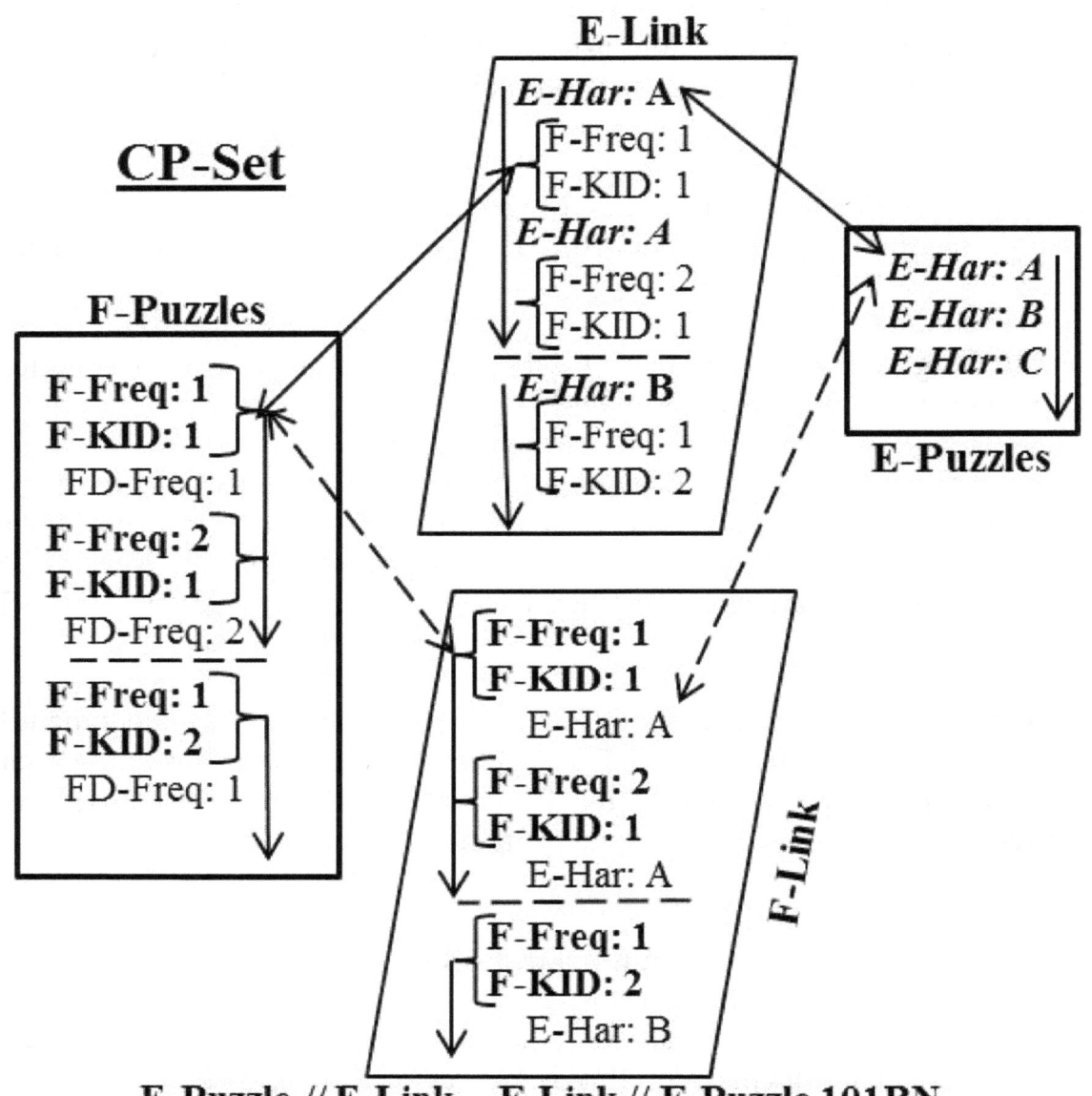

E-Link enables rapid retrieval of associated F-Puzzles when an E-Har is known; whereas F-Link enables rapid retrieval of the E-Har when an F-Puzzle is known. Specifically, E-Link establishes the relationship between a single E-Har ('right' solid line) and therefore its many associated {F-Freq // FD-Freq} group members ('left' solid line).

Cooperatively, F-Link solidifies the relationship between a single F-Puzzle F-Freq (left dotted line) and a single E-Puzzle E-Har (right dotted line). These features will become vital as complexity increases.

Initialization-Processor has one remaining task: alert following mechanisms about the new CP-Set. Notification is accomplished by creating a join relationship between the original TEA-Dat and the created CP-Set E-Har notated as {TEA-Dat // E-Har} and instilling it into P-Pend. There will be much discussion further along regarding the implications of this action. To reduce clutter a connecting line between Initialization-Processor and P-Pend is not shown on the illustration.

**Resolution Processor: Match-Condition**

For 'Match-Condition' discussions, the working TI-Inbound scenario has evolved: it expands to include both the initial CP-Set (created by 'No-Match' processes) plus the arrival of a new TEA-Dat.

> Conspicuously, Figure-It-Out evaluation practices deviate substantially from Soma-Self Components, whose design was to determine either 'same' or 'not-same'.

In other words, Body-Self mandates were dichotomously tuned to either recognize identical frequency-signatures then deal with them or pass-on 'not-same' to the next evaluator.

> Forwarding-on was certainly the case when Body-Self created the ultimate 'pass-on' - the Cognitive-Alert - which epitomizes Body-Self's bearing: "I cannot resolve this data-stream, so get Mind-Self to assist".

TEA-Dat is a trigger-event. As its arrival in DM-Alert instigates Equivalency-Processor to evaluate the TEA-Dat against CP-Set E-Puzzles, TEA-Dat is therefore deemed the 'comparator'.

> Recall the initial TEA-Dat was propagated to the 'No-Match' channel, which resulted in the creation of the first P-Cluster 'CP-Set' (E-Puzzle plus multiple linked F-Puzzles). On delivery of the second TEA-Dat however, CP-Set is not empty: thus providing Equivalency-Processor with a 'comparatee'.

Significantly, Equivalency-Processor evaluation ('comparator' to 'comparatee') is not to uncover 'same', but instead determine 'substantial-similarity'. Resultantly, 'substantial-similarity' is implemented as the functional meaning of 'Equivalent' in Equivalency-Processor.

> 'Substantial-similarity' then is the new comparative standard because 'same' can never become a TEA-Dat in the first place

Here is why. Body-Self discussions determined 'recognized' (and minimally intense) events as 'same'. Notably, for one bombardment event to be the 'same' as another, an involved SLID Tag must be of nominal intensity and already exist as a Body-Self Bracket.

> Notably, 'Soma-same' event types pervade much of our day - not raising any flags. They are nicely handled by Body-Self habitual responders and never become Cognitive-Alerts. Resultantly, 'same' never enters the Cognitive-Self domain.

However, exceptions do. Notably then, every encountered 'first-time' Body-Self 'Event-Condition' is not 'same' but new. Except for the most unimaginably banal situations, listening to some speakers drone on or escaping in deep sleep for instance, 'ongoing-same' is not as likely, as slightly-to-very different: especially when young or doing something new or in a new way.

> So, whether sparked by a Cognitive-Alert or by Cognitive-Sensor processors (visual) recognizing a 'remarkable-feature', 'not-same' is the impetus for cognition

Consequently, it is the ongoing millions of first-time 'not-same' Event-Conditions gradually accumulating through new bombardment combinations, which populate Data-Matrix, P-Cluster and (subsequently) more advanced reference data-repositories yet to be discussed.

This means Equivalency-Processor comparison must be redefined as 'new-to-similar-old': i.e., DM-Alert 'TEA-Dat' to an E-Puzzle 'E-Har' (respectively). As they cannot be 'same', Figure-It-Out 'Match or No-Match' determination must therefore evaluate the closest frequency-match to resolve whether a TEA-Dat is 'substantially-similar' to an E-Puzzle.

Following this reasoning, a challenging question looms: "If Event-Conditions are so discretely defined, how does 'similarity-matching' work?"

The answer involves several contributing dynamics spanning from foundational E-Puzzle "Bracketing-roots" to the ultimate involvement of more complex comparative constructs yet to be presented: such as, "M-Bundles", "M-Links", "P-Groups", "P-Links", "E-Cluster" and "C-Cluster".

Let's begin the path to understanding "How-We-Work" by defining the basis for the existence of everything

First, our Universe: let's call it "Universe-H" because Hydrogen is not only by far its most common element but also the basis for all elements, which are created in stars and through their explosions distribute elements throughout our Universe-H realm.

Additionally integral, all compositions within our Universe-H, regardless of how subtle their differences, rely on the constancy of a frequency-scale called the Electromagnetic Spectrum for discrimination.

Every recognizably different particle and/or energy is only able to be distinguished because of its specific, immutable frequency assignment, which therein provides two integral characteristics: a unique vibrational signature; and a compelling propensity to snuggle-up with 'same'.

Literally, for our species in our Universe-H, if it doesn't vibrate, it doesn't exist.

Consequently, as we are part of our Universe-H and composed of its stuff, then so too does every aspect of our being equally rely upon frequency variances for stability and recognisability.

Not surprisingly both Body-Self sensors and Cognitive-Sensors frequencies employ a portion of Universe-H's "Master-Frequency-Array".

The very nature of this truth thereby also encapsulates and integrates us into the 'big-picture' as well.

With this in mind, the 'Bracketing-Roots' part of the answer unfolds where frequencies transition. Although from one point-of-view the Electromagnetic (Frequency) Spectrum is seemingly continuous, there are actually extremely small micro variances transitioning its millions of 'frequencies'.

> By default then, changeover from one frequency to the next must occur by default. This transition event, exhibiting characteristics of both frequencies, is termed "Waveform-Overlap".

A familiar example of frequency transition has probably been experienced by most. Think of a trip where your destination was three or more hours away, perhaps the next town or into the mountains.

You depart your residence, get into your car, turn on the radio and start to drive. About 2 hours into the journey your favorite radio station begins to break-up while another radio station begins to sputter in and out. Gradually, if you bear with the entire hissing and static filled transition or Waveform-Overlap, the new radio station (its frequency) takes over completely and the original station becomes lost.

In this scenario, the duration of Waveform-Overlap was fairly long for a few reasons: radio station frequencies are quite far apart in Electromagnetic Spectrum terms; standard radio receivers are neither calibrated nor sufficiently sensitive to completely isolate a single frequency during transition; and your vehicle is slow compared to near speed-of-light radio transmissions.

> Regardless, consumer electronic design normally allows for experiencing the Waveform-Overlap instead of the alternate, which would be unacceptable radio silence until full transition occurs.

Equivalency-Processor is similarly designed to permit frequency overlap without immediate rejection. Differently, Figure-It-Out utilizes its perpetually updated 'Gradient-of-Acceptability' to determine 'substantially-similar': also at near light speed.

> In other words, Figure-It-Out ascertains, almost instantaneously, if the inbound 'TEA-Dat to E-Puzzle' Waveform-Overlap is within acceptable limits to conclusively process {TEA-Dat // E-Har} as 'same'.

This is an excellent species enabling methodology as it eliminates both debilitating alternatives: 'silence' and/or ambiguous cognitive 'static'. Both would result in unworkable data-flow, which would either cause inaction or propel disastrous actions.

This being so it is imperative to understand: "Under what 'originating conditions' could one TEA-Dat be considered 'substantially-similar' to another?"

Even though potential combinations and permutations of Cognitive-Alert Tag-Clusters forming a Pooled-Assembly are enormous, they are not operationally infinite: i.e., within daily 'routines' they are reduced because even 'slightly new' daily events tend to produce repetitive SLID activities.

In fact, one Event-Condition harmonic (morphed Pooled-Assembly) can very closely approximate another when there are only slight 'Tag' variances (such as holding a pen versus holding a pencil).

Of course, it is those slight 'Tag' variances, which can be responsible for driving the data-package to Mind-Self via Cognitive-Alert in the first place. Reasonably then, one should expect close approximations to potentially be considered as 'substantially-similar'.

This is so because if every TEA-Dat was considered unique, they would always be unmatchable to E-Puzzles. Cognitive chaos would thereby ensue resulting in the "cognitive-assistive-process" being rendered useless.

Fortunately, Figure-It-Out can and regularly does evaluate 'Waveform-Overlap' as 'same': thereby enabling assumption, best-guess and approximation (dealt with more thoroughly further on).

This Figure-It-Out competency, to evaluate 'close frequencies' as 'acceptably-similar', is a defining hallmark of our species. It is the fundamental factor responsible for 'seeing things differently'.

Waveform-Overlap is the foundation upon which ingenuity, invention, assimilation and many other cross-integration capabilities are enabled

On a subjective level, all realize it takes years of experience (less time when experiences are highly intense) before one is capable of evaluating how a slight information shift might provide greater utility. A few new data-element combinations may be the only requirement to initiate Waveform-Overlap, thus prompting comparison of the 'established-way' to a 'possible-new-way': thereby spawning significant change.

By providing the smallest tidbit of new information then, those with vast experience can inspire revelation. As an example, expert negotiators present options in tiny increments because they know this will afford their best chance for 'acceptable' outcome.

This is because 'new' initiates a cascade across multiple E-Puzzles, which can dramatically shift ones points-of-view within 'higher' constructs (discussions to come). A perspective shift, which positively enhances the utility of 'the old', is ingenuity at its best.

One can actually experience the 'shift' occurrence. Think of a situation where you were presented new information, which at first seemed correct but then was quickly dismissed as preposterous (many jokes use this juxtaposition).

Although explained in greater detail below by incorporating more comprehensive constructs, awareness of the transition is possible because an E-Har (previously established as the emotional driver), actually elicits a change in harmonic-potential (an 'electrical surge' if you like) when link-resources members are reorganized; i.e., unlinked and relinked by Figure-It-Out.

The 'driver' can be experienced because harmonic-potential changes, coupled with instigated hormonal adjustments within the neural-mass, are primary awareness triggers.

It is no surprise puzzles of all kinds from Jigsaw-to-Sudoku have such appeal: They play into our reorganizational cognitive strong suit. Resulting 'transition-awareness' often enables experiencing resolution progress as the more complex 'C-Cluster' constructs of satisfaction and accomplishment

In summary, Tag-Clusters of a Pooled-Assembly, although differently morphed by Data-Matrix into IA-Facets, Distinct-Episodes and a single EA-Harmonic, are the common origin for both an E-Puzzle 'summary' (E-Har) as well as its many F-Puzzle 'details' (F-Freq's).

Additionally, as an Event-Condition is synonymous with both an EA-Harmonic and an E-Har, it thereby establishes the pivotal touch-point for cognition.

Critically for all that follows, F-Puzzles form the common threads, whose invariable F-Freq frequency-signatures directly tie neural acceptance location Identifiers (SLIDs) to an Event-Condition; thereby providing immutable and precise connection between a 'question' and the 'answer' as well as between 'body' and 'mind'

## Match-Condition Process

Admittedly, shaping the second TEA-Dat to be 'substantially-similar' to the (only) CP-Set E-Puzzle was contrived to facilitate unambiguous 'Match' discussions. By so doing Equivalency-Processor is obliged to evaluate a 'Match-Condition' between the second (new) TEA-Dat and the only available (old) E-Puzzle 'E-Har'.

Equivalency-Processor communicates its 'Match' findings to next step "Resolution-Processor" by instilling pertinent data-elements into the pending or holding "R-Pend" hopper-resource located on the 'Match' channel: thereby allowing Resolution-Processor to uptake the information when ready.

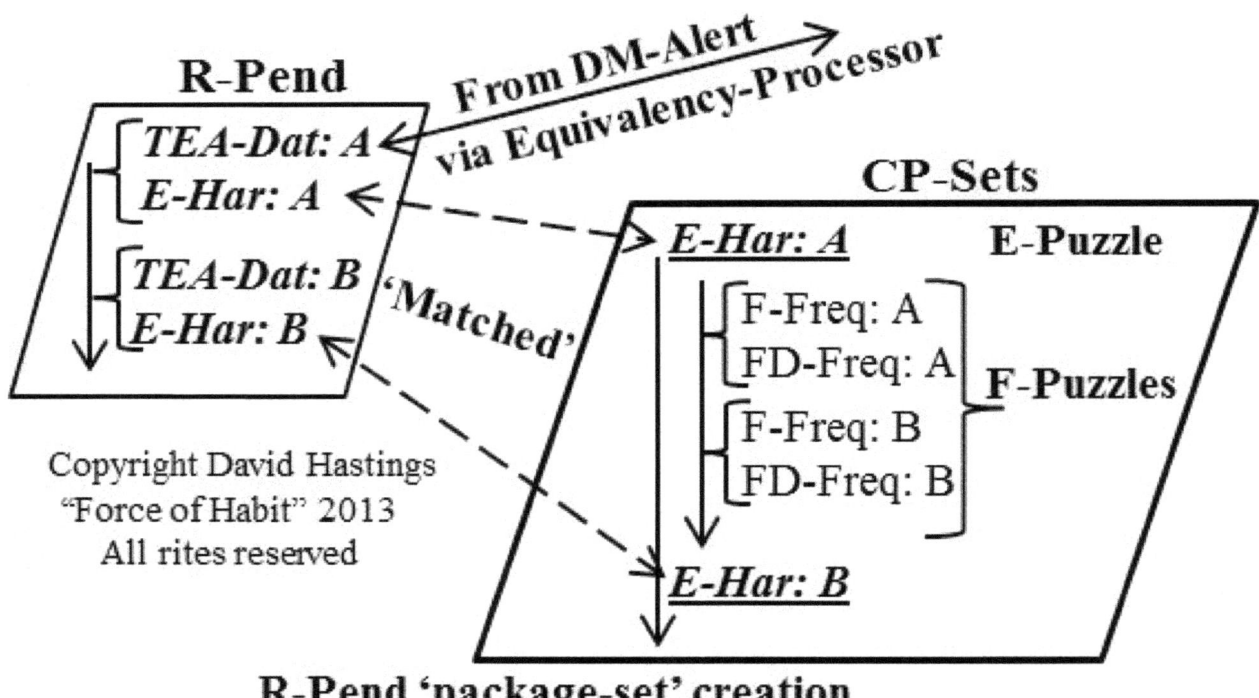

R-Pend 'package-set' creation

Specifically, Equivalency-Processor creates an "R-package" with a one-to-one relationship combination key-identifier, written as {TEA-Dat // E-Har}, by utilizing both the 'TEA-Dat' and the 'Matched' CP-Set E-Puzzle 'E-Har'; and then instills it into the R-Pend hopper-resource (see illustration above).

Responsibility for 'Matched' TEA-Dat disposition is thereby transferred to Resolution-Processor. Such data-resource division-of-responsibilities has been emphasized as beneficial on many previous occasions, especially in high volume bombardment situations, because the functioning processor is thus enabled to independently manage and control its own capacity, instead of being force-fed data by a previous mechanism.

Whether initially prompted by a Cognitive-Alert or by Cognitive-Sensor processors identifying a 'Remarkable-Feature' thereby instigating Body-Self action, Initialization-Processor creates CP-Sets, which unequivocally define the base-level Figure-It-Out 'question' to be resolved or 'answered'.

This being the case: What then delivers the 'answer'?

158  Dr. David J. Hastings PhD

## Resolution-Processor: Current-data Processing

Resolution-Processor provides two discrete functions: Current-Processing and Background-Processing. Current-Processing manages the 'in progress data-stream' (R-Pend) by polling, loading and processing "RP-packages"; whereas transparently operating Background-Processing (discussed below), continually evaluates the 'resolution-status' of P-Cluster 'CP-Sets' in order to locate, transfer and remove those,

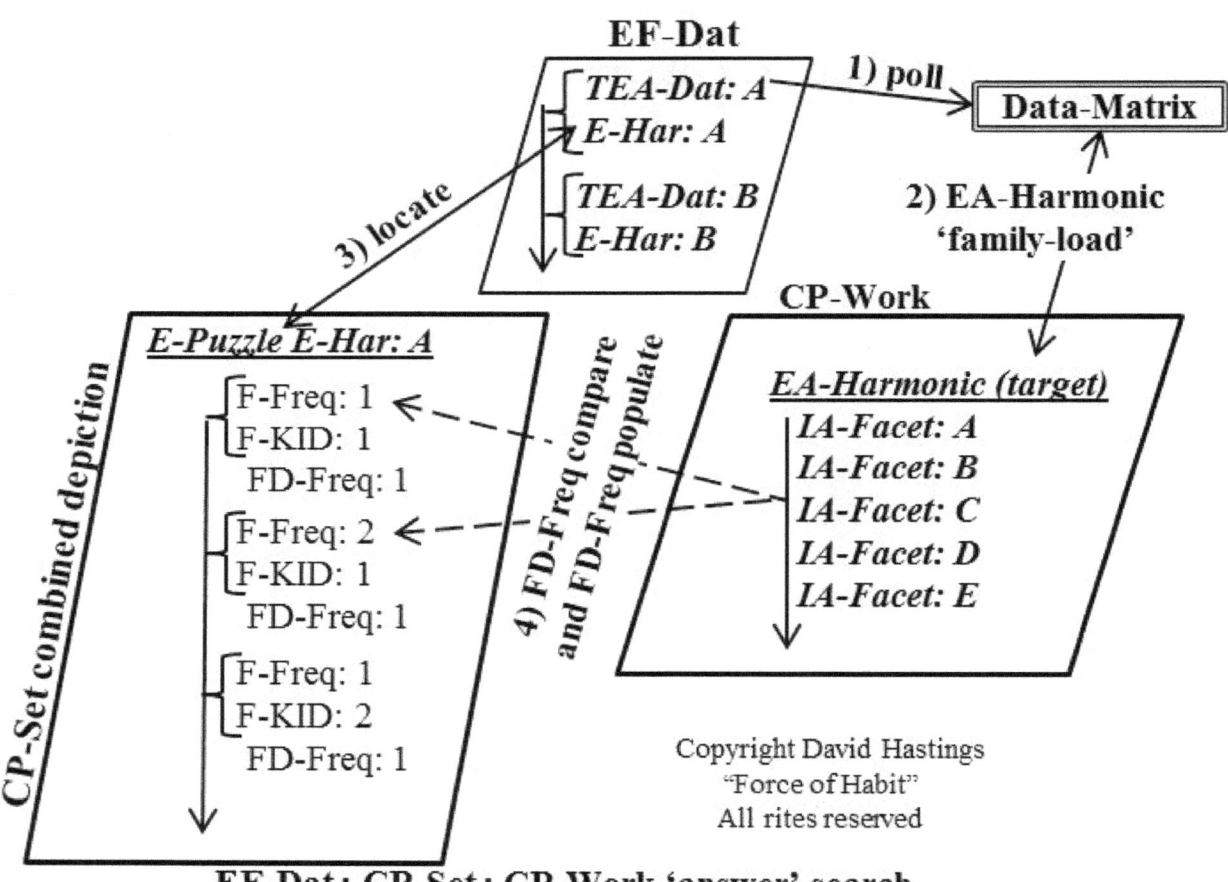

EF-Dat : CP-Set : CP-Work 'answer' search

which are resolved.

Current-Processing deploys several phases to fulfill Resolution-Processor mandates (see illustration numbering above). "Polling-Phase" initializes its involvement by continuously scanning R-Pend for a new 'package-set', which when apprehended, is removed and instilled into EF-Dat ('E', for E-Har; 'F' for F-Puzzle).

This transfer is necessary so each data-resource can discretely fulfill its role without overlap: R-Pend, as a feeder or hopper; and EF-Dat, as the current fodder for 'current' Resolution-Processor activities.

Although both elements of the dual EF-Dat key-identifier (TEA-Dat //E-Har) are utilized to ensure retrieval of correct 'Match' data, individual retrieval outcome and purpose are different: TEA-Dat is employed to supply potential 'answers' from Data-Matrix (illustration item #1); whereas E-Har is exploited to target the correct CP-Set unresolved 'question' (illustration item #3).

The next phase seamlessly utilizes the EF-Dat 'TEA-Dat' as a locator-beacon to not only identify the E-Har equivalent Data-Matrix EA-Harmonic (illustration item #2) but also locate all EA-Harmonic associated IA-Facets. Consequently, both the EA-Harmonic and each IA-Facet are replicated and instilled into a "CP-Work" transitional-resource.

Next, "Resolution-Phase" continues interrogation by utilizing the E-Har portion of the EF-Dat assess-key to establish connectivity to the implicated E-Puzzle in CP-Set. Using 'frequency-matching' to establish 'significant-similarity' or not, Resolution-Phase compares all replicated IA-Facets within 'CP-Work' to the F-Freq's of the target E-Puzzle in CP-Set (illustration item #4).

> Stated differently, evaluation is designed to determine if any 'answer' (IA-Facet) is 'acceptably-similar' to any 'question' (F-Freq) instilled previously in the 'No-Match' phase.

Specifically, this Resolution-Phase cross-matches all CP-Work facet-elements (loaded IA-Facet replicants), which can potentially provide 'answers' to F-Puzzle F-Freq 'questions' of the implicated 'Matched' E-Puzzle.

A 'match' results in each CP-Work IA-Facet's intensity being accrued into the appropriate F-Puzzle FD-Freq 'answer' within the target CP-Set: CP-Work IA-Facets determined not 'significantly-similar' are simply dropped from CP-Work.

> This strategy effectively takes new input (TEA-Dat) and uses it to target Data-Matrix IA-Facets (experiences) to fill in some of the FD-Freq 'blanks' of a 'significantly-similar' CP-Set (previous unresolved input)

F-Puzzle population and ultimate resolution are foundational; without which higher process would not exist.

> Two conditions must be satisfied to resolve an F-Puzzle: an FD-Freq must be provided for each F-Freq (i.e., an 'answer' for each 'question'); and the FD-Freq intensity must at least match that of the F-Freq.

In other words, all FD-Freqs must be populated with intensities at least equal to companion F-Freqs.

For instance, if one F-Freq intensity was '9' and its mate FD-Freq only '6', even though all other {F-Freq // FD-Freq} 'companion-sets' fulfilled criteria, E-Puzzle resolution could be hampered. E-Puzzle resolution consequences will be discussed a little further along.

When some of the companion-sets fall short, what are available options for their fulfillment? Firstly, unlikely the next arriving random TEA-Dat will either accomplish population of all unresolved FD-Freqs of the target CP-Set or provide correct intensity at least equal to its F-Freq counterpart.

> This means CP-Set must wait for another 'significantly-similar' TEA-Dat to top-up FD-Freq intensities, before it can be resolved.

Two options are available for acquiring the additional needed TEA-Dat(s): continuing random Bombardment and/or Test-It requests (discussed below). Notably then, as will be soon revealed, creation of the latter (a Test-It) is an incredibly enabling proactive capability.

> "Facet-Resolution" is clearly where the-rubber-hits-the-road so to speak because each 'significantly-similar' evaluation (F-Freq // IA-Facet) where FD-Freq intensity is at least that of its corresponding F-Freq will result in single F-Puzzle resolution potential.

Remember, unmatched F-Puzzles or F-Freq's where its corresponding FD-Freq either remains unpopulated or of insufficient intensity will remain unresolved.

Of major benefit, one other option is possible: i.e., when 'enough' FD-Freqs sufficiently exceed the intensity of their companion F-Freqs (such as a '9' FD-Freq with a companion '6' F-Freq).

> When these occurrences cascade by also involving 'enough' significantly-similar E-Puzzles as well, this condition can be incredibly enabling because it can propel one into inspiration: sometimes far beyond the limitations of the original Bombardment E-Puzzles. This will be expanded upon as more complex features are uncovered following.

In other words, although there are other factors, FD-Freq capability to capture greater intensity than its companion F-Freq is incredibly excellent as it permits an outcome greater than the original driving 'question'

Concurrent to the above activities, as each FD-Freqs intensity is being incremented within its F-Puzzle, Resolution-Processor populates the "FEP-Pend" transitional-resource.

In the illustration below FEP-Pend is demarcated as the transitional-resource to the left of the vertical dotted line.

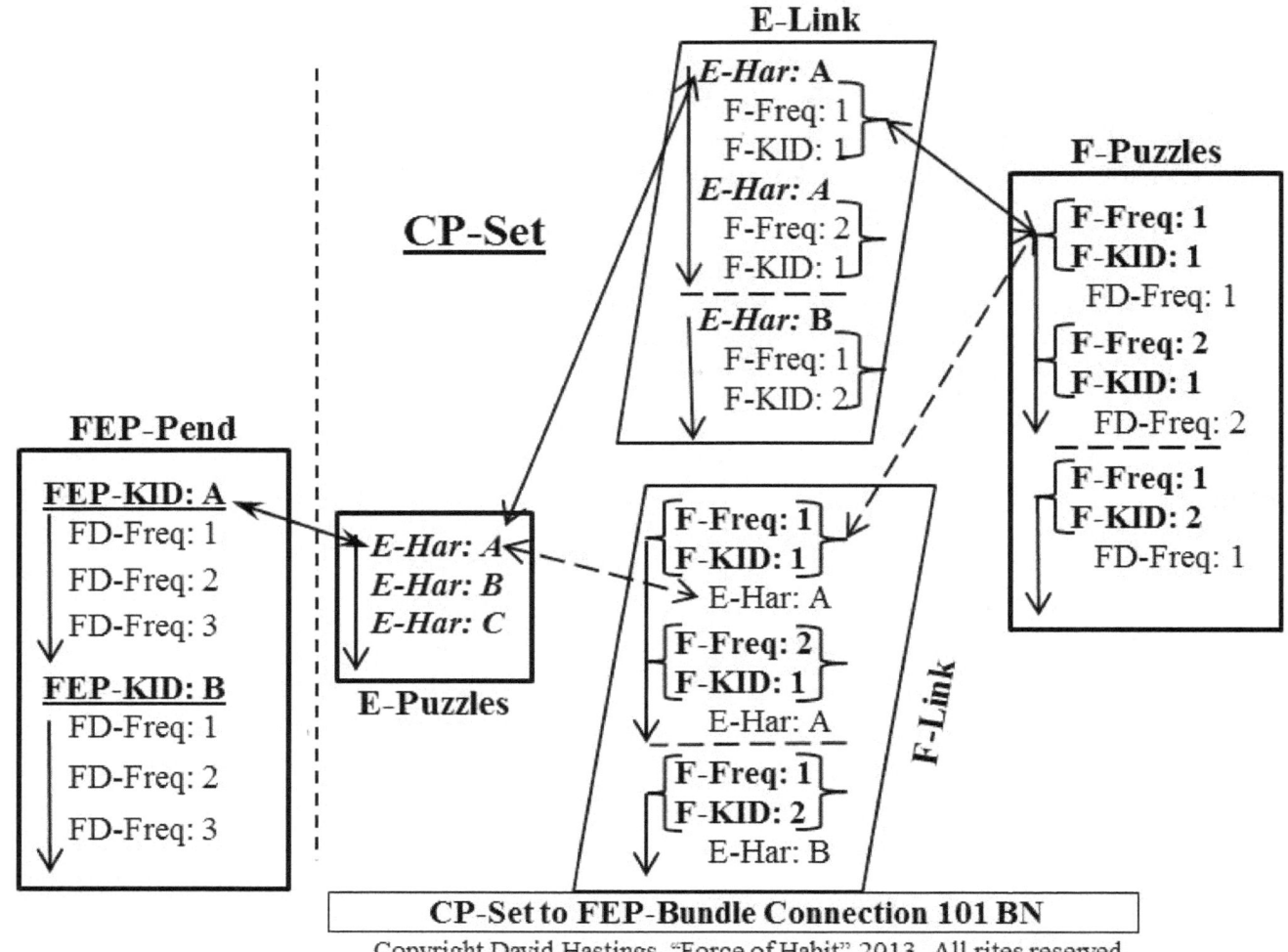

Copyright David Hastings "Force of Habit" 2013 All rites reserved

The CP-Set diagram is provided below to not only accent it as the source but also indicate the target E-Har was instilled as the FEP-Pend key-identifier, thereby preserving connection to CP-Set: in this case 'FEP-KID: A' and the target E-Har are synonymous.

Two population possibilities exist: FEP-KID will either already exist in FEP-Pend or not.

If not, a new FEP-KID record is created and the appropriate FD-Freqs are added.

However, when FEP-KID already exists, two processes are necessary: add new FD-Freqs and update existing ones.

Updating in this case requires the intensity of the arriving FD-Freq to be added to that of the resident FD-Freq: i.e. if the resident was '3' and the arrival was '2' the result would be '5'.

Until CP-Set is determined resolved by "Background-Processor" (discussed further along) any new TEA-Dat will cause the intensities of its retrieved FD-Freqs to be added to existing FEP-Pend 'FD-Freq' intensities. It is this circumstance, which enables inspired outcome.

Following discussions will explore how FD-Freq 'base-level' building-blocks provide the critical stratum for cognition. They are enablers because higher-up-the-chain of complexity various processors manage interlacing their continually morphing harmonic mix, identified as an "FEP-Har" (discussed below), into more robust constructs.

> From humble FD-Freq beginnings to the relocation of high-level 'Solutioned' "M-Bundles" to 'hardened' neural real-estate, FD-Freqs thus 'fodder' referenceable repositories of concluded events for ever-more comprehensive assessments: although in a completely different modality than Data-Matrix (variances will be discussed in detail as we progress).

---

## P-Bundle Broader-Scope Introduction

Previously, by simplifying data-flow into two inbound TEA-Dats, it was possible to allay the usual tumultuous quantity of continually flowing Bombardment complexity to ensure clarity of new concepts and functionalities: The first provided an engineered 'No-Match'; the second a 'Match' condition.

Abridged data-flow, though useful for introductory discussions, does not properly showcase Figure-It-Out's extreme capabilities.

> Perhaps then, either slightly niggling or possibly overtly nagging, your Figure-It-Out is poking at awareness, intuiting there must be more to 'The-Ways' than just the above…Figure-It-Out is correct: there so is.

Indubitably our conceptualization of an event is much grander than any single Event-Condition (E-Puzzle E-Har) with its associated details (F-Puzzle F-Freq's).

Therefore, cognitive mechanisms must be available enabling "Broader-Scope".

> Not surprisingly, it is Figure-It-Out which provisions the next (but not the final) plateau of cognitive complexity, which moves data-integration up the cognitive 'complexity-chain' by variously integrating previously discussed building-blocks and some yet to be presented.

To aid in conceptualization, the P-Cluster data-repository depiction (cross-hatched in grey below) has been updated and reorganized to include two additional data-arenas not shown on 'The-Ways: Solutioning' illustration.

> P-Cluster purview now provisions four 'zones', which are indicated as larger white areas, each containing various data-and link-resources.

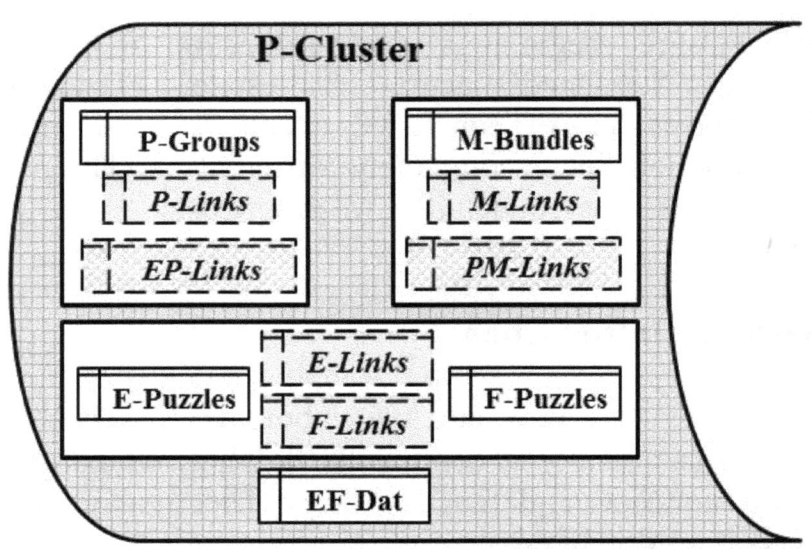

Copyright David Hastings "Force of Habit" 2014 All rites reserved
V2014-PCluster-101BM

Indicated on the 'lower-half' of the illustration are two previously discussed zones imparting distinctive attributes: CP-Set (E-Puzzles; F-Puzzles; E-Links; F-Links) and EF-Dat.

Focus for this sections discussions however will be on the remaining two P-Cluster 'upper-half' arenas: i.e., the 'left' zone, which houses 'P-Groups' ("Phase-Groups" data-resource and its two link-resources, namely "EP-Links" and 'P-Links'; and the 'right' zone, which houses 'M-Bundles' ("Macro-Bundles") data-resource and its two link-resources, namely "PM-Links" and 'M-Links' (discussed following).

These data-resources together with their essential data-link connectivity provide the structure for increasingly complex or 'broader-scope' functionality.

---

## Transition to Cognition

> Explaining various cognition characteristics as well as its extreme ranges from 'background-unaware' to 'inspired-aware', somewhat describes the goal of following sections.

To this juncture Mind-Self discussions have been tailored for defining the fundamental building-blocks necessary to enable cognition by defining CP-Set origins, creation, integration, functionality, handling, etc. As the groundwork has been completed, it is now possible to focus on how CP-Set 'foundational-elements' enable higher cognitive function.

> Mind-Self's pervasive larger purpose is to proactively enable survival or maximum benefit

Proactive capability requires two aspects: early "broad-event" similarity detection earmarked and queued by rapid, multiple and continuing significantly-similar sensory acceptances; and the ability to devise and deploy some plan, which appropriately moderates occurrence.

> In other words, first recognize event-groupings, which exhibit the potential to either cause harm (or at least not be optimal according to one's reference library of gained 'broader-scope' experiences) and then do something about them.

Although proactivity is partly enabled by maintaining detailed referenceable Data-Matrix data-archives, it flourishes due to Figure-It-Outs capability to recognize unfolding patterns by queuing-off amalgamations of multiple sensory clues or Bombardment "event-fusions".

> Proactive recognition of 'event-fusions' ranging from simple to complex facilitate a huge cognitive leap as requirements for this incredible capability to function are extensive. Incredibly, as one gains experience, proactive capability enhances.

The novice will not be able to make connections to event possibilities the expert will 'sense' as obvious: the deduction (event-fusion) capabilities of several popularized detective-types fall within this scope.

The experts 'sense' is the direct consequence of the rapid availability of copious 'higher-level' cognitive constructs, which are utilized as comparatives to scope out "patterns-of-similarity" against coalescences of new sensory information provided by TEA-Dats

As experience expands familiarity, dependence on Data-Matrix as an (initial) recognition strategy (when inexperienced) declines, while reliance on 'higher-level' cognitive constructs grows.

'Higher-level' is a foddering process where ever larger amalgams of previous 'base-level' data-element collections enable 'broader-view' by coalescing significantly-similar 'harmonic-frequencies' to not only create referenceable "harmonic-archives" but also yield other interactive 'broader-scope' capabilities such as "recognition-sense".

Previous discussions clarified CP-Sets exist to answer granular or base-level 'questions'. Once answered, they are destined to participate as elements of 'broader-scope' or higher cognitive functions. Importantly, next stage "Cognitive-Puzzles" are recognizable and sensed on a much larger basis: i.e., one becomes aware fairly quickly, has a 'recognition-sense' if you like, when there is a 'significant' puzzle in need of 'Solution'.

That being said, 'broad-event' puzzles present neither efficiently grouped nor in their entirety. Seldom a homogeneous single flawless presentation, 'recognition-sense' is usually a composite: comprised of an overall "Macro-Sense" coupled with some-to-many related "Phase-Senses": neither is necessarily clear.

In other words, one gets some "Macro-Sense" of the overall 'Hot-Fat' event "Macro-Puzzle" (something is wrong) as well as some sense of variously related and accumulating 'aspect-puzzles' or "Phase-Senses" (smell; skin burning; noise; etc.).

Stated differently, puzzles typically stratify as a global puzzle with some to many smaller loosely linked puzzles. The hot fat spitting on skin provided focus for the Macro-Puzzle - I am getting burned; whereas the connected smaller puzzles assess why: in order to inspire solutions for each 'Phase' (heat too high; too close; pan not covered) and ultimately therefore the Macro-Puzzle as well.

Additionally compounding complexity, ones "recognition-sense" is also not 'neat' but instead subject to wide assessment variability ranging from totally wrong to somewhat accurate.

> For instance, while driving the highway on a very hot day, ones 'recognition-sense' may warn of wet road ahead due to sensory information yielding incorrect assessment. Even more confounding, radical 'recognition-sense' morphing can occur as new pertinent information assimilates into CP-Sets.

Unaware or transparent 'experience' retrieval to date focused on Data-Matrix as the archive-resource of choice. However, P-Bundle and M-Bundle sections discuss a new type of "experience-amalgam" developed for current or unresolved "puzzle-events": i.e., those which remain un-Solutioned in P-Cluster as P-Groups and M-Bundles.

Amalgamated from potentially thousands of FEP-Har impressions they are constructed and maintained to provide extreme proactive capability by enabling a sophisticated 'recognition-sense' early-warning-system, which manifest as aware 'feelings' or 'senses' about situations in need of Solution.

Complexity for P-Group and M-Group is enabled by both the integration of F-Puzzle 'FD-Freqs' and the coordination of their joined E-Puzzles.

> FD-Freq assimilation into these higher constructs starburst the utility of a Deluge inspired E-Har into a dynamic Event-Condition fusion, whose morphing enables both a granular and overall current 'sense' of 'what-is-going-on' as well as an ever expanding 'recognition-sense' reference library

## FEP-Sets

FEP-Pend demarcates a significant functionality change from 'answering' building-block 'questions' to 'broad-scope' puzzle 'Solutioning'. This is because FEP-Pend provides the 'fodder', which impacts 'higher-processes'. "FEP-Processor" activates when FD-Freqs impact FEP-Pend.

> Regardless of either update or addition, FEP-Processor harmonizes the FD-Freqs of the affected FEP-Pend 'FEP-KID' thus creating a virtual "V-FEP-Har". It is

then used to create or replace an existing FEP-Har (in "FEP-Set") as targeted by its identical FEP-Pend 'FEP-KID' counterpart.

By examining the illustration below it is evident an update at the FEP-Sets level will roll-up or cascade to higher-levels as well. For this section, P-Group will be the terminus for explanations. This is only a discussion convenience though, as following discussions will attest.

Note the illustration is divided into two areas by a vertical dotted line: it is intended to provide demarcation between P-Bundle and its FEP-Sets feeder. P-Bundle is comprised of two link-resources ("FEP-Link" and P-Link) and one data-resource (P-Group).

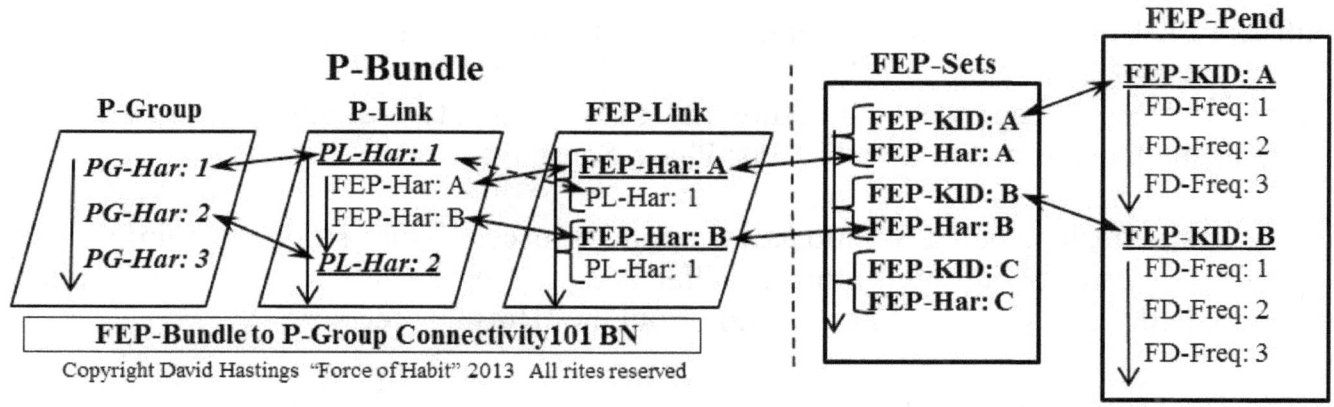

Discussions will start with P-Group and explain implications in reverse order as this will hopefully provide more clarity.

PG-Hars, synonymous to individual Phase-Senses (Phase recognition-senses), are maintained within the P-Group data-repository (see illustration above).

As such, a PG-Har is the stable outcome of a dynamically morphing "PL-Har", which was in turn created by FEP-Processor harmonizing amalgamations of "FEP-Hars".

> As previously stated, an FEP-KID (whether in FEP-Pend or FEP-Sets) is synonymous to the target E-Har which creates it. Therefore it is the E-Har, which ensures the correct allocation of the FD-Freq 'answers' within FEP-Pend. Resultantly, when FEP-Pend 'FD-Freqs' are harmonized to create an FEP-Har, ensured is not only up-link symmetry to 'higher-constructs' but also down-link integrity to originating Bombardment conditions.

Consequently, just as E-Hars can be associated when evaluated as 'significantly-similar', so to can FEP-Hars combine into assemblies. Importantly, PL-Har intensity increases in proportion to the intensities of the FEP-Hars, which were harmonized to create it: sometimes exponentially in survival situations.

To maintain the integrity of 'significantly-similar' E-Hars, now housed in FEP-Sets as FEP-KIDs, FEP-Processor associates significantly frequency-similar FEP-Hars and then harmonizes them to form a P-Link 'PL-Har' or 'working' Phase-Sense.

Once the update-cycle is finalized (FEP-Pend 'FD-Freq' harmonizing into V-FEP-Har; V-FEP-Har transfer into FEP-Set as an FEP-Har along with its associated FEP-KID; FEP-Har harmonization to form a PL-Har along with creating appropriate FEP-Link entries), PL-Har is replicated and replaces the existing previously joined PG-Har.

> PG-Hars independent structure is critical as its autonomy ensures both instantaneous and non-ambiguous Phase-Sense retrieval

As a Phase-Puzzle is being Solutioned everyone 'senses' texture-shifts from unfamiliar-and-nervous (unsure) through more familiar and 'getting-it-under-control' to familiar-and-satisfied. Let's take one Phase-Puzzle from the 'Hot-Fat' scenario.

When the event was unfolding and the Macro-Puzzle (being burned) was recognized, Figure-It-Out solutioning of 'what-to-do' to rectify the situation created additional possibilities or Phase-Puzzles: one being 'turn the heat down'.

> It rolled from the initial point of being unsure such an action would help through feeling it would be useful to being satisfied it was one part of the Solution as the fat-spitting subsided.

Phase-Senses or 'feelings' of change occur as a result of sensory input delivering waves of FD-Freq answers, which get grouped and intermittently rolled-up to FEP-Sets, then to a PL-Har and then to a PG-Har Phase-Puzzle.

> When PG-Har is replaced with a PL-Har replicant the change in electrical potential caused by the intensity variance additionally initiates an endocrine response, which is 'sensed' as a feeling.

Furthermore as FD-Freqs cease no further changes in electrical-potential or hormonal mix occur for the involved PG-Har and one 'senses' completion or resolution. Further up-the-line Macro-Senses will also be affected (discussed in its section: next).

## M-Bundle

Even though a PG-Har, because it is comprised of vast quantities of variously resolved CP-Set questions, forms an essential awareness ingredient, its major purpose is to provide 'fodder' for even more comprehensive constructs.

> Assembled into significantly-similar groups, each coalesced companion cluster is harmonized to form a 'Tier-Three' M-Bundle MB-Har or 'Macro-Sense'.

Notably, to be established as a PG-Har in the first place, a Cognitive-Alert and therefore TEA-Dat data-flow must have occurred to spirit 'broad-scope' involvement.

However, many CP-Set and subsequent PC-Har and MB-Har creations do not contain sufficient intensity (small quantities of PC-Hars with small quantities of PG-Hars) to raise conscious awareness (future discussions describe what does) and are handled transparently or without aware intervention.

Other grouping of event intensities range on the 'awareness-fringe': where mindfulness is fleeting. One's day is peppered with these 'minimally-aware' events, form deciding on a beverage to pathing ones way through a busy crowd: characteristically, these types of 'Puzzles' arise and quickly Solution.

## P-Group integration into M-Bundles

As we are enthusiastically attempting to Figure-It-Out, by receiving new and discharging not-useful information, our 'feeling' about progress toward the 'Solution' of the 'big-puzzle' changes.

> This makes sense as one is driven to solve puzzles in direct proportion to one's interest (event intensity): therefore 'sensing' puzzle-status essentially guides 'broad-scope' Solutioning.

How does the continual shift in our 'feeling' about 'how the whole event is going' actually manifest? Surprisingly, we can tap into this 'feeling' and provide a swift, brief answer.

> "How is it going" someone may ask? This translates to "how do you feel about progress so far"?

M-Bundle provisions a 'big-picture' data-resource housing many "MB-Har" residents (from which it is named). MB-Har and Macro-Puzzle are synonymous with its "Macro-Sense", which was in turn coalesced from many PG-Hars (and so on down the chain to CP-Sets).

There is no question when some Macro-Puzzle (MB-Har) is 'brought-to-mind' (recalled) one has a 'sense' of its current status.

Additionally, if it has some complexity and one focuses on only one subordinate Phase-Puzzle, a slightly different 'sense' of its nature is obvious. In other words, all phases consciously 'feel' separate yet connected, as you strive to Figure-It-Out and Solution the overall issue.

For instance (and very simplified), let's consider 'preparing a bacon-and-egg breakfast' a Macro-Puzzle. Consequently, its Phase-Puzzle constituents might be scrambling eggs, cooking bacon and cutting up a tomato.

> If asked, "How is preparation going", you would have an overall 'feeling' (Macro-Sense) of the current state of affairs, which might be conveyed as "no issues". However, if asked about a single part of the preparation such as, "how are the eggs coming along", your 'feeling' (Phase-Sense) would definitely be different; yet still connected to the overall Macro-Sense. How is this possible?

### P-Group to {PM-Link ~ M-Link} to M-Bundle

Now clear is PG-Hars were created by the harmonizing of multiple FEP-Hars. Additionally uncovered was {PG-Har // FEP-Har} inter-relationship integrity was provided by two link-resources: P-Link and FEP-Link.

Similarly, not only are MB-Har M-Bundle residents the culmination harmonizing multiple PG-Hars but also {MB-Har // PG-Har} inter-relationship integrity is established and perpetuated by two data-link resources as well: "PM-Link" and "M-Link" (see depiction below).

Previous discussions also determined the inclusion of an FD-Freq from FEP-Pend would 'up-link' cascade or re-harmonize both the updated and non-updated FEP-Har members to PL-Har, thereby ultimately shifting PG-Har 'Phase-Sense'.

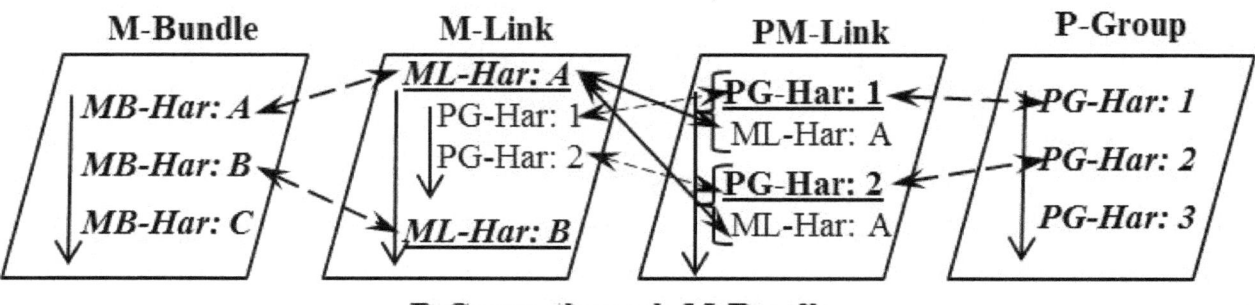

P-Group through M-Bundle
Copyright David Hastings "Force of Habit" 2013 All rites reserved

So too is this the case for an MB-Har: except its members are PG-Hars, instead of FEP-Hars. Resultantly, due to up-link cascading, an MB-Har Macro-Sense is the harmonic created from the coalition of all significantly-similar PG-Har constituents whose inclusion is re-evaluated at the time of up-link processing: thereby enabling not only updated PG-Hars but also their addition or removal to affect 'Macro-Sense'.

    Stated more succinctly, just as PG-Hars are affected by FEP-Hars, so too do MB-Hars synchronously morph as affected by PG-Har regroups and 'up-link' cascading.

M-Link is charged with providing the resource for managing the connectivity between many individual PG-Har 'drivers' and their harmonization into a single MB-Har 'driver'. Two stages are necessary though because Figure-It-Out's MB-Har Macro-Sense processor must, upon PG-Har update, be able to quickly 'up-link' from PG-Har to MB-Har. The illustration above shows the data-pathway from P-Group to M-Bundle.

Specifically, the PM-Link intermediary utilizes elements of both P-Group and M-Link to define first-stage inter-connectivity. Resultantly, the target PG-Har is employed as PM-Link's primary key-identifier (also called PG-Har), which is connected to its associated second-stage pointer: the M-Link primary key-identifier, termed "ML-Har".

Similarly, M-Link employs elements of both PM-Link and M-Bundle to accomplish its second-stage requirement. Differently though, it becomes the storehouse for not only the transitional 'Macro-Sense', called ML-Har, but also all current PG-Har contributors.

In this way any PG-Har update will register in M-Link and thereby morph the ML-Har to a new configuration (via M-Link update processors) and therefore possibly provoke a new "Macro-Sense" of the situation.

> M-Bundle forms the final-point-of-contact for all individual Macro-Senses. Each MB-Har is intimately connected to its corresponding M-Link 'ML-Har'.

As such, MB-Har is the streamlined go-to 'final' word, so to speak, for the status 'sense' of a Macro-Puzzle (MB-Har). Even though M-link processors may be actively updating in the background, MB-Har structure ensures a stable, instantaneous and non-ambiguous Macro-Sense.

**P-Cluster Discussion Review**

The initial outcome, when Equivalency-Processor cross-compared the first TEA-Dat to E-Puzzle, was a 'No-Match' condition. Consequently, Initialization-Processor was invoked to fulfill its mandate of establishing the first CP-Set in P-Cluster, which thereby also represented the first E-Puzzle 'question'.

> A CP-Set, inspired by a 'No-Match' condition, is characterized as an E-Puzzle 'question' because all associated F-Puzzle F-Freq's remain unresolved: i.e., all FD-Freq's within the {F-Freq // FD-Freq} F-Puzzle structure are initially unpopulated.

In 'No-Match' situations CP-Set 'question' creation is the norm because 'resolution' is only possible with a 'Match' condition. In other words, only when a new TEA-Dat is evaluated as 'significantly-similar' to an (existing) E-Puzzle is the stage set for possible 'solution'. Specifically, E-Puzzle 'resolution' is only possible by an acceptable quantity of associated F-Puzzle {F-Freq // FD-Freq} intensity matchups, which thereby 'resolve' them.

> Therefore as a corollary, there must first be a 'No-Match' condition providing a 'question' against which future 'significantly-similar' 'Match' data can be utilized to provide the 'answer'.

Alternately then, the effect of a 'Match' circumstance, rather than engaging Initialization-Processor, recruits Resolution-Processor, which engages its three stage 'resolution-protocols' in an attempt to 'answer' the questions associated to the 'Match'.

Resolution-Processor initializes first stage by exploiting the new TEA-Dat as an EA-Harmonic 'locator' to focus data-mining efforts on retrieval (finding and replicating) of the new TEA-Dat Distinct-Episode 'contributors' from Data-Matrix.

Following successful capture, second stage processors attempt to frequency-match each (current-data) 'replicated-member' (possible answer) against each (prior-data) F-Freq (F-Puzzle) 'question' of the target E-Puzzle. Final stage processors are responsible to not only instill 'equivalents' into applicable F-Puzzle FD-Freq's but also ensure any unmatched replicants are discarded.

> Favourably, when an F-Freq and its corresponding FD-Freq mate, {F-Freq // FD-Freq}, are populated with adequate intensity, the F-Puzzle is potentially 'resolved' or 'answered'.

E-Puzzle 'resolution' however requires a different set of competencies. An E-Puzzle will persist as a 'question' until either 'acceptable' quantities of its F-Puzzles get 'resolved' or the overall intensity of its FD-Freqs at least matches E-Har intensity. Resultantly, it is possible many E-Puzzles could 'kick-around' P-Cluster for extended periods awaiting 'resolution'.

It is notable E-Puzzles will persist within P-Cluster until disposition of M-Bundle (the third-tier) is accomplished (discussed in the E-Cluster section below). E-Har persistence is noteworthy because the purpose of much Figure-It-Out neural real-estate is to provide an off-line arena for 'mulling'.

> This capability requires maintaining granular data-elements (CP-Sets, P-Groups and M-Bundles) as readily available building-blocks for ever more complex data-arrays.

When an MB-Har Solutions though, due to the resolution of its down-line constituents, it is replicated and instilled into the "E-Pend" data-resource of "Reference-Complex". It is this action which triggers next process (future discussion).

## Background-Processor

As its name suggests Background-Processor works transparently or in the background. It continuously scans CP-Sets to assess F-Puzzle completeness: i.e., it evaluates FD-Freqs to determine satisfactory FD-Freq intensity has been attained for each companion

F-Freq of an E-Puzzle. This task is accomplished by evaluating all F-Puzzles of each E-Har to determine if sufficient F-Puzzles are satisfactorily fulfilled to also resolve the E-Puzzle.

Notably, having both 'question' (F-Freq) and 'answer' (FD-Freq) available in not only an independent data-resource but also a single Facet-Puzzle (F-Puzzle) are of major benefit for rapid assessment.

As Background-Processor need only locate an F-Puzzle with either a 'null' or lower than F-Freq intensity to move on, it can rapidly parse the F-Puzzle data-resource. This strategy ensures processing-capacity is not squandered on parsing unresolved issues but only utilized for evaluating and resolving CP-Sets.

---

**P-Cluster 'Big-Picture'**

Clearly, Figure-It-Out 'puzzle-solving' methodologies are designed for the 'big-picture'; not as a responder to minutia. In other words, to truly Figure-It-Out, when the 'It' is whatever we desire and the 'desire' is whatever we 'feel' is worthy, there must be 'cognitive-facilities' with bodacious processing competencies provisioning not only impetus for action but also referenceable data-resources providing 'expansive-scope'.

At the hub of expanded "cognitive-facilitation" are up-link mechanisms: CP-Sets through M-Bundles.

> 'Broader-scope' understanding, awareness and the opportunity for conscious intervention are all foddered by these capabilities.

'Up-link' processors cascade FD-Freq 'answers' into 'amplified-drivers': specifically FEP-Hars, PG-Hars and MB-Hars. The two tiers of resultant Puzzle-Senses, 'Phase-Sense' and 'Macro-Sense', not only provide the impetus for Figure-It-Out actions but also dramatically facilitate finding 'The-Ways' by enabling 'resolution-senses', which drive puzzle completion.

So, even though the CP-Set facility and entwined multifaceted processors are incredible in every way, its ultimate objective is but to 'fodder' even more complex data-resource matrixes, which are created to be utilized by Figure-It-Out proactive "Mulling-processors" as 'broader-scope' reference-sites.

In that regard, the P-Cluster neural-arena is an instrumental contributor for sentience: both feeling and cognition connotations.

## P-Cluster Consequences

Simultaneously with 'up-linking' to P-Group and subsequently to M-Bundle, the strategic 'escalation-condition' for Cognitive-Pathway 'choice' was also established.

In other words, because FEP-Har drivers (Event-Conditions) provide cumulative effect, 'Puzzle-Sense' now embodies intensity coordinated to original sensory acceptance but incredibly may be greater than the original Bombardment conditions creating the original 'drivers'.

> Therefore, due to PG-Har formation (harmonizing) from FEP-Hars and consequent MB-Har formation (harmonizing) from 'pooled' PG-Hars, intensity-escalation is once again achieved as it was with 'Tags' when they were similarly 'pooled' to create an Event-Condition.

Specifically, the greater the similar sequential bombardment activity, the greater becomes the quantity of TEA-Dats; therefore, the greater the quantity of significantly-similar FEP-Hars: The greater the quantity of 'pooled' FEP-Hars, and so the intensity escalates up the line to 'Puzzle-Senses'.

> Incredibly, although PG-Hars and MB-Hars display broad-gradients of 'Puzzle-Senses', they are always in direct proportion to the sensory-activity, which instigated them

As multiple PG-Har 'Puzzle-Senses' are the 'building-blocks' of an MB-Har so too is MB-Har correspondingly affected by the quantity and intensity of its various P-Group members.

Therefore, activities in which you more fully engage are loaded with FEP-Hars, which thereby cascade to yield more robust 'Puzzle-Senses'…when massive these are therefore re-designated "Passion-Senses".

> The most excitement for a project will be elicited when all of its elements have high 'Passion-Sense'. So strive to fully engage in whatever you are doing and enjoy the pleasure

P-Group and M-Bundle support two classes of "Puzzle-Events": 'active-puzzles' and 'passive-puzzles'. Although both are recruited by Figure-It-Out find 'The-Ways', 'active-puzzles' form 'notable' and therefore conscious events whereas 'passive-puzzles' remain transparent or unaware.

> There is an extremely significant reason, which highlights why one should seek to fully engage in all endeavours: because Solutioned MB-Hars and their building-blocks get transferred to the hardened neural real-estate of the Reference-Complex to be relived for a lifetime

## Reference-Complex

When 'Solutioned', M-Bundle along with its "data-chain" connections fodders two 'broad-scope' 'Reference-Complex' data-archives: "Event-Cluster" or "E-Cluster" and "Concept-Cluster" or "C-Cluster". These Mind-Self data-resources are also designated 'Fourth-Tier' and 'Fifth-Tier', respectively.

> Excitingly, Reference-Complex data-resources provide a significant "Cognitive-Edge" by changing the balance of survival power in our favor: From being a bombardment target to proactively choosing parameters of engagement with the Deluge

Although many species display various aspects of structures and processes so far discussed, the depth and breadth of the human Reference-Complex is unique in neural quantity, variety and complexity.

> Resultantly, 'Enhanced-Solutioning' becomes possible via Cognition-Complex mechanisms, which among other marvels can devise ostensibly unlimited ingenuity or "solutioning-scenarios".

Its primary data-retrieval mandate is accomplished by accessing extensive Reference-Complex archives to locate applicable "harmonic-drivers", which thereby enable access to appropriate Data-Matrix details and associated visual imagery.

Incredibly, retrieval is even reasonably accurate with regards to not only pertinent detail targeting but also temporal-juxtaposition.

Everything we 'know' or believe in is derived from sensory experiences: We simply do not 'know', what our sensors have not accepted

Beyond the miracle of detail and image retrieval, we possess the capability to not only realign disparate experiences into stories, jokes, inventions, intuition, imagination, etc. but also develop and store multiple "Value-Senses" with personalized 'gradients-of-acceptability'.

Such tailored variances are evident in beliefs such as: what we like and what we do not like; what is acceptable to us and what is not; what is correct; what is going in the right direction according to our own "Cognitive-Values"; explaining why and what we value; developing strong cases for our beliefs; evaluating another's explanations of their values against ours; deciding to reject or incorporate some or all; and so on.

Even though mostly taken for granted, we perform miraculous feats of recall: Just to have the capacity to "…remember when…" is beyond amazing!

---

## Event-Cluster Foundations

As revealed so far, substantial resources were commanded by Figure-It-Out to accomplish its exactingly precise and repeatable P-Cluster data-acquisition. Astonishing Filtering-and-Slotting manipulations culminated in incredibly detailed event-storage as well as precise inter-connections for not only sensory events occurring relatively simultaneously but also similar events temporally far-removed.

> Without the capability to accumulate to and retrieve from 'Reference-Resources' (see 'The-Ways: Solutioning' depiction) 'broad-scope' events would seem new all the time: This would not be useful for survival.

Fortunately, genetic design has significantly boosted survival-potential by extending Figure-It-Out purview to not only encompass multiple compounding layers of data-capture but also utilize previously acquired 'broad-scope' experiences as comparative-references against which to evaluate current-data.

> Thereby Figure-It-Out is enabled to determine current new event status as 'familiar' or 'foreign'.

Notably by providing previous 'broad-scope' experience data a 'familiar-condition' (significantly-similar) will fast-track responses. Fortunately for experience acquisition however, an 'unfamiliar-condition' does not cause disaster because it initiates yet another set of competencies, which drive "TI-Outbounds" to gather specifically probed for data from ones Bombardment-Sphere (detailed "Test-It" discussions further along).

To this juncture, Figure-It-Out has been dedicated to managing 'P-Cluster'. Specifically, by involving its multiple specialized processors: From initial No-Match // Match determinations through F-Puzzle, E-Puzzle and P-Group formation; culminating in M-Bundle creation.

> It may therefore not be surprising Figure-It-Out will continue providing the impetus to determine disposition of 'Solutioned' P-Cluster data-element groups or "Puzzle-Packages".

**182**    Dr. David J. Hastings PhD

## Event-Cluster Formation

E-Cluster formation from 'Puzzle-Packages' exhibits compound challenges. Resultantly, more complex multiple-stage manipulations are necessary to satisfy successful outcome beginning with E-Pend 'polling', which kicks-off the progression.

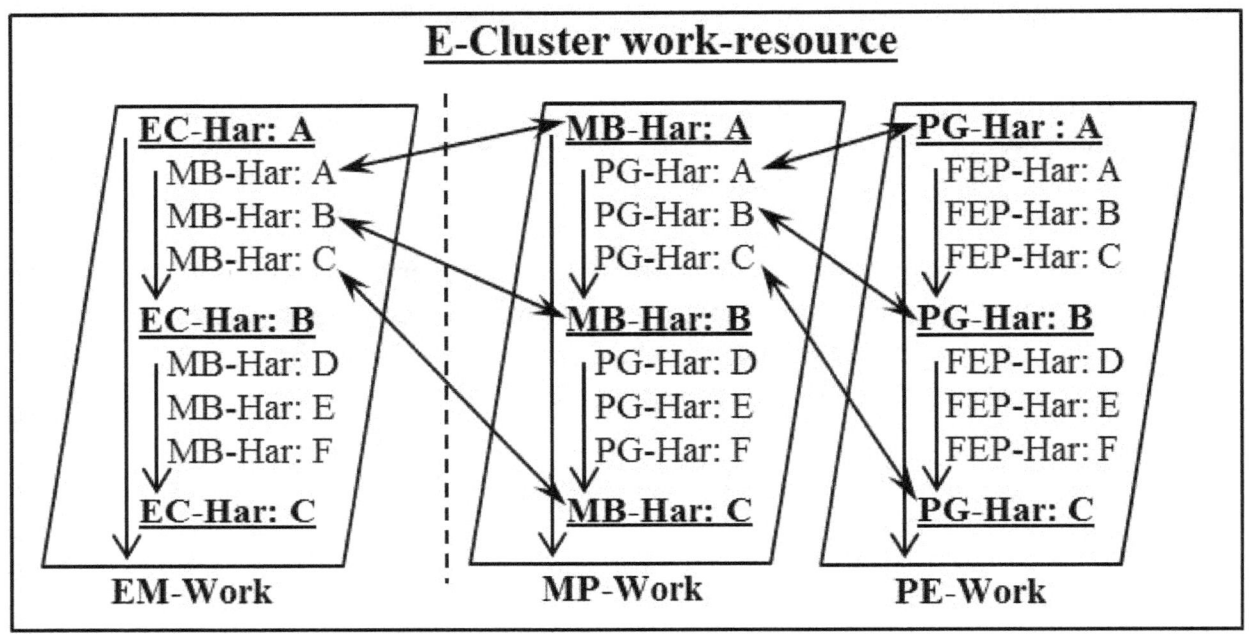

At the forefront Figure-It-Out utilizes a temporary "E-Cluster work-resource", whose design mimics the E-Cluster data-resource format (see depiction below). A working-resource is necessary to accumulate the needed data-elements prior to instilling the formed E-Cluster ("EC-Har") into non-volatile neural-real-estate.

The dotted line in the illustration below is meant to indicate "PE-Work" and "MP-Work" (to the right of the line) as emulating P-Cluster P-Groups and M-Bundles, respectively: whereas "EM-Work" to the left of the line will house the assembled E-Cluster. Each is designated for the accumulation of specific Puzzle-Package elements.

The first stage acquires an MB-Har from E-Pend and then replicates it as an MB-Har/R ('/R' designates replicant). As the MB-Har/R is equivalent to its (P-Cluster) M-Bundle key-identifier counterpart, it is used for M-Bundle targeting.

Three tasks comprise stage-two: replicate all MB-Har 'PG-Hars'; replicate all PG-Har related FEP-Hars; and populate 'MP-Work' and 'PE-Work'. Inter-relationship integrity is achieved by utilizing two previously discussed P-Cluster link-resources in 'down-link' mode: M-Link is used to locate all PG-Hars and P-Link to locate all FEP-Hars.

The third stage 'pools' all 'MP-Work' MB-Har's and then harmonizes them into an EC-Har, which it loads into the 'EM-Work' thereby completing the set. Once validated the 'E-Cluster' work-resource is instilled into the E-Cluster data-resource.

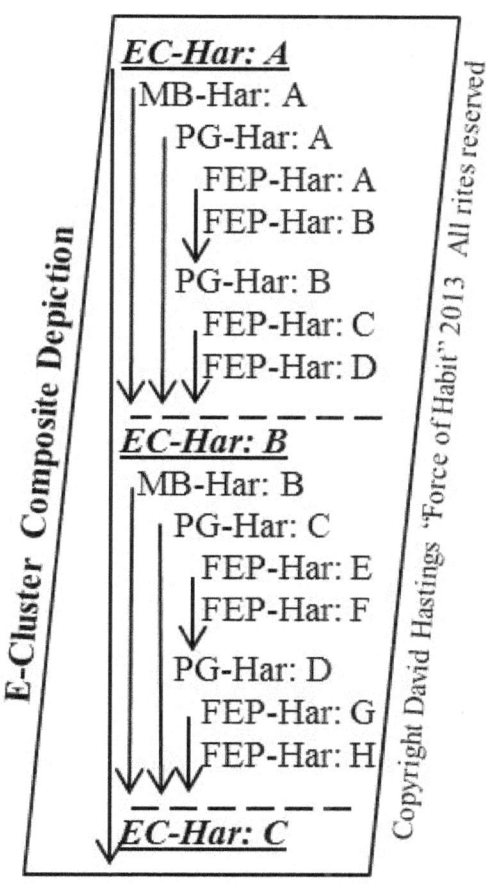

The illustrations present two different depictions: the one below a relative view of all data-elements and their relationships; the other (side) a segregated more classical data-resource view.

'Reading' the "E-Cluster Composite Depiction" (right) beginning from the first horizontal dotted line (intended to indicate the 'EC-Har: A' record-set) upwards should help to clarify what is related to what.

First though note the vertical arrows all indicate many-more-records within their particular purview. Thus by analyzing 'PG-Har: B' one can see there are two (2) FEP-Hars (C and D) as well as a down arrow beside them, which is intended to indicate many more FEP-Har data-elements belong to the 'PG-Har: B' group.

Likewise 'PG-Har: A' also contains many FEP-Hars as indicated by the vertical arrow beside them. Similarly, the longer vertical arrow traversing beside 'PG-Har: A' and 'PG-Har:

B' indicate many more PG-Har data-elements exist; as does the vertical arrow beside 'MB-Har: A' mean many additional MB-Har records exist. The longest vertical arrow transcends the dotted lines to indicate there are many more EC-Har records.

The "E-Cluster Data-and-Link resource Depiction'" (below) displays a different view, however. It provides comparative connectivity between data-and-link resources by displaying only a very small data-element and sampling. For instance, PE-Link displays only two (denoted by 'PG-Har: A' and 'PG-Har: B') of the many thousands of its PG-Har residents.

## *WayBetter* Your L.I.F.E$^2$.: **Mind-Self**

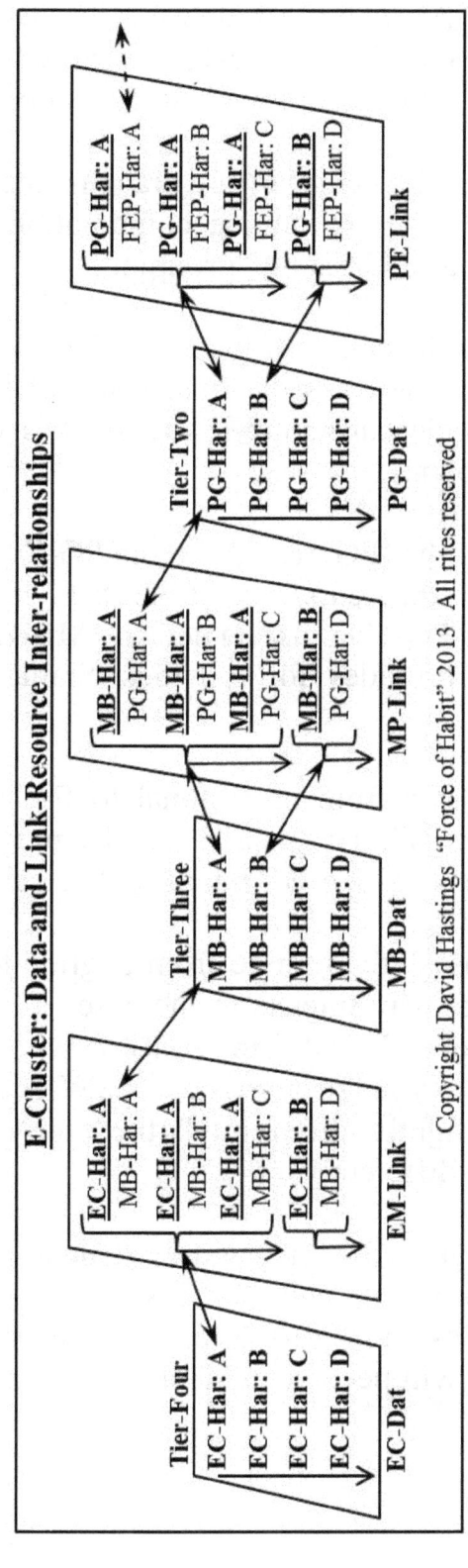

By singling out 'PG-Har: A', a large brace can be seen encompassing three of its illustrated 'PG-Har: A's'. A different FEP-Har (denoted FEP-Har: A, 'B', and 'C') is associated with each 'PG-Har: A', thereby showing its one-to-many relationship.

> The down arrow from the center of the brace is intended to show many hundreds of {'PG-Har: A // FEP-Har} unique combinations exist, which thus form the members of its discrete 'PG-Har-A' grouping.

The acute-angle arrow from the center of the first PE-Link brace to a single 'PG-Har: A' in the PG-Dat data-resource indicates the final result of the amalgamation of the 'PG-Har-A' grouping into a single harmonic: Likewise it is with 'PG-Har: B' and all the 'PG-Har' groupings not shown.

The acute-angle arrow from the 'PG-Har: A' in the PG-Dat to the MP-Link 'PG-Har: A' indicates it as not only subordinate to the 'MG-Har: A' in the 'MP-Link' repository but also one-of-many different PG-Hars associated to 'MB-Har: A'. This pattern is stable throughout E-Cluster and provides for previous characteristics and capabilities and those yet to be discussed.

> The moment of transfer from provisional to E-Cluster data-resources causes a shift in "driver-potential". This 'shift' thereby potentially enables the 'Solution' to be not only 'cognitively-sensed' but also physically rendered.

Resulting "Experience-Senses" then range from negligible in the case of a transparent passive-puzzle shift to extremely intense in the case of a highly active-puzzle shift. A resounding "YES…I Figured-It-Out" in concert with several exuberant physical responses may alert others to your strong Experience-Sense recognition. When you hear someone say, "I see it slightly differently" the 'see' is Experience-Sense; i.e., 'I experience-sense it slightly differently'.

"Clean-up" is the final stage. It is delegated to remove all 'Puzzle-Package' elements (including F-Puzzles) from not only P-Cluster data-and-link resources but also transitional data-resources as well. Further along when recall is discussed, aside from reusing neural-resources, it will become evident why 'clean-up' was essential.

## Concept-Cluster Introduction

The process is incredible…a significant bombardment event series triggers recall of similar 'broad-scope' occurrences or cognitive Experience-Senses. These 'drive' us to Figure-It-Out by not only instigating immediate mental and hormonal alertness but also synchronously testing or prodding the 'out-there' by directed information feedback requests designed to instigate physical responses

As we now appreciate, sentience 'roots' originate in sensor-accepted bombardment events. Gathered and harmonized into ever more complex constructs, they ultimately form incredible Experience-Senses. These culminate as "Concept-Cluster-Harmonics", which remain directly tuned to their sensory origins. Maintained in Concept-Cluster or just C-Cluster within the Reference-Complex repository, its members form our highest-level 'emotional-drivers'.

> Incredibly, 'Experience-Senses' evolve to become the primary Figure-It-Out 'go-to' rapid-response Cognitive-Habit 'survival-strategy': directly validating and/or augmenting Soma-Responses.

Not implanted genetically, "CC-Harmonic's" or "CC-Hars" (C-Cluster members) gradually through interactions with the Deluge (experience), become THE principal front-line 'event-evaluators' by providing the 'trigger-points' or "cognitive-expectations" for new event 'Filtering-and-Slotting': i.e., from recognition to initial response processes.

Understandably then, the shift to utilizing Cognitive-Habits as THE go-to first 'driver-sense' is gradual.

> In fact, 'Experience-Senses' come to provide instant evaluations, whose 'gradients-of-acceptability' define the boundaries of each person's perceptions, anticipations or Cognitive-Habits

In other words, C-Cluster storehouses a comprehensive array of Cognitive-Habits, whose mosaic characterizes individual uniqueness. Its members provide 'emotional-driver' initiating touch-points for language, speech, labeling-concepts, self-image, beliefs, point-of-view, preferences, likes, dislikes, etc.

'Experience-Senses' also spirit dig-down capability purposed to support the pro-active Mind-Self mandate. Almost instantaneously, not only does a small scoop of associated information 'attach' to an 'Experience-Sense' but also, more often than not, so do images.

Depending on originating 'event-driver' (FEP-Har) intensities, duration and quantity, "Recall-Packages" can manifest into awareness from 'brief-minimal' to 'lengthy-extensive'. Regardless, subsequent processing is accomplished by deliberations expedited in Cognition-Complex: discussed in a following section.

Following from previous discussions, 'Recall-Packages' will never contain 'same' but instead 'significantly-similar' as this is the nature of not only Reference-Complex harmonics but also Data-Matrix.

> Therefore, when experience with an 'event-genre' is minimal the result can be wildly inappropriate responses, which can also, as we are all too familiar, manifest as irrational fears or 'feeling out of your depth'

Notably then, follow-up recall is seldom straight forward but mostly requires various amounts of "Mulling" to shake additional details and images loose. This is because Cognitive-Habits have a 'hardened' nature due to several factors. Firstly, Reference-Complex does not reside within the dynamic elastic or malleable neural real-estate of Figure-It-Out but instead in much less elastic Mind-Self territory.

> Also compounding significant data-resource structural variance are radically different processing proclivities: Figure-It-Out is designed as the most active and responsive; whereas Mind-Self, configured for data-repository reliability and steadfastness, is not.

Reference-Complex data-resources have also been 'stocked' over decades. Resultantly, if we try to figure-out why we believe something in a particular way it is difficult because of the elevated position of these Cognitive-Habits at the top of a long line (four tiers) of foddering processes.

> 'Elevated position' then, although enormously beneficial, also poses a significant issue because recall actually requires CC-Hars to undergo 'inverse-engineering' in order to extract details.

As 'Experience-Sense' initializes the recall process, 'recall-flow' must therefore proceed from general (CC-Har) to specific (Data-Matrix) by utilizing 'down-link' processing. Although recall processing will be addressed further along, suffice it to say for the moment the detail-recovery process, as we all realize, is neither instantaneous nor always easy.

Cognitive-Habits are by their nature then, due to the reasons discussed above, not 'elastic' but 'hardened'. As matter-of-fact, vast amounts of new, different yet complimentary data, would be required to spirit even a slight Cognitive-Habit variance. Consequently, once formed Cognitive-Habits are difficult if not downright impossible to change.

> As we have all no doubt experienced, no matter how hard one tries to 'change' a Cognitive-Habit, not only is the likelihood of success minimal but also the effort necessary to cause any shift is huge

Moreover, confounding any desired 'change' are the Cognitive-Habits themselves. This is because Figure-It-Out uses them as THE initial filters through which all new data is accepted for additional Cognition-Complex testing; or not. Cognitive-Habits rule perceptions from the shoes you 'choose' to the hairdo you 'like': useful for rapid response but not so useful for choice. Stated differently, without significant intervention "Your Habits are Creating You": i.e., keeping you in place.

However, the Force-of-Habit subtitle, "Create Your Own Habits: Don't let your Habits Create You", provides good news. A quick, successful and easy alternative is available to enable choice: intimated by the 'Create your own Habits' portion of the sub-title. Specifically this phrase means disregard the Cognitive-Habit you are finding 'not-useful' and create a new "Go-To-Habit".

> In this way you get control to build 'the-new-habit' from the get-go from current desires and information instead of trying to update 'the-old-habit', which was instilled in you through many years of domestication

Unrelentingly, Cognitive-Habits have dictated your "lifetime-to-date". They ensure your perspectives are their perspectives by either denying any new 'significantly-similar' data-elements, which are considered radical by their assessment or incorporating only supportive elements. Thus perpetuate biases.

Notably, we have several worst Cognitive-Habits: such as, "The-Way-We-Think"; "The-Way-We-Speak"; and "The-Way-We-Hide". These will be discussed more fully later. However, by choosing to create a new puzzle through the 'mulling' process (to be discussed) whose solution seeks new information, a fresh cycle is supported by Figure-It-Out, which results in a new "Go-To-Habit" of your authentically 'chosen' creation.

> As a Toastmaster, I have encountered many who by gentle persuasion to come to a meeting (thereby starting new puzzles) have bypassed their domesticated negative speaking habit perspective and become great speakers by creating new 'Go-To-Habits'

> Be warned though, those old cognitive-habits do not go away but tenaciously remain as pesky survivors trying, as habits do, to be at the forefront forcing their will

## Concept-Cluster Creation

Commencing with TI-Inbound 'foddering' of P-Cluster and culminating with E-Clusters creation, Figure-It-Out deployed multiple processers whose stratagems focused on data-acquisition. In other words, Figure-It-Out mechanisms were instrumental throughout: from TEA-Dat handling through F-Puzzle extreme detail 'gathering' - designed to provision very specific 'answers' for very specific 'questions' - to the establishment of E-Clusters multiple data-resources and inter-connecting data-links.

> Figure-It-Out responded to E-Cluster creation challenge in two stages: evaluating M-Bundle 'Solutioned' status (by assessment of the 'resolution' statuses of its constituent down-line P-Groups); and then passing a "data-cue" (MB-Har) to a transitional data-resource (E-Pend in this case) thereby enabling next Concept-Cluster processes.

Congruently for the formation of a CC-Har, Mind-Self utilizes similar strategies to some deployed by Figure-It-Out. In order to keep apprised of current conditions as part of the survival mandate, EC-Hars are also continually evaluated for 'significant-similarity' (as were predecessor P-Cluster elements by Figure-It-Out).

Likewise, EC-Hars matching Mind-Self criteria are loaded as an "EC-pool" into the "C-Pend" transitional data-resource (see 'The-Ways: Solutioning' illustration). From here,

EC-pools will be grabbed by subsequent processors, mandated to either update or create a CC-Har.

C-Cluster thereby houses a remarkable, expandable and updatable reference data-resource. Its CC-Har members are the culmination of the harmonic-integration of 'pooled' E-Cluster (EC-Har) members specifically evaluated by Mind-Self as significantly-similar.

> FEP-Hars are the foundational 'fodder' for both E-Cluster and C-Cluster harmonic key-identifiers

The illustration below provides a pictorial or analytic portrayal of 'Tier-Five' C-Cluster structures and the "CE-Link" relationship necessary for up-link processing from 'Tier-Four'. This illustration will be updated to incorporate additional factors in the 'Recall Section' following.

The illustration below provides a very small C-Cluster sampling: it includes both data- and-link structures as well as their interdependencies.

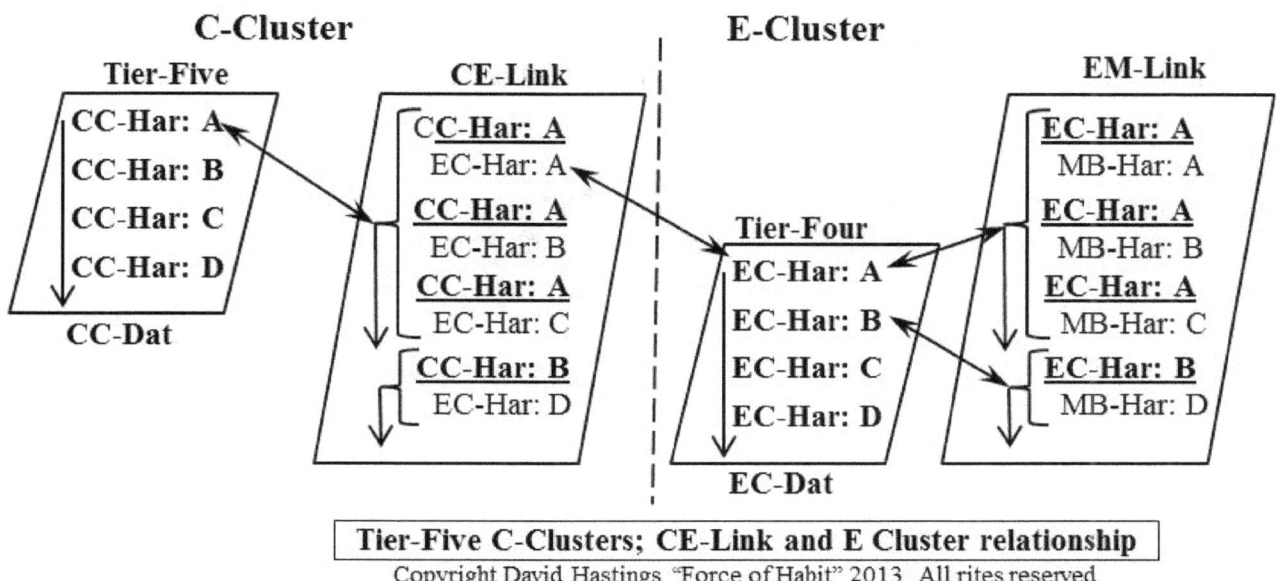

Tier-Five C-Clusters; CE-Link and E Cluster relationship
Copyright David Hastings "Force of Habit" 2013 All rites reserved

For instance, CE-Link displays only two of the many thousands (denoted by 'CC-Har: A' and 'CC-Har: B' brackets and down arrows) of its CC-Har residents.

By singling out 'CC-Har: A', a large brace can be seen encompassing three of its illustrated 'CC-Har: A's'.

A different EC-Har (denoted EC-Har: A, 'B', and 'C') is associated with each 'CC-Har: A', thereby showing its one-to-many relationship. The down arrow from the center of the brace is intended to show many hundreds of {'CC-Har: A // EC-Har} unique combinations exist, which thus form the members of its discrete 'CC-Har-A' grouping.

The left acute-angle arrow from the center of the first CE-Link brace to a single 'CC-Har: A' in the CC-Dat data-resource indicates the final result of the amalgamation of the 'CC-Har-A' grouping into a single harmonic frequency: Likewise it is with 'CC-Har: B' and all presumed (but not shown) 'CC-Hars'.

---

Our Figure-It-Out data-gathering journey has taken us from TI-Inbound to P-Cluster formation and through Reference-Complex culminating in highest level Concept-Cluster 'Experience-Senses'. In one way this is the end of a journey and in another, just the beginning.

> The 'beginning' because Data-Matrix, P-Cluster and Reference-Complex experience data-archives are variously integrated by Cognition-Complex Components with current sensory information for the creation of our "Living-Story"

Resolution-Processor provided two outbound pathways: to E-Pend and to P-Pend. As the E-Pend journey was documented above, it is now time to turn attention to P-Pend and see what amazing features it enables.

---

## Parameter-Processor

'The-Ways: Proactive' illustration below serves to not only summarize previous Figure-It-Out discussions (albeit in a different format) but also highlight remaining Figure-It-Out topics. It is intended to provide not only a diagrammatic reconfiguration of previous processes but also the final expansion of the 'Cognition-Complex' zone depicted on 'The-Ways: Solutioning' illustration.

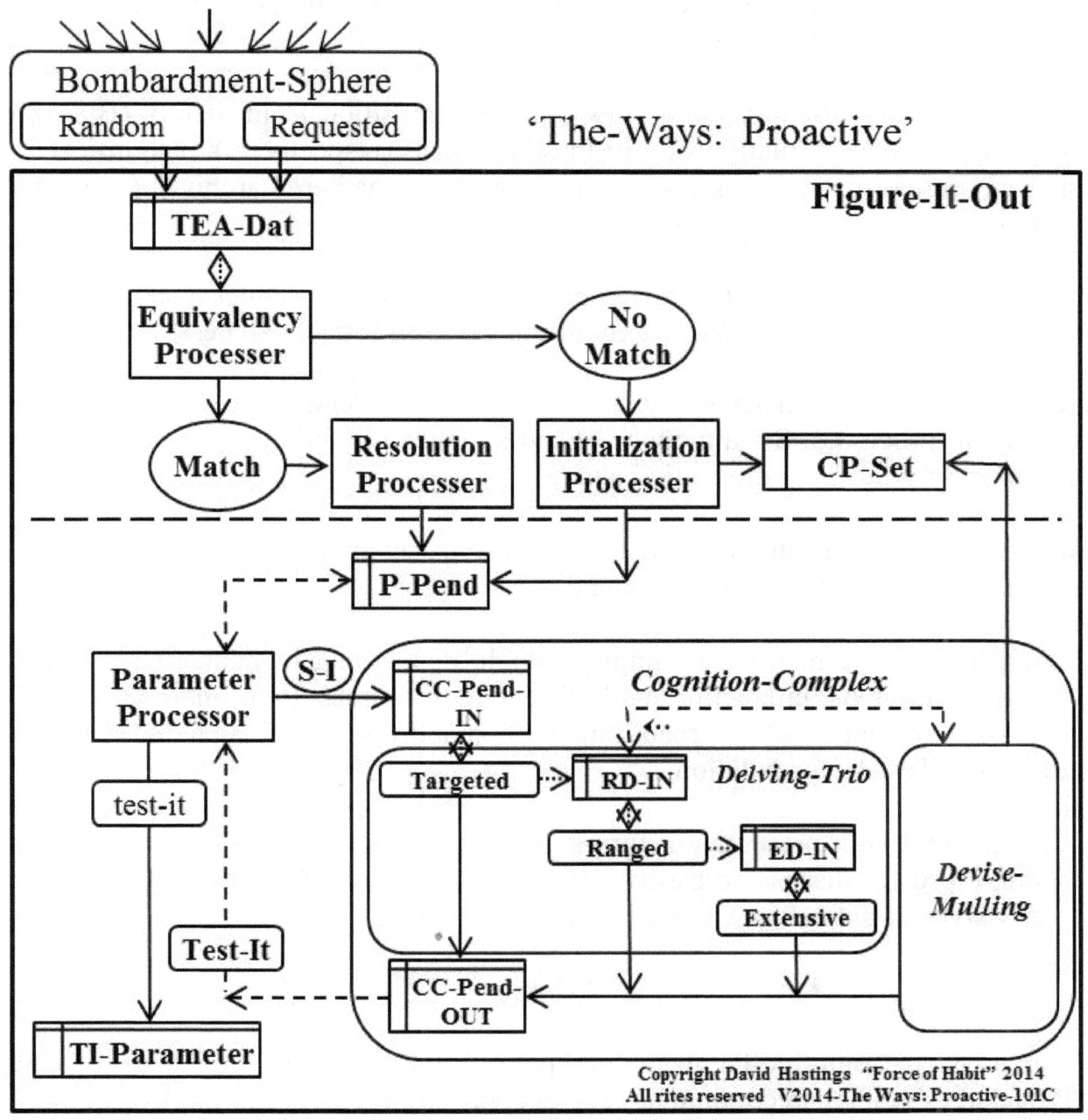

The 'P-Pend' inbound hopper-resource, located near the center of the graphic, provides the launch-point for further discussions.

> As has been the case so far, 'hopper' data-resources remain an ideal solution because they permit the accessing mechanism to regulate its own capacity by extracting only what it can handle.

The horizontal dotted line just above P-Pend is meant to distinguish previous functions (above) from new scope (below).

In a very real sense P-Pend demarcates a pivotal transition from merely 'Bracketing' sensory-experience to actually using it: In other words (respectively), a significant shift from archiving current happenings to comparing those gathered archives (experiences) to current 'broad-scope' events (bombardment).

> This is a really big deal as this comparative capability enables a species defining leap from reactive to proactive cognition processes and awareness

More specifically, Parameter-Processor 'polling' of P-Pend initializes all remaining Figure-It-Out processes. So, although P-Pend supplies the fodder, Parameter-Processor is the controlling-hub (see illustration above).

It alone provides final integration between not only TI-Inbound and TI-Outbound but also Cognition-Complex and TI-Outbound.

Although this at first may seem simple enough, demanding mandates need fulfilling, including: continuous interaction with five data-resources (two inbound and three outbound); and supply of a broad range of support services such as, assessment, blending and 'Test-It' formulation.

> Consistent with presentation format to date, a single event stream will again be employed for discussion clarity. Of course in ongoing Cognitive-Pathway terms, massive variant activity is continuously inundating.

## P-Pend

By storehousing Cognitive-Pathway 'raw-parameters', P-Pend inbound data-packages or "P-packages" establish continuous crucial connection to not only the Deluge but also

P-Cluster and therefore precise CP-Set puzzles. Consequently, P-package evaluation and manipulation (Filtering-and-Slotting) by Parameter-Processor bodes serious implications for following mechanisms, as they in turn depend on best information being deposited into their 'inbound-hoppers'.

Recall from previous discussions a P-Pend 'P-package' was shaped from two sources: the originating Deluge data in the form of a TEA-Dat plus the implicated (P-Cluster CP-Set) E-Har, which was either created or matched by Equivalency-Processor as a consequence of TEA-Dat evaluation.

> Therefore, a P-Pend 'P-package' enfolds a specific join format: {**TEA-Dat** // E-Har}: where the TEA-Dat portion forms the primary 'element' or key-identifier.

Element usage has crucial implications in the ongoing search for 'answers': especially accented because Cognition-Complex is the last stop to assist in "Finding-the-Ways" for Bombardment events.

At this juncture, Parameter-Processor is charged with implementing Figure-It-Out's mandate by deploying two simultaneous processing functions, which differently utilize P-package: one, evaluation to determine "intensity-value"; the other, immediate Parameter-Processor Test-It creation. Additionally, if "sufficient-intensity" (SI on the illustration) is concluded, Cognition-Complex will be simultaneously engaged to assist.

**Parameter-Processor Test-It creation**

The Parameter-Processor track will be discussed first because, regardless of 'intensity-value', Parameter-Processor must always expedite Test-It creation; thereby ensuring not only data-flow remains ostensibly uninterrupted but also actions are not jerky but fluid. Due to this rapid deployment mandate the source for Test-It configuration must also be restricted to a single CP-Set.

> Here are the strategic data-flow events, which brought us to this point: Figure-It-Out was initiated by a TEA-Dat; TEA-Dat was subsequently transformed into an unresolved CP-Set; P-package was created; and Parameter-Processor has acquired the P-package from P-Pend.

TEA-Dats are continually arriving: some create new CP-Sets and some contribute to the resolution of existing CP-Sets (specifically its E-Har F-Puzzles). As we know, new CP-

Sets are mostly created from random Bombardment-Sphere (TEA-Dat) events: such as, the sound of a passing car. What then inspires match-condition or 'significantly-similar' TEA-Dats?

As potential combinations of bombardment (the SLID mix – Soma Location IDentifiers) are enormous, one can therefore conclude most 'matches' are not random as this condition would not allow for resolution within a useable time-frame: instead 'matches' must result from directed activities. What then is the primary inspirator to direct the creation of significantly-similar TEA-Dats?

> There must be mechanisms, which can amass pertinent unresolved issues (relating to current P-package events), then generate a relevant outbound request to physical response systems, which thereby elicit specific Bombardment-Sphere interactions.

'Request' design would require sufficient detail to applicably direct specific physical interaction, to generate 'match' feedback, to provide 'fodder' for directly expediting the resolution of unresolved CP-Set issues. Of course, this section is purposed to present Parameter-Processor as the first mechanism to generate the first type of "rudimentary-request" branded and written as 'Test-It'.

Specifically, Test-It creation is accomplished by Parameter-Processor utilizing the 'P-package' E-Har to accesses P-Cluster to first locate its CP-Set // E-Har counterpart then locate all E-Har unresolved F-Puzzles; i.e., those FD-Freq's with null or lesser intensity than their companion F-Freq (recall F-Puzzle F-Freq's emulate the original Sensory Location ID's or SLIDs).

As located, each unresolved F-Puzzle (of the target E-Har) is replicated and compiled into a "collection-resource". When complete, collection-resource data is hierarchical arranged by SLID frequency into a Test-It data-bundle. In this way, unresolved sensory bombardment information (F-Freq's with 'unanswered' FD-Freq's) forms the outbound Parameter-Processor Test-It; thereby driving bombardment-pertinent feedback.

### Reactive-Cycle

The 'Reactive-cycle' encompasses the following stages: TI-Inbound receives a TEA-Dat; 'Match' prompts the creation of a 'P-package' data-bundle and inserts it into 'P-Pend'; Parameter-Processor retrieves the 'P-package'; P-package is evaluated; a Test-It is created by Parameter-Processor and sent to TI-Parameter; and follow-up Components (potentially) implement physical activations, which can result in minor positional adjustments within ones Bombardment-Sphere; thus providing directed new sensory feedback.

> Of the two P-package 'elements', {**TEA-Dat** // E-Har}, E-Har was utilized to pinpoint the corresponding CP-Set. Its unresolved or 'unanswered' F-Puzzles were replicated to create a Test-It to thus inspire feedback for the unresolved 'questions'.

Additionally, at the point when Parameter-Processor 'P-package to E-Har to F-Puzzle' evaluation establishes the implicated CP-Set as resolved, no additional Test-Its will be issued and therefore the reactive-cycle will end.

> Therefore, 'reactive-cycle' Test-It creation activities not only prompt specific feedback but also remain transparent (unaware). As will be evidenced, 'quiet' outcomes is not necessarily the case when Cognition-Complex is brought on-line.

### Sufficient-Intensity Concurrent Evaluation

Parameter-Processor has another immediately deployed parallel duty besides apprehending and utilizing a 'P-package' to create a Test-It: What really 'lights-us-up' is when it assesses "sufficient-intensity". Intensity computations are vital as they dictate the creation of either both a Test-It and a CC-Pend-IN or just a Test-It (directed to TI-Outbound).

Populating CC-Pend-IN (as it did for Cognitive-Alert) inspires an incredible set of specialized capabilities.

> Cognition-Complex, by being alerted to bombardment events, is enabled to provide an array of proactive "Delving" contribution based not only on current Deluge but also on experience as well: **this capability is a major game-changer**

Sufficient-intensity therefore induces Parameter-Processor to alert Cognition-Complex by inserting a replicated P-package into CC-Pend-IN (the Cognition-Complex inbound hopper). The replication strategy allows Parameter-Processor to continue working while enabling Cognition-Complex to initiate its simultaneous processing.

Notably, Parameter-Processing 'intensity' evaluations closely parallel Cognitive-Pathway distinctions, which of course inherently incorporate intensity-gradient. 'Tepid' to 'Survival' (CP-5 through CP-1) Cognitive-Pathway escalation fundamentally signifies a corresponding upsurge in F-Puzzle quantity. Resultantly, CC-Pend-IN notification would be the rule when 'Hot' (CP-2) or 'Warm' (CP-3) pathways initiate the P-package.

Parameter-Processor intensity evaluation is fairly straight forward. The resulting intensity-value is simply the quantity of unresolved F-Puzzles (those targeted by the use of the 'P-package' E-Har as above): i.e., greater quantities of unresolved F-Puzzles evoke higher intensity-value. When gauged by Figure-It-Out, intensity-value will occupy a point on the intensity-gradient as either sufficiently-intense or not.

This makes sense as 'more-unresolved' F-Puzzles (higher intensity-value) should get the larger proportion of processing attention. For instance the initial TEA-Dat, used for the 'No-Match' condition scenario, resulted in 100% unresolved F-Puzzles.

Parameter-Processor therefore would not only impose a higher intensity-gradient but also usurp proportionate processing resources: i.e., more resource allocation for higher intensity-value events. There is perfect symmetry to this strategy: when feedback provides F-Puzzle resolution so too will intensity-value decline, thereby uniformly reducing demands on processors.

There are two other aspects though, which directly impact the volume of F-Puzzles: bombardment intensity and the quantity of involved Sensory-Location-IDs (SLIDs). In a more massive bombardment situation, like jumping into cold water, are not only many Soma-Locations involved but also substantially more receptor neurons engaged. Both conditions therefore deliver many more 'Tags', therefore larger 'Tag-Clusters' and resultantly, a larger quantity of F-Puzzles.

Consequently, more F-Puzzles will also require 'more' sensory feedback to resolve. Fortunately two wild cards are available, which provide situational scalability by quickening resolution duration (i.e., adapt to the wax-and-wane of Deluge events): more processing power can be brought on line; and additional feedback can be requested via Test-Its. These will be discussed below in context with their application.

---

**Cognition-Complex**

If we did not continuously move around like a storm wave within our Bombardment-Spheres causing conditions to continuously morph (thereby actually begging for trouble) our copious Mind-Self Filtering-and-Slotting activities (evaluations, manipulations, data-archiving, retrieval and re-evaluations) would not be necessary.

> For instance, we could stay very, very still - like a clam perhaps. Although this alternate would be substantially less interesting, it would serve to minimize bombardment experiences and therefore serve to allay requirements for receiving and processing complexity.

I think our mobility design not being so limited is incredibly fortunate. However, to balance the riskiness caused by the extremely broad array of possible physical interactivities (thereby instigating a potentially huge array of bombardment scenarios), powerful integrating, evaluating and actioning compensators, capable of utilizing and integrating current-data (bombardment) with reference-data (experiences), need to be available.

> In other words, to ensure we do not have to 'reinvent-the-wheel' each time a repeat event-sequence occurs interactive counterbalancing mechanisms are imperative.

Here are a few: an expandable resource tool-set capable of determining if 'same-or-nearly-similar' has previously occurred; processes to proactively enhance survival conditions by locating and interacting current events with similar storehoused 'broad-scope' experiences; methodologies to assess and deploy 'uncovered-parameters' and enact previously determined 'safe' tried-and-true responses; and there are more.

Cognition-Complex nicely fulfills strategic 'living' and critical survival requirements. It is designed to support finding 'The-Ways' or 'Figuring-It-Out' by: delving into ones experience base and mixing in appropriate (similar) current activity; creating bombardment interaction experiments (Test-Its); gathering requested feedback; re-evaluating; re-delving; creating adjusted experiments; and continuing to cycle until 'The-Ways' are uncovered (i.e., CP-Set questions are resolved).

P-Pend supplies inbound intense 'bombardment-fodder' to Cognition-Complex: whereas, Cognition-Complex sends designed proactive experimental Test-Its outbound, purposed to define that very 'fodder'.

Notably, Test-It 'requests' are fundamental to sending outbound 'best-guesses' to impact ones Bombardment-Sphere by instigating physical action. Supporting mechanisms on the other hand are mostly evaluative: designed to not only determine Test-It effectiveness but also redeploy Test-It's if necessary.

Stated differently, 'requests' would not be useful unless two other capabilities were not also possible: evaluate the effectiveness of deployed Test-It bundles; and issue new Test-It's for remaining unresolved aspects.

There is however a potentially deal-breaking issue. As complexity increases due to delving deeper and interacting more data, locating and integrating the resulting vast experiences with bombardment requires more time than provided by the 'fast' data-flow channels: such as, Parameter-Processor.

Fortunately, Cognition-Complex "breakout-facility" comes to the rescue by not only providing multiple enhanced strategy sets but also provisioning additional processing time.

Cognition-Complex thereby tends more toward "mulling" than rapid-processing and rapid-deployment strategies utilized by the Parameter-Processor feeder mechanism.

Figure-It-Out focus to date has been on Filtering-and-Slotting and data-retention; notably in ever more comprehensive data-and-link resources.

Engagement of Cognition-Complex earmarks the transition from storage-centric archiving to proactive-centric 'Solutioning'. Its mandate is to variously assess current data-resources against experiential data-repositories, then 'fodder' specialized Test-Its purposed to assist finding 'The-Ways' by inspiring additional directed actions.

Importantly, the Cognition-Complex extended tool-set is only engaged when bombardment is evaluated as 'sufficiently-intense' by Parameter-Processor. 'Extended' is vital to highlight because whether 'sufficiently-intense' or not, Parameter-Processor always crafts its own Test-It thereby fulfilling the 'rapid-deployment / processing' mandate spoken of above.

For instance, while enacting daily tasks (CP-4) Parameter-Processor will handle all "nominal-intensity" data-flow (initiated by a Cognitive-Alert) without demanding "Delving-Trio" assistance: whereas in more exciting CP-3, extreme CP-2 or life threatening CP-1 conditions (i.e., hand-to-hand combat), it must engage them.

> Parameter-Processor is simply not equipped to design more complex requests, especially when intensity escalates to sufficiently-intense.

Importantly though, 'sufficient-intensity' is not a single point but a range stretching from 'just-sufficient' to 'extreme-threatening'. Resultantly, 'Solutioning' processes must also be scalable. Nicely accommodating broad variability is Delving-Trio with its three 'escalation-layers': "Targeted-Delving"; "Ranged-Delving" and "Extensive-Delving".

> Significantly, Delving-Trio layers do not necessarily all engage. Even if individually conscripted into action, all do not simultaneously but instead progressively turn-on based on intensity. Thereby, they (respectively) furnish ever-more complex capabilities to accommodate 'sufficient-intensity' ranges (from adequate through extreme).

Supporting Delving-Trio enhanced strategies are two substantial augments to Parameter-Processor capabilities: intensity assessment methodology is no longer dictated solely by P-package (thus by bombardment); and a data-resource, "PT-Assembly", dedicated for Delving-Trio use has been provided.

> PT-Assembly data-resource design supports many advanced features including not only transitional stability between Cognition-Complex Delving-Trio participants but also a dynamic information "data-pool" utilizable for Test-It creation.

For instance, the first trio-members (Targeted-Delving) inbound CC-Pend-IN data-hopper has only P-package from which to assess intensity-value. However, Targeted-Delving additionally (as well as with P-Package) loads results of its 'delving-activities' into PT-Assembly.

> Specifically, the 'delving' enhancement gathers storehoused similar sensory accepted events or experience (what has 'gone on' before) and then loads

collected 'fodder' into PT-Assembly. This process permits intermingling current bombardment with experiences in order to maximize survival potential.

Thereby, evaluation of its gathered data-elements provides the basis for re-definition of 'sufficient-intensity' into a new Cognition-Complex intensity-currency termed "delving-intensity": from which escalation / de-escalation between Delving-Trio members is determined. Notably then, either current sensory events and/or combination with 'experiences' (provided from delving into various data-resources) can provide impetus for escalation.

> Targeted-Delving alert is provided by Parameter-Processor when it evaluates P-package as sufficiently-intense. Therefore, although P-package assessment determined initial magnitude, which may not inspire additional Delving-Trio escalation, its 'delving' activities could very well upgrade intensity, thereby resulting in the additional engagement of the next layer whose mechanisms are capable of proactively compelling us to safety.

This is powerful because one does not have to be repetitively pounded by Deluge to respond by getting to safety. Rather than continuously having to endure each severe tempest exposed, one can proactively evaluate current climate conditions by delving into and incorporating experience and thereby choose to seek appropriate shelter prior to storm arrival.

> To be truly proactive then 'sufficient-intensity' must be handled progressively because swelling 'delving-intensity' may be the harbinger of pending higher intensity event-streams with serious survival implications.

PT-Assembly data-resource has another benefit besides stowing retrieved (i.e., selected and replicated) data-elements: it supports efficient transition from one level to the next. As well it also makes 'delving-work' accessible to the next trio-member: thereby minimizing processing redundancy.

Regardless of which trio-member is active, assessment of PT-Assembly to evaluate delving-intensity is only performed after tailoring a 'Test-It' sensory-feedback request. In other words, prior to Targeted-Delving determining delving-intensity by evaluating PT-Assembly, it will always utilize PT-Assembly to create a **Test-It** (specific notation for Targeted-Delving use).

If sufficient to require escalation, Ranged-Delving will be alerted next. Similarly Ranged-Delving, once its **TEST**-it is created will also assess PT-Assembly (now updated by its delving activities) to evaluate delving-intensity. If delving-intensity is again assessed as sufficient, escalation will be effected to Extensive-Delving. Thus each Delving-Trio member progressively aids resolution.

Escalation is accomplished by moving P-package to the next trio-members inbound hopper-resource: if not required, P-package and applicable PT-Assembly data-elements are removed, thereby ending the current P-package(s) 'activity-stream'.

As an example of a current *external* events causing escalation, let's say you are familiar with hiking a particular trail in the forest. You set out fairly late; it is getting dark. A few minutes into your walk, you round a bend heading to a favorite spot by the creek below.
However, just then you encounter a black bear on the trail about 30 steps ahead. It notices you.

Escalation from peaceful to survival needless to say is rapid. Devise-Intensity can escalate as a result of feedback inspired by the additional Test-It's created by each of the Delving-Trio, which resultantly produces many additional unresolved F-Puzzles.

Knowing your survival protocols you look down and slowly back away until the bear is out of sight: then you run.

> Some months later you are on the same trail. Enjoying the hike, it begins to get dark. As hiking in the dark is not ideal, "Devise-Mulling" (dealt with below) always busily at work, *internally* alerts of the previous similar situation by not only sending **Test-IT**s but also creating CP-Sets.

These additional puzzles result in substantially enhanced scrutiny of surroundings. You become anxious as memory and visions of the 'bear encounter' are cascaded into awareness. Test-It's literally stopped you in your tracks and proactively gets you out of there before a 'bear' occurrence repeat.

As a rule then, whenever CC-Pend-IN is not utilized processing is 'reactive; whenever engaged, it is 'proactive'. Importantly, Cognition-Complex 'proactive' engagement is only initiated due to 'sufficient-intensity' assessment by Parameter-Processor, which thereby populates CC-Pend-IN.

Notably, Parameter-Processor will always evaluate an Initialization-Processor issued P-package as 'higher-intensity' because no F-Puzzles are resolved: From another perspective, because the associated CP-Set 'question' is 100% unresolved.

The mechanics of how the 'Delving-Trio' works to fulfill its mandate to integrate data-flow and suggest actions to influence interaction with the 'out-there' will be addressed first. Expanded implications of these processes, such as how one actually comes to be able to think and speak etc., will be addressed in the 'Devise-Mulling' section.

## Targeted-Delving

When Parameter-Processor determines P-package ({**TEA-Dat** // E-Har}) conveys 'sufficient-intensity', it transfers P-package to the CC-Pend-IN hopper-resource: thereby alerting Targeted-Delving. This first 'Delving-Trio' member delivers the primary layer of expanded strategies designed to assist 'Solutioning' by handling Cognitive-Pathway Three intensity ranges.

Targeted-Delving enhancements are threefold: encompass broader scope 'delving' activities; provide a dedicated 'Delving-Trio' PT-Assembly data-resource (see model illustration below); and ultimately notify TI-Parameter of its **Test-It** parameters.

> Similar to Parameter-Processor, Targeted-Delving utilizes the 'P-package E-Har' to locate its specific CP-Set E-Har counterpart.

However, there are two differences: investigation (delving) is enlarged to also include a restricted quantity of frequency-similar E-Hars from the 'CP-Set' P-Cluster data-resource; and both the associated P-package and located information are now stored in PT-Assembly.

However, by the very nature of retaining 'delved' information two complications exist in relation to Deluge-events: they do not occur as one-at-a-time discrete events, nicely sequentially organized one-from-the-next, but all jumbled together; and their diverse data-flow is continuously arriving in large to massive volumes.

> This is a huge issue for Cognition-Complex as it is purposed to assess and inspire feedback for related event-trends: requiring similar occurrence grouping instead of individual event handling.

## PT-Assembly Structure

Differentiation or "data-grouping" pertinent items within PT-Assembly therefore become a Targeted-Delving responsibility. Notably, if a simple scenario such as talking on the phone while washing dishes were not segregated one would not only perceive an undefined mush of sensory input but also therefore be rendered impossibly confused and ineffective.

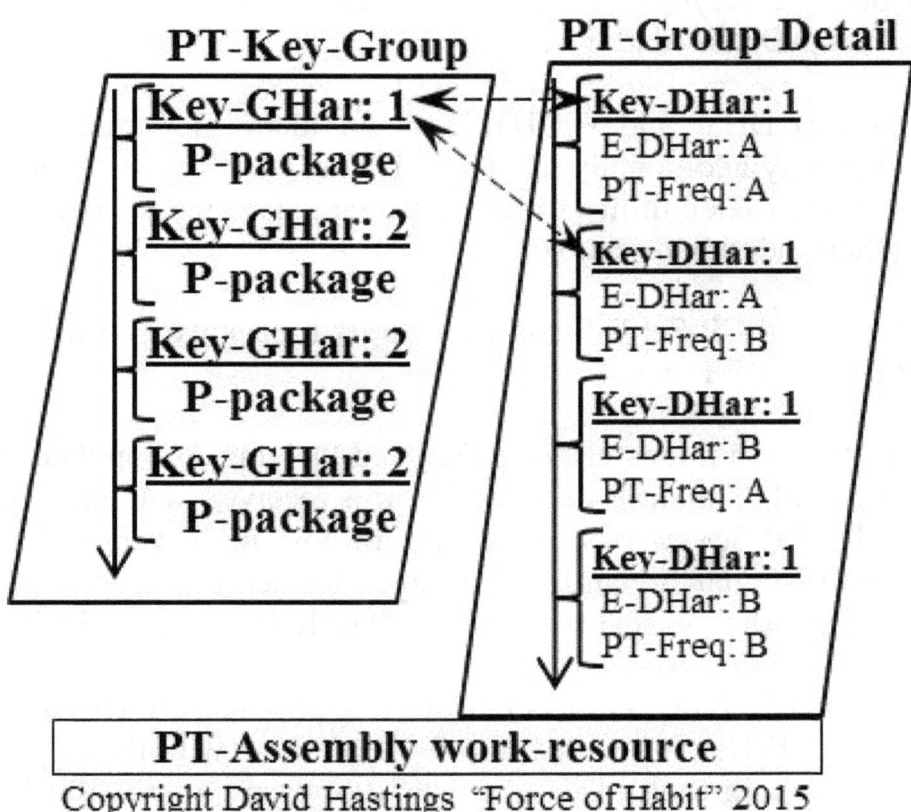

Copyright David Hastings "Force of Habit" 2015
All rites reserved

Significantly, the P-package E-Har is exploited to spawn a "PT-Key-Group" key-identifier, called a "Key-GHar", which provides for needed 'similar-event' recognition and rapid grouping. Employed by each member of the Delving-Trio, Key-GHar is additionally pivotal as each point directly to a specific CP-Set E-Har as well as the initiating the instigating P-package.

The PT-Assembly work-resource is utilized for five purposes: event similarity recognition; a 'holding-tank' for temporarily accumulating applicable replicated data-elements; a source for **Test-It** creation; providing an up-to-date 'data-pool' for use by the next Delving-Trio member if escalation is required and storehousing P-package.

Differentiation is possible because a new P-package E-Har will either be significantly-similar (harmonically) to an existing Key-GHar or not. When created initially (i.e., when the P-package E-Har does not have a corresponding significant 'match' to a Key-GHar) PT-Assembly is populated by first replicating and then instilling the P-package E-Har into not only PT-Key-Group as a Key-GHar but also Key-DHar as an E-DHar within the "PT-Group-Detail" data-resource.

> Populating Key-DHar and E-DHar with an identical harmonic to Key-GHar serves to not only additionally identify this duo as a "key-set" within PT-Group-Detail but also provide utility for other Delving-Trio members if engaged (more on this in their individual sections).

Finally, each unresolved CP-Set F-Freq of the target P-package E-Har is replicated and additionally instilled as PT-Freqs.

There are two further conditions causing Targeted-Delving to populate PT-Assembly: when a new significantly-similar P-package E-Har is received; and when delving locates significantly-similar CP-Set E-Hars, either during post initialization delving or upon locating significantly-similar E-Hars. It is assumed located E-Puzzles will have at least one unresolved F-Freq; otherwise the resolved E-Puzzle would not exist in P-Cluster.

In both cases Targeted-Delving requires two steps to populate PT-Group-Detail. First, a replicant of the target E-Har is instilled into E-DHar along with the original Key-GHar as Key-DHar; and each unresolved CP-Set F-Freq of each target E-Har is instilled as a PT-Freq. Dissimilar to the E-Har identical 'key-set' instilled during 'group' initialization though, Key-DHar and E-DHar now contain different harmonics. This critically discriminates them as 'delved' data-elements rather than 'key-sets'.

---

## Data-Compounding

Notably, receipt (determined from the P-package E-Har) and/or retrieval (by CP-Set delving processes) of 'harmonically-similar' E-Puzzles is a first-step toward Trend-Analysis, as 'exact' E-Har match is no longer a limitation.

> Extended-reach thus enables more robust 'Solutioning' assistance as broader 'recognition' provides more fodder (F-Freqs // PT-Freqs) for the next **Test-It**: from not only related {TEA-Dat // E-Hars} flowing in ongoing bombardment but also significantly-similar CP-Set E-Puzzle delving.

Resultantly, resolution assistance is significantly incremented due to 'similarity-compounding', which causes broader data accessibility due to an expanded range of 'feedback-activity' than was provided by a single P-package.

Strategically, this methodology additionally satisfies both conditions for shortening resolution duration spoken of earlier: i.e., the compounded **Test-It** contents simultaneously not only stimulate more feedback but also usurp additional processing power.

'Similarity-compounding' makes sense because one is not cognitively aware of event seriousness in the beginning stages of what might become an intense situation. However, in the rapid world of sensory acceptance, it is a proactive necessity because early warning, provided by rapid and 'delved' **Test-It**s inspiring appropriate avoidance responses are both mandatory for best-chance outcome.

> Keep in mind a **Test-It** is utilized to inspire Bombardment-Sphere interactions purposed to deliver 'close-approximation', best guess if you like, sensory-feedback information in order to resolve CP-Sets. Therefore, the compounding process does not have to be precise because **Test-It** driven feedback will continue to hone until F-Freq resolution, a P-Cluster responsibility, is achieved by exact F-Freq matches only.

Thus, although intensity-value was initially sufficient to alert Targeted-Delving, additional escalation (to Ranged-Delving) would not be possible if {TEA-Dat // E-Har} events remained unrelated. Fortunately, by data-compounding, yet unresolved similar event 'Trend-Analysis' is achieved by accumulating significantly-similar unresolved

SLID (Soma Location IDentifiers) data-elements (F-Freq's with null FD-Freq's) into PT-Assembly.

Events clearly symmetrically overlap. Their association is of course dictated by SLID frequency mix as well as temporal proximity. In other words, a few taps on the back of the hand will involve hundreds of SLIDs activating reasonably concurrently and therefore belong to the same event group (PT-Key-Group). Conversely, a similar occurrence yesterday or those involving other Soma location-mixes should not; although repetition could trigger a different process discussed in the future Devise-Mulling section.

P-packages are incessantly arriving at Parameter-Processor, which define same, similar and different events. Targeted-Delving must therefore have a way of discriminating or grouping one type of event from another within PT-Assembly: otherwise all events would mush together and be meaningless.

Groups are comprised of significantly-similar E-Hars because by very definition E-Hars are joined to specific sensory impact SLID data (F-Freqs). Stated differently, one would expect simultaneously stubbing your toe and bumping your head to be recognized as different events occurring at the same time.

Discrimination occurs because the "SLID-packets" (TEA-Dats) from the two events, even though they occurred simultaneously, are not substantially frequency-similar. As such, 'packets' retain discrete integrity as a result of substantially-different harmonic content, which resultantly creates different PT-Key-Groups.

Targeted-Delving therefore Filters-and-Slots all new incoming significantly-similar E-Hars from a P-package and utilizes them as a group key-identifier. In other words, the 'toe subbing' event (indicated above) provided tens of thousands of P-packages, which determined their being grouped as the same event: rather than as hundreds of different individual and disconnected data-elements.

As previous significantly-similar E-Hars would have already formed CP-Sets, this consequently furnishes the opportunity for Targeted-Delving to not only populate PT-Assembly with unresolved F-Puzzles (F-Freq's) gleaned from a broader array of frequency similar E-Hars (from the E-Puzzle data-resource) but also build an expanded **Test-It** (forwarded to "CC-Pend-OUT") from the F-Freqs within the PT-Group-Detail data-resource.

The implication for Targeted-Delving, where escalation to Ranged-Delving is not necessary, is the significant bombardment events which prompted its engagement have become resolved or satisfied by tapping into significantly-similar P-Cluster E-Puzzles (via CP-Set resolution from **Test-It** initiated feedback).

---

'Resolved' outcome is excellent. This means the 'questions' resulting from Deluge events are Solutioned (answered) by the cyclical interaction between new P-package E-Hars foddering **Test-It**s to inspire feedback and P-Cluster frequency-matching new sensory data. Incredibly these small resolution victories result in E-Puzzles also being resolved, amalgamated, Solutioned and uploaded to P-Cluster and possibly C-Cluster: thus providing a vast experience base enabling higher cognitive function.

Once all F-Freq replicants and corresponding E-Hars have been apprehended, intensity re-assessment is performed on the accumulated PT-Assembly E-Har data-elements in order to gauge a 'devise-intensity' value. Recall, reassessment is necessary because retrieval of significantly-similar E-Puzzles (Bracketed sensory information) can additionally cause an intensity increment.

---

Remember, once one of the Delving-Trio is engaged, a Test-It will always be deployed. This is true even when engagement of the next level is required. For instance, even though Extensive-Delving was initiated by Ranged-Delving, and Ranged-Delving initiated by Targeted-Delving, all three would have created a specifically tailored Test-It: however, with increasingly complex content.

If Targeted-Delving deems devise-intensity is sufficient, the target P-package will be transferred into "RD-IN" after **Test-It** and CP-Set creation (below): thereby effectively notifying Ranged-Delving of its additionally required involvement.

Ranged-Delving will have a jump-start though, because PT-Assembly already contains critical information, upon which next-steps can build.

If devise-intensity was not sufficient, Targeted-Delving would continue to satisfy P-package demands without escalation. This would result in purging both the applicable PT-Assembly entries (groups and details) and the target P-package from CC-Pend-IN after **Test-It** and CP-Set creation.

## Internally-Driven 'Question' Creation

The capability to create CP-Set 'questions' from internally-driven 'mulling' enables another huge leap toward proactive management.

> This is because resolution is dramatically expedited by both creating CP-Set 'questions' and organizing coordinated **Test-IT** feedback action-plans to inspire 'answers'. As this strategy ensures a one-hundred percent 'match' condition for requested feedback, it allays the need for relying on processors to associate significantly-similar from what would otherwise be random bombardment.

Thus both ends are covered so-to-speak: the questions and the suggested motions to provide the answers. This is additionally beneficial in high-intensity Cognitive-Pathway One situations where non-match data-elements become identifiable thereby permitting fully occupied processors to ignore them without consequence. This is why one does not remember much detail outside the intense event; everything else was simply ignored as 'static'.

> 'Tailored' Test-Its funneled from Cognition-Complex via CC-Pend-OUT to Parameter-Processor and beyond are expressly fabricated to inspire specific sensory-feedback.

However, it would not be useful for quick precise action if the 'requested-feedback' was not discernible from the ongoing volumes of background bombardment 'noise'.

In other words, 'No-Match' by Equivalency-Processor would unacceptably eliminate any chance at synchronising Deluge to 'requested-data', which is the purpose of a Test-It in the first place: thereby rendering Test-Its minimally effective.

> As 'hit-or-miss' does not fall into the Figure-It-Out mandate, a superior alternate must be found: because best would be a 'Match' condition for 'requested-feedback'.

Figure-It-Out has an elegant strategy: create Test-It equivalent CP-Sets to ensure a 'Match' condition (not new) will result for 'requested' feedback. In other words, the only way of ensuring a 'Match' condition is to create CP-Sets, which mirror Test-It parameters.

Fortuitously, PT-Assembly has what is required: Key-DHars to parallel E-Puzzles; and PT-Freqs to parallel F-Puzzles.

> Recall Tag constituents are perfectly aligned to yield F-Puzzle frequency specific data, which can exactly emulate a bombardment event. After all, bombardment Tags presented as a TEA-Dat enabled Equivalency-Processor action in the first place.

Resultantly, regardless of Test-It origins (Delving-Trio and/or Devise-Mulling), Cognition-Complex executes two steps for CP-Set creation. First, by utilizing PT-Assembly Cognition-Complex accesses the appropriate Key-GHar to retrieve and replicate its E-Hars and associated F-Freqs., Secondly, it engages Initialization-Processor to perform the creation process.

---

## Forward to Continuity-Controller

On the 'Cognitive-Pathways Model' illustration a horizontal arrow has been placed midway between TI-IN and TI-OUT to represent "TI-Notify". Although not labeled on the illustration it populates Continuity-Controllers CC-Match as does DE-Notify.

TI-Notify evolves a critical step because it enables Continuity-Controller to assess incoming Deluge by immediately cross-comparing Cognition-Complex Test-It data-elements in order to correctly determine intensity and therefore appropriate Cognitive-Pathway.

Regardless of Test-It origins, either Delving-Trio and/or Devise-Mulling, TI-Notify is formed by arranging the target PT-Assembly Key-DHar 'PT-Freqs' by hierarchically descending frequency.

> Where Test-Its have provided huge 'fodder' and Deluge is still significant, escalation can thus be appropriately gauged. Without feedback from Cognition-Complex at this point, early warning escalation would not be possible.

## Ranged-Delving

When 'Ranged-Delving' is initiated, devise-intensity is notably elevated. As elevated intensity defines Cognitive-Pathway Two (2) activities, Ranged-Delving can therefore be thought of as the default mechanism accommodating this pathways intensity-range.

## Recap

> Recall TEA-Dat was the primary P-package informant utilized by Parameter-Processor to disclose sufficient-intensity. Salient increases in bombardment (i.e., significant rises in receptor neuron activity) were required to instigate escalation to Targeted-Delving: whereas 'banal' did not.

Once Targeted-Delving was engaged, both P-package elements (TEA-Dat and E-Har) provided sources from which PT-Assembly populating was made possible. Specifically, E-Har provided the critical transition to P-Cluster CP-Sets, which as we now know are not only the precursors to established experiences but also one of the fundamental inducements for following actions.

Transition to Delving-Trio (from Parameter-Processor to Targeted-Delving) thereby permitted both unresolved/unanswered 'question' targeting (E-Puzzles) and consequent PT-Assembly population.

Important because evaluation of the resulting PT-Assembly composition defines a new 'devise-intensity' benchmark by utilizing PT-Assembly: created by the integration of both current (TEA-Dat) and previous bombardment data being retained in CP-Sets. Devise-Intensity is critical as its 'devise-value' is employed to determine whether escalation to Ranged-Delving is needed (or not).

The 'one-data-package-at-a-time' approach has been frequently utilised to enhance discussion clarity. However, the true state-of-affairs within Cognition-Complex is 'multitudes-of-data-at-a-time': thus providing the quantities of progressive data-flow necessary for the decryption of trends. The Cognition-Complex capability to handle trend analysis or data-compounding is mandatory not only for successful avoidance of continuing noxious bombardment but also to conjure best-case suggestions (Test-Its).

For instance in high bombardment conditions, dozens if not hundreds of significantly-similar E-Hars (recognizable due to PT-Assembly structure) as well as their unresolved F-Freq replicants are being buffered by Targeted-Delving into PT-Assembly from frequency-similar CP-Set E-Puzzles. Notably, greater intensity bombardment, especially when focussed on the same array of SLID sites, provides an increased magnitude of 'significantly-similar' data-events upon which to draw.

Bear in mind, F-Freqs (each identifiable by a unique SLID frequency) define not only the most granular sensory impact information, which is the primary building block for determinations, sentience and actions but also exacting frequency signatures, which are symmetrical within Distinct-Episodes, F-Puzzles and outbound Test-Its.

Detailing the 'Hot-Fat-Scenario' should offer step-by-step clarity to processing stages. In the initial 'fat-spitting' stage (about the first hundred milliseconds), insufficient significantly-similar P-package E-Hars existed to spur Parameter-Processor to engage Cognition-Complex: i.e., Parameter-Processor was coping just fine.

However, due to ongoing 'significantly-similar' Deluge dramatically incrementing intensity (about three hundred milliseconds in) transition to

Targeted-Delving occurred. In other words, as a consequence of intensity exceeding Parameter-Processor operational range, P-package was inserted into CC-Pend-IN: thus achieving escalation.

Ongoing high intensity spurred Parameter-Processor to continue alerting Targeted-Delving. Resultantly, the ongoing (albeit less than one second) SLID 'significantly-similar' saturation caused rapid significantly-similar 'group' (PT-Key-Group) data-accumulation in PT-Assembly, which quickly pushed Targeted-Delving to its upper intensity-handling extreme. Specifically, this was due to the many SLID frequency appropriate time-frame 'data-compounding' elements being inserted into PT-Assembly.

Therefore, upon performing its characteristic evaluation of PT-Assembly (after deploying **Test-It**), Targeted-Delving evaluated devise-intensity as 'sufficiently-intense' to request additional assistance from Ranged-Delving: escalation was thus effected by inserting P-package into RD-IN.

Such 'recognition' of ongoing 'significantly-similar' is a major step toward sophisticated Trend-Analysis, which is one hallmark of Delving-Trio. In this case, trends were indicated because PT-Assembly was being rapidly populated by CP-Set frequency similar unresolved E-Har F-Freqs within a limited time-frame causing 'group' data-upsurges in PT-Assembly, which resulted in increased devise-intensity and thus escalation.

> As a precursor for higher readiness at this juncture, one would probably be aware of an 'unsettled' feeling niggling at the fringes of consciousness. Incredibly one begins to become 'event-aware', as a consequence of Ranged-Delving being activated: due to devise-intensity prompted alerting of a continuing sufficiently-intense event series (i.e., higher than 'normal' SLID activations).

---

'Ranged-Delving' responds to escalation by expanding delving activities beyond P-Cluster. Its leap to increase delving-activities into Data-Matrix is the first step in bringing previous experiences to bear on current bombardment conditions: specifically to uncover and utilize information established as pertinent in prior similar situations.

Significantly, provision of superior 'fodder' underlines the fundamental purpose of data-repositories in the first place. Clearly then, when previously accumulated related information augments a Test-It, control of Bombardment-Sphere physical interactions will certainly morph from less useful 'random-attempts' to more useful 'guided-attempts'.

> Recall, Test-It inspires feedback by defining sensory-linked conditions specifically designed to impact physical positioning within and therefore interaction with one's Bombardment-Sphere.

Stated differently, greater experience (Information-Assemblies with their integrally joined Distinct-Episodes) equates to more comprehensive Test-It formulations. Resultantly, superior 'fodder' tempered by experience will in turn dramatically enhance "Response-Component" ability to physically interact in a more useful way.

In other words, physical action outcome will critically not only be experientially aligned but also address the correlated granular demands of current (TEA-Dat) bombardment as well. In fact, once Data-Matrix becomes populated with tens-of-thousands of granularly similar (Distinct-Episode) entries contributed by repetitive practice, actions will become appreciably enhanced.

Consider any sport you like to play: You practice-and-practice building up those data-archives so when it comes time to get into action, Ranged-Delving is there to tap into (recall) experience in relation to the very specific "Deluge-moment" requirements.

> Generally, the more practice the better the performance, because of much 'larger' Information-Assembly Brackets feeding better information to Test-Its.

Either if very young or the sport is new, required data-archives are minimal; and so therefore is fine motor skill. Fine-point physical juxtaposition within ones Bombardment-Sphere is accomplished by creation of rapid-fire Delving-Trio Test-Its created from PT-Assembly: the more exacting their information, the more precise will be the outcome as these 'fodder' Response-Component performance patterns (more on this later).

> Specifically, 'Ranged-Delving' augments 'Solutioning' by targeting Data-Matrix Distinct-Episodes (within targeted Information-Assembly Brackets) by using accumulated PT-Assembly E-Hars provided from both the 'P-package' E-Har (provided by bombardment) and current CP-Set E-Hars (provided by Targeted-Delving investigations).

On the 'Cognitive-Pathways Model' illustration, CP-3s Data-Matrix is represented as a rectangular graphic, whose contents on CP-2 are similar to the following: {VS}..EA><{IA}.

Its purpose was to depict a character string indicating interactions between Visual-Scape (VS), EA-Harmonic (EA) and Information-Assembly (IA), where the braces "{}" indicate 'many', the dash ".." depicts a 'Link' condition and the facing arrows "><" represent a 'Join' condition.

> {VS}..EA><{IA} put into words becomes "many Visual-Scapes **can be** 'Linked' to a single EA-Harmonic to which many Information-Assemblies **will always** be 'Joined' (note the 'can be' and the 'will always be')".

Although acceptable for the illustration, Ranged-Delving discussions require the following expanded format:

$$\{VS\}..EA><\{IA\{DE\}\}$$

Putting this final version into words updates the last section of the 'statement' above: from "many Information-Assemblies **will always** be Joined"…into "many Information-Assemblies **will always** be Joined…' and within each Information-Assembly many Distinct-Episodes **will always** be bundled".

Important to re-clarify is both EA-Harmonics (EA) and Information-Assemblies (IA) reside in independent data-repositories. However, they are inseparably integrated due to the 'Joining' of myriads of associated events in turn resulting from billions (even by age 5 or 6) of previous Bombardment occurrences.

> Although EA-Harmonics compositions are theoretically unlimited due to vast variances in Deluge combinations, Information-Assemblies are finite because they represent SLIDs (Soma Location IDs).

Additionally, 'Distinct-Episodes' are also theoretically unlimited because they represent a 'same' Information-Assembly bracket segregated with a different time-stamp. It is both the time-stamp and the EA-Harmonic to which IA is associated, which makes each Information-Assembly Distinct-Episode a slightly different 'sensory-experience' when sourced in relation to current bombardment.

Distinct-Episodes also account for why practice works; it provides a deep storehouse of referenceable granular SLID events, which can be ported via Test-It and patterned by 'Response-Component' to accommodate wide ranges of physical movement necessary to accommodate and mitigate Deluge events (more on this in Template-Component and Response-Component section discussions following).

Ranged-Delving provisions an enhanced strategy to retrieve (locate, replicate, accumulate and instill into PT-Assembly) Distinct-Episodes for the specifically matched {E-Har // EA} event from the F-Freq matched Information-Assembly Bracket group, which has a frequency-matched counterpart (PT-Freq) in PT-Assembly.

More simply put, its delving purpose is to retrieve a broad array of Distinct-Episodes, which match the unresolved or 'unanswered' F-Puzzles, which are represented as PT-Freqs within the PT-Assembly target array.

> Specifically, each PT-Assembly E-DHar (loaded by Targeted-Delving) is utilized to locate its EA-Harmonic Data-Matrix exact counterpart.

Once located each PT-Assembly E-DHar associated PT-Freq is cross-matched to each EA-Harmonic><Information-Assembly (IA) bracket. Exact frequency matches (PT-Freq to IA) result in the creation of a single PT-Freq replicant for each sourced Distinct-Episode from within the target IA bracket.

All recoveries are temporarily held within a transitional 'Recall-Package' data-resource. When completed the Recall-Package is extracted into the appropriate PT-Assembly 'data-group'.

> Spectacularly, when Visual-Scape links are attached to target EA-Harmonics, many Visual images will cognitively manifest: from fleeting to longer lived; vivid to elusive.

Obviously more experience (i.e., greater quantities of Distinct-Episodes) will provide richer 'fodder' for **TEST**-its than was available to Targeted-Delving. Resultantly, Data-Matrix with tremendous quantities of EA-Harmonics and associated Information-Assembly Distinct-Episodes will provide substantially more comprehensive data for **TEST**-it creation.

Thus, 'deeper-reach' sourcing of storehoused experiences (Bracketed Distinct-Episode sensory information) aids in 'Solutioning' because it inspires more feedback, thereby resolving more 'questions' and finding 'The-Ways' faster.

Ranged-Delving is the first process-set then which integrates bombardment with targeted experience by gathering a range of inter-related pertinent archived data, which is used to populate PT-Assembly data-resources.

Resultantly, from those accumulated Distinct-Episode replicants, a much expanded **TEST**-it action plan can be created and forwarded to CC-Pend-OUT. Recall also, CP-Sets get created and DE-Notify alerted.

Lastly, if evaluation of PT-Assembly by Ranged-Delving determines sufficient 'devise-intensity', P-package will be inserted into "ED-IN" thereby effectively notifying Extensive-Delving of its required involvement: otherwise appropriate data-elements will be purged.

Targeted-Delving and Ranged-Delving, although absolutely essential, only partially explain our proactive capability, ingenuity and the 'Way-We-Work' as a sentient being creating our "living-scenario" by ejecting perpetual granular 'choices' into the 'out-there': However, 'Extensive-Delving' and 'Devise-Mulling' do.

**Extensive-Delving**

> Mundane will not invoke Extensive-Delving's participation:
> but extreme excitement or danger will: Thus, we feel most
> aware and conscious when the stakes are high.

'Extensive-Delving' only engages when (bombardment-driven) devise-intensity, determined by Ranged-Delving assessment of PT-Assembly, is extreme.

Therefore it is obligated to perform its mandates within a tremendously challenging environment: because not only does no loftier support system for bombardment-driven data-flow exist but also within this extreme make-or-break environment it must seamlessly and rapidly handle 'Cognitive-Pathway One' highest-intensity ranges.

> Recall, PT-Assembly was populated utilizing two independent sources: P-package, which provisioned inbound bombardment-data; as well as Targeted-Delving and Ranged-Delving, whose independent research achievements provided CP-Set and cursory experience data, respectively.

Creating a **TEST-IT** action-plan by combining Deluge with extended 'similar-to-bombardment' experiences is a fundamental Extensive-Delving mandate. In other words, only with recommendations ensuing from interlacing bombardment with related experiences are safety and survival provided best possible outcome during these maximum load situations by providing best-guess external **TEST-IT** action-plans.

Generally speaking then, Extensive-Delving fulfills its mandate by implementing data-repository delving for significantly-similar E-Hars. Additionally, processing capabilities permit simultaneous rather than sequential (as for Targeted and Ranged-Delving) handling of multiple P-packages, thereby vastly incrementing throughput.

Extensive-Delving's data-and-link resource retrieval strategy (locate, replicate, accumulate and instill into PT-Assembly) extends its reach much further than Ranged-Delving by not only having substantially more E-Hars to process as a consequence of Ranged-Delving activities but also including a small range of significantly-similar E-Hars as well.

In other words Extensive-Delving processes not only Information-Assembly Distinct-Episodes for the specifically targeted (E-Har // EA) event but also for significantly-similar E-Hars.

As for Ranged-Delving, Distinct-Episode targets are accumulated from associated Information-Assembly Brackets, which have a frequency-matched F-Freq counterpart (PT-Freq) in PT-Assembly. More simply put, Extensive-Delving's purpose is to retrieve Distinct-Episodes from a broadened EA-Harmonic array, which matches the unresolved or 'unanswered' F-Puzzles, which are represented as PT-Freqs within the PT-Assembly target array.

Specifically, each PT-Assembly E-DHar (loaded by Targeted and Ranged-Delving) is utilized to locate its EA-Harmonic Data-Matrix exact counterpart.

Once located each PT-Assembly E-DHar associated PT-Freq is cross-matched to each EA-Harmonic><Information-Assembly (IA) bracket. Exact frequency matches (PT-Freq to IA) result in the creation of a single PT-Freq replicant for each Distinct-Episode as sourced from the target IA bracket.

All recoveries are temporarily held within a transitional 'Recall-Package' data-resource. When completed the Recall-Package is extracted into the appropriate PT-Assembly 'data-group'.

Obviously more experience (i.e., greater quantities of Distinct-Episodes) will provide richer 'fodder' for **TEST-IT**s than was available to Ranged-Delving.

Resultantly, Data-Matrix with tremendous quantities of significantly-similar EA-Harmonics and associated Information-Assembly Distinct-Episodes {IA{DE}} will provide substantially more comprehensive data for **TEST-IT** creation.

Thus, 'deeper-reach' sourcing of storehoused experiences (Bracketed Data-Matrix sensory information) aids in 'Solutioning' because it inspires more feedback, thereby resolving more 'questions' and finding 'The-Ways' faster.

Spectacularly, when Visual-Scape links are attached to target EA-Harmonics, many Visual images will cognitively manifest: from fleeting to longer lived; vivid to elusive.

Extensive-Delving comprehensively integrates bombardment with targeted experience by gathering a range of inter-related pertinent archived data, which is used to populate PT-Assembly data-resources.

> Resultantly, from those accumulated Distinct-Episode replicants, a much expanded **TEST-IT** action plan is created and forwarded to CC-Pend-OUT. Recall also, CP-Sets get created as well as DE-Notify alerted.

**Devise-Mulling**

Devise-Mulling is not only home-base for intuition and awareness but also engenders 'who we are', our unique personifications: how we think and speak, make conscious choices and so much more.

> Inexorably, Devise-Mulling must provide dramatically enhanced capabilities than do either other Mind-Self or Body-Self mechanisms: four engender extensive implication.

First, Devise-Mulling dispenses three "mulling-modes" discriminated by divergent processing imperatives: Overt (focussed/aware); Passive (transparent/unaware); and Transitional (dreams/visions).

Generally, 'mulling-modes' achieve both delving and outbound goals by selectively and variously deploying from a kit of interactive methodologies, which include: intensely combing data-repositories to populate "DM-Assembly" work-resource (DM = Devise-Mulling) with its 'finds'; retaining DM-Assembly key-group arrays for extended periods; effecting Trend-Analysis; creating multiple **Test-IT**s for a single event-group; and controlling **Test-IT** introduction timeframes.

> The DM-Assembly work-resource structure (below) parallels PT-Assembly in most ways but is dedicated for Devise-Mulling use.

DM-Assembly enables four enhancements: autonomous information control; cross-pollination due to the same key structure (allows both it and PT-Assembly data-resources to be used for **Test-IT** creation); extended retention timeframe without conflicting Delving-Trio requirements within PT-Assembly; and an "ES-Pool" sub-Key explained in the 'Experience-Sense' section below.

## Overt-Mode

As we have all experienced when seeking answers, solutions will not be attained by simply acquiring particulars by random trial-and-error but by asking better questions. This serves to not only make interactions more precisely directed but also usefully group acquired details and less obviously, instigate meaningful feedback from 'out-there'.

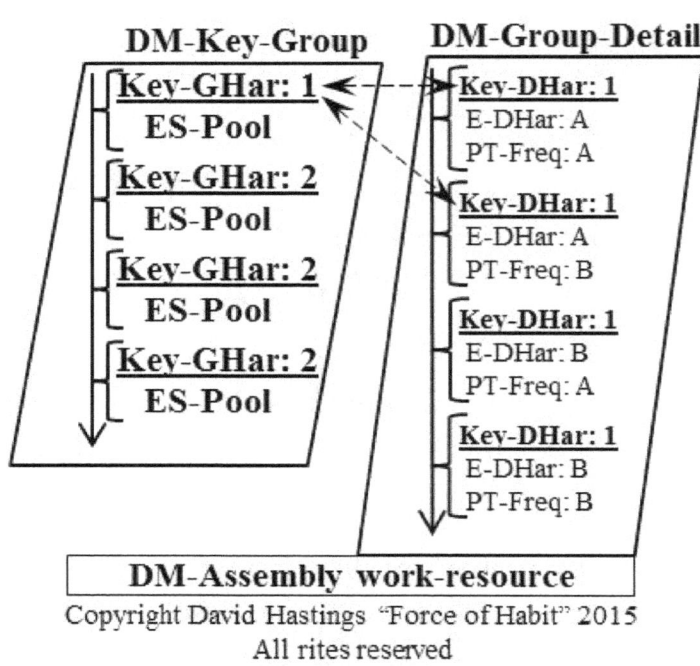

"Overt-Mode" takes the lead during critical event-stream onslaughts by deploying simultaneous functionality layers, which dramatically enhance Delving-Trio actions. It utilizes the RD-IN alert to ensure its activities are in alignment with the Cognitive-Pathway One (CP-1) Deluge event-stream: essential to coordinate, expedite and resolve the occurring intense 'episode'.

However, Overt-Mode is an internal-mulling process designed to supplement the externally-driven Delving-Trio.

Therefore, it has the 'luxury' of an extended time-frame for: evaluation of multitudes of P-packages; performing extensive delving; loading DM-Assembly; and creating as many **Test-IT**s as seems appropriate to acquire necessary 'answers'.

> There must be a 'question' before there can be an 'answer'

Probably not surprising, CP-Sets provide primary delving focus. This makes sense as investigating CP-Sets will provide access to 'questions' as well their resolution or 'answer' statuses: i.e., quantity of F-Freqs without companion FD-Freqs.

Devise-Mulling is unique by enabling experiences to be inserted between sensory acceptance and responses thereby changing existence from "Habitual-Reactive" to "Solutioning-Proactive".

Retrieval of reference experience-data requires several stages. As a first stage a CP-Set E-Har (pointed to from a P-package E-Har) is utilized to locate its EA-Harmonic match in Data-Matrix. Stage two employs the 'Recall-Cascading' methodology (see previous section by the same name) to uncover other EA-Harmonics joined to each significantly-similar Distinct-Episode.

By exploiting the EA-Harmonic of a located Distinct-Episode, it is possible to cascade to a different EA-Harmonic in order to additionally search out its significantly-similar associated Distinct-Episode 'matches'.

> Resultantly, significantly-similar Distinct-Episodes from EA-Harmonics, which may be very different harmonically from the originating E-Har, provide a substantial upsurge in available DM-Assembly fodder.

This process is not designed to grab everything: Instead, only Distinct-Episodes within 'Information-Assembly' are utilized where a located Distinct-Episode is 'significantly-similar' to the target CP-Set F-Freq.

The resulting 'Recall-Bundles' (also see the previous section by the same name) will thereby contain possibilities from a huge time and occurrence range. As each EA-Harmonic pathway exhausts its experience-data [EA><{IA{DE}}] channel, Recall-Bundles are loaded into DM-Assembly.

> As both Delving-Trio and Devise-Mulling may be at work independently, mulling-modes can instigate multiple Test-Its by combining data-elements from both DM-Assembly and PT-Assembly. **Test-It** launch into CC-Pend-OUT ultimately inspires 'requested' feedback.

As the Devise-Mulling process can be extensive, many **Test-IT**s will normally be created during its ferreting activities. These of course, produce granular physical variances (enabling fluid rather than 'jerky' motion) variably impacting the 'Out-There', which in turn inspire new TEA-Dats (feedback).

Proactivity thereby produces precise detailed feedback, which alerts to either the incremental success of **Test-IT** suggestions and/or required adjustments. So the episode mulling cycle continues until one has Figured-It-Out and 'The-Ways' are uncovered.

The Overt-Mode cycle continues until gradual resolution is achieved, which is evidenced by de-escalation to Ranged-Delving, then Targeted-Delving and then to Parameter-Processor when all activity has returned to 'Tepid' (CP-4).

Completion of an Overt-Mode cycle does not mean either Passive-Mode or Transitional-Mode have finalised contributions: this is because external events do not directly affect their diligence.

Data-repository maximization, designed to ensure 'working' data-resources are 'clean' and data-elements are organized and rapidly retrievable, is one purview of the background "Passive-Mode" work-horse.

More specifically, it provides transparent or unaware support functions, which continuously ferret and evaluate to ensure the contiguity of 'working' data-resources, such as: purging extraneous data-elements from PT-Assembly and DM-Assembly during de-escalation.

"Transitional-Mode" functions as Overt-Modes longer-term processing companion. It continues to work even during quieter times (sleep; meditation), toward Solutions to 'questions' left unresolved once the imperative has passed and Overt-Mode has 'moved-on'.

Purposed to provide 'wrap-up' CP-Sets 'answers', it delves differently than Overt-Mode by seeking data-similarities across divergent Data-Matrix Distinct-Episodes. Its 'boundary-leaping' activities within Information-Assembly data-resource invariably engage many different Information-Assembly joined EA-Harmonics, which when linked to Visual-Scape, can elicit vibrant dreams and or waking visions.

## Recap

Feeder mechanisms, whether initial sensory receivers or follow-on processors, were solely activated by receipt of new data. Although this is also the case for

Overt-Mode, the nature of its two associates is to 'mull' whether or not CC-Pend-IN provides a new external alert to activate Cognition-Complex.

Functionally, when the alert sounds indicating the RD-IN gateway has been populated, Devise-Mulling 'Overt-Mode' and Delving-Trio's Ranged-Delving concurrently activate. Importantly though, Delving-Trio and Devise-Mulling remain autonomous: each providing unique contribution to 'Figuring-It-Out'.

Although each Devise-Mulling mode delves deeply, 'Overt-Mode' is specifically designed to handle critical Cognitive-Pathway One (CP-1) ongoing events (those escalating beyond Targeted-Delving), whereas Passive-Mode and Transitional-Mode, operate more surreptitiously and are not dependent on receipt of P-package to deploy.

> They are thus considered 'internally-driven': i.e., their methodologies do not rely on Deluge to spur them into action (more on this below) even though Devise-Mulling may have inspired the instigating TEA-Dat by deploying **Test-IT**s in the first place.

---

Second, unlike precursor Figure-It-Out data-stream processors, which Filtered-and-Slotted (realigned) a previous mechanism's bombardment 'fodder' for their own restricted purpose, Devise-Mulling seizes unlimited reign to retrieve from all Mind-Self data and/or link-resources, remix and evaluate using whatever 'mulling' time-frame is necessary to accomplish Solution.

---

Third, although enhancing survival potential is the principal reason all mechanisms exist, Devise-Mulling expands 'survival' purview to encompass external-condition proactive management as well.

> This is a key game-changer because expansion of 'purview' upgrades the game-plan from passively taking a bombardment-hit to proactively assessing Deluge events against "experience-archives".

Deep delving enables Devise-Mulling to recombine broad scope pertinent experiences in order to formulate recommendations or ideas (**Test-IT**s) for maximizing 'survival' potential.

Unrestricted, 'spoils' can be recombined based on every delved fragment of experience, perceptions manifested and "devised-conditions" sent outbound via **Test-IT**s to exact a significantly elevated variety of feedback.

> In other words, Devise-Mulling can instigate, investigate and formulate ostensibly unlimited proactive "intuition-scenarios" then deploy them using its outbound **Test-IT** suggestion-vehicle to inspire new experiences: rather like a 'try-this-best-guess-(idea)-and-see-what-happens' experiment.

In this way by choosing to specifically affect our 'Out-There' positioning and therefore our inter-activity with the Deluge, Devise-Mulling truly instigates ones moment-by-moment 'living-story'.

Internal-processing competencies can by unrestricted data-repository delving, devise essentially unlimited new combinations and permutations or ideas, which can, in specific circumstances, spawn awareness and sentience.

> Restated to emphasize the critical driving nature of Intuition, 'ideas' is altered to 'I.D.E.A.S.': meaning,

**I**ntuition **D**rives **E**xperiences, **A**wareness and **S**entience

---

Finally but not trivially, Devise-Mulling Overt-Mode is simultaneously charged with fulfilling 'internally-driven' awareness and sentience by utilizing 'Experience-Senses' as comparative 'expectation-yardsticks' to focus and coordinate Deluge-to-experience retrieval: it becomes the comparative criteria onto which data is reflected.

> Distinguishing 'bombardment-driven' as opposed to 'internally-driven' awareness and sentience is important, as the former was the purview of Delving-Trio.

Experience-Senses are also utilized to provide extensive fodder into DM-Assembly: thus **Test-It**s, responses and therefore feedback. Recall also, CP-Sets get created as well as DE-Notify alerted.

> In the introduction to the Concept-Cluster section, a declaration was promised clarification during Cognition-Complex discussions: (paraphrasing) it was stated

"… CC-Hars… (Cognitive-Habits / Experience-Senses)… become THE principal front-line Filtering-and-Slotting event-evaluators"...

### 'Experience-Sense' Deployment

> Although facts are the foundation of rational thought and emotion (sensory intensity) the energy sustaining information retention: it is feelings or Experience-Senses, which provide the impetus for recalling, filtering and reconstituting archived substance.

Important for following discussions is to reiterate C-Cluster is a Tier-Five data-repository. It is populated by multitudes of CC-Hars; also termed Cognitive-Habits or Experience-Senses. Harmonically, CC-Har experiences epitomize both the copious data-detail and intensity of myriads of 'Solutioned' CP-Sets, which were formed from a disparate array of sensory accepted building-blocks or SLIDs (Soma Location IDentifiers).

Theoretically, SLID combinations are enormous. SLID groupings (TEA-Dats) have the potential to incorporate broad SLID diversity, which would normally form multitudes of dissimilar CC-Hars. However, due to the restricted nature of motion within ones Bombardment-Sphere as a consequence of habitually existing in familiar surroundings, substantial quantities of closely-similar (harmonically speaking) CC-Hars get created as well.

> This adheres exactly to the "Bracketing-Principle" for data-repositories; such as Data-Matrix. It states (during seemingly repetitive activities) 'accumulated closely-similar' provides not only detailed comparative knowledge and/or wisdom but also granular experience fodder ultimately directing precise movements within ones Bombardment-Sphere.

Understanding this corollary is critical as 'accumulated closely-similar' plays a key role when Devise-Mulling delves C-Cluster data-repository. By so doing it acquires and populates "CC-Bundle" virtual-resource (labels are for descriptive clarity) with not only the closest significantly-similar CC-Har 'match' but also a small range of 'harmonically-closest' CC-Hars as well.

As will be evidenced below, this broadened CC-Har 'grab', the norm for Cognition-Complex data-retrieval, is particularly critical in highest-intensity situations.

Actually, without Experience-Senses in these conditions, not only would bombardment-data jumble but also retrieval would be non-specific and confusing as a consequence of insufficient delving-focus.

Experience-Senses are critical for advanced Solutioning as they provide parameters, which critically correlate Bombardment events with appropriate data-repository experience (data-element) retrieval. Stated differently, Experience-Senses maintain internal "solution-focus" by providing a delving Filtering-and-Slotting guide, which enables discrimination between essential and spurious experience-data.

When an ongoing high-intensity Deluge event is transpiring, Overt-Mode launches two progressive phases: initial and cyclical.

Although both phases 'grab' Experience-Senses, the initial-phase (when Devise-Mulling is solicited by RD-IN population) is constrained by the originating contents of PT-Assembly: populated by the restricted capabilities of Targeted-Delving plus concurrent contributions being provided by Ranged-Delving of course.

Therefore, although sufficient information is not initially available to precisely 'grab' Experience-Senses, enough is obtainable for an approximation. Thus our first sense (Experience-Sense) of an unfamiliar event (ones initial assessment) is typically diffuse, non-specific and most times minimally accurate.

### Initial-Phase

"Initial-phase" is mandated to populate a virtual 'pool-resource' with a "blended-harmonic". As PT-Assembly storehouses both Bombardment and Delving-Trio data, it is pivotal to acquiring the appropriate data-elements. Fortunately by design, PT-Assembly is comprised of many E-Hars (stored as E-DHars) and vastly more associated F-Freqs (stored as PT-Freqs).

It is specific Key-GHar group E-DHars for the current bombardment scenario, which however provide the means to locate both the primary CC-Har and a small cluster of significantly-similar ones. Using these in a specific way enables targeting C-Cluster to retrieve a preliminary set of CC-Hars (Experience-Senses).

So to accomplish initial-phase Experience-Sense targeting, Devise-Mulling utilizes the initiating P-package E-Har to accesses PT-Assembly PT-Key-Group to locate its 'matched' Key-GHar (there must be a 'match' as Targeted-Delving created it). Once revealed, Key-GHar is applied to access its Key-DHar array. When located each of its E-DHars are replicated and populated into a virtual-resource.

> When gathering is completed its E-DHar members are "harmonically-blended", then virtually maintained in "EDH-Pool" (label is for descriptive clarity) as a new unique harmonic.

The blended-harmonic is then used as a 'harmonic-template' to mine C-Cluster for the closest significantly-similar CC-Har (Experience-Sense). When located, it and a small group of significantly-similar CC-Hars are replicated and stored in a virtual-resource, termed "CC-Group" (again for descriptive clarity).

Experience-Senses house significant intensity: Consequently upon populating CC-Group, each CC-Har independently turns-on large numbers of specialized Cognition-Complex neurons, which one "Cognitively-Senses" as awareness.

> Critically, when the primary CC-Har (within CC-Group) is harmonically similar to the EDH-Pool harmonic, one will feel clarity: when dissimilar, confusion.

In situations where one does not have much experience, a lag between the unfolding event and response to it is usual. Resultantly, first responses are tentative. Gradually however by continued involvement, do not only actions become more specific as event-interactions (responses) become more tailored (by **Test-IT**s) but also our Experience-Sense(s) or feelings about what is going on, becomes clearer.

> One's initial feelings/expectations about an unfamiliar event will not be accurate.

However, as Devise-Mulling begins its 'down-link' Experience-Sense delving to comprehensively access related experiences, DM-Assembly becomes ever more populated. When the upload of initial Experience-Senses data is complete, a **Test-IT** (for Deluge feedback) is created and sent to CC-Pend-OUT.

> This suggestion-box format ultimately provides sensory feedback, which in turn enables the next Experience-Senses 'grab' to be more honed.

Consequently, these are down-link processed as well: thus not only additionally populating DM-Assembly but also providing additional fodder for a new **Test-IT**: This cycle continues until CP-Set resolution provides M-Bundle Solution and/or intensity reduction no longer inspires Cognition-Complex engagement.

## Recap

It is important to note Devise-Mulling processes take time: One experiences this 'lag' as being 'frozen' in place or unable to move.

First responses are tentative because Devise-Mulling either has just been alerted (therefore only PT-Assembly is available to divulge the initial non-specific Experience-Sense packet) or Ranged-Delving is in the first stages of down-link processing.

In either case, Ranged-Delving has neither had sufficient time to additionally populate PT-Assembly nor create a new **Test-IT**: therefore has not acquired additional sensory feedback.

For instance, in a new Deluge event-stream (as in the first attempt at water skiing) significantly-similar 'Experience-Senses' will invariably be few and therefore unreliable: the novice will thus typically feel (Experience-Sense) this as confusion, stress, fear, difficult, etc.

Alternately, when ones Deluge experience is vast (i.e., driving to score-a-goal while playing a favorite sport) the experts 'Experience-Senses' will be quite precise and targeted; therefore feel 'clear' and attainable.

## Cyclical-Phase

Guidance by "experiential-expectation" though is not the only use for Experience-Senses. They are also employed to deliver copious experience-driven fodder into DM-Assembly to power maximally tailored requests (**Test-IT**s) for very specific additional feedback.

**Test-IT** precision is dramatically accelerated by "Cyclical-Phase" because it down-links Experience-Sense core information to exponentially fodder DM-Assembly.

Designed to populate DM-Assembly with Experience-Sense (CC-Har) fundamental information, the "Cyclical-Phase" employs down-link processors to extract related 'experiences' from Data-Matrix. Extraction is possible because Devise-Mulling employs several 'link-resources' (see previous C-Cluster and E-Cluster illustrations) to source the many E-Hars from which CC-Hars were originally composed.

> This is a demanding task because search complexity rapidly increments due to the quantity of E-Hars: thereby requiring not only mulling-time but also multiple simultaneous processors.

First, CC-Har associated E-Hars (probably tens-of-thousands) are each utilized to target a corresponding Data-Matrix EA-Harmonic mate. Once located, EA-Harmonic 'joined' Information-Assemblies, which fall within a flexible match-range of existing Key-DHar PT-Freq frequencies, are determined. These Information-Assemblies are then repurposed to reveal 'core information' in the form of Distinct-Episodes.

A single replicant is created for each, which is then instilled into DM-Assemblies PT-Group-Detail as PT-Freqs: with the sourcing E-Har as an E-DHar and the group E-GHar as Key-DHar. Once all the E-Hars of each CC-Har have provided their contribution to PT-Freq population within DM-Assembly, a **Test-IT** created. This cycle continues until all CC-Hars (potentially hundreds plus) have been processed.

> Experience-Senses thereby provide rich fodder to suggest more tailored-to-bombardment physical interactions: i.e., more precise feedback via **Test-IT**s.

As feedback rolls-in Experience-Senses morph in symphony with the changing bombardment landscape (which it prodded via **Test-IT**s): thereby enabling 'feeling' shifts in relation to changing Deluge. This is possible because new Experience-Senses (feelings) provide additional Distinct-Episodes to DM-Assembly, which fodders additional **Test-IT**s, whose feedback elicits additional Experience-Senses, and so on.

> One can actually feel the 'sense-of-something' change as more information arrives. If you have ever excitedly thrown a bowling ball down a lane when a strike was critical, then watched its progress with ever more anticipation (morph of feelings) you have experienced the transition caused by new information (ball progress) empowering the cascading and morphing of Experience-Senses.

This is possible because the EDH-Pool harmonic-blend is stored with each contributing DM-Assembly DM-Key-Group Key-GHar as an "ES-Pool". This is why for a short while, until the DM-Key-Group is deleted due to resolution, one can remember how the transition previously felt.

**TI-Parameter Outbound**

TI-Parameter, the last Figure-It-Out Component prior to Cognitive-Filter taking over, has several duties. Its initial task channels two independent Test-It data-streams, one produced by Parameter-Processor and one arriving from Cognition-Complex (via CC-Pend-OUT), into a single "inbound-buffer", while ensuring receipt sequencing is maintained.

TI-Parameter's second intermediate assignment accesses inbound-buffer in order to grab the next Test-It. Once acquired, TI-Parameter hierarchically reorganizes (Filters-and-Slots) Test-It data-elements into descending SLID (Soma Location Identifier) frequencies. The task is not simple because TI-Parameter must manage not only large spontaneous volume fluctuations from sleep to survival but also wide ranging variances in Test-It complexity.

Recall, although Parameter-Processor creates only a single, fairly simple Test-It, Cognition-Complex can send up to four Test-It types of escalating complexity (from Test-It through **TEST-IT**). Complexity is significant in this stage as more complex means longer reorganizational processing times: nicely accommodated by TI-Parameter's elastic processing capabilities.

Notably, reconfiguration will directly affect not only Template-Component (next section) but also "Cognitive-Response", which follows it. Resultantly, both require TI-Parameter to enforce a best-case consistent data-configuration strategy enabling their rapid patterning and unambiguous interactivity with pertinent physical responders, respectively. Once manipulated, each Test-It is sent to "pending-buffer".

The third 'Outbound' stage utilizes 'pending-buffer' as a holding tank. By retaining reconfigured Test-Its until 'grabbed', TI-Parameter accommodates Template-Component throughput capabilities by allowing it to determine appropriate flow-rate. Once acquired a Test-It becomes one integral data-element within "TI-Flow" (explained in Template-Component section next).

> Test-Its must connect both sensory input and physical output utilizing a common 'language' format. 'Language' in this context means "Tag-Language".

'Language' provisions a data-format relevant to both the originally implicated sensory locations (SLIDs) as represented in 'P-package' and following Components: Template-

Component and Cognitive-Response. Only recognizable and applicable data is useful for relevant Bombardment-Sphere interaction.

If it wasn't, stepping on a tack with a bare foot might mean reaching for and attempting to pull the tack from your cheek.

> Alignment between occurrence and response is obviously indispensable

Test-It configuration is of paramount significance because it is decoded by Template-Component, which in turn enables Cognitive-Response: together they form a significant portion of our feedback-loop.

This is because outbound Cognitive-Response instructions instigate solicited sensory feedback through activating physical interaction with the 'Out-There', which thereby provides the additional sensory-data (ultimately TEA-Dats) utilized for resolving unresolved F-Puzzle F-Freq's and therefore potentially their E-Hars, and so on.

> With sufficient feedback, both Phase puzzles and Macro puzzles (P-Groups and M-Bundles) can also become 'Solutioned' then uploaded to Event-Cluster and possibly form a new Concept-Cluster: perhaps thereby slightly changing the 'way-one-perceives-something'

---

**Devise-Mulling Implications**

Cognition-Complex provides two definitive, yet diverse Figure-It-Out mechanisms: Delving-Trio, whose actions are mostly transparent, unaware or consciously imperceptible (accepting certain Extensive-Delving interactions); and Devise-Mulling, which facilitates conscious or aware participation when specific conditions persist.

> Notably, awareness is characterized not by a point but instead by a gradient from 'fringe' through 'overt'.

As you might recall, for unsolicited externally-driven events (Deluge) conscious or aware interaction is possible only when significant intensity coexists presenting particular circumstances: unrecognized, ongoing and/or complex. Alternately, internally-driven Devise-Mulling delving can define its own awareness-level, which can span the entire possible 'awareness-gradient'.

Devise-Mulling enables conscious or aware interaction by transforming action parameters from reactive to proactive.

To so accomplish, two cyclical methodologies couple to instigate specific 'feedback-requests': data-archive research, which initiates to uncover a range of experiences pertinent to a current Deluge or 'delving' event; and Test-It configurations, which solicit feedback utilizing the mined data-elements.

Additionally, to ensure tailored and not random interaction with feedback, Devise-Mulling deliberately not only creates pertinent CP-Sets but also retains corresponding DM-Assembly groups: thereby ensuring direct connection to its uniquely formulated Test-Its.

Implications of Devise-Mulling capabilities are enormous. Understanding how Devise-Mulling "proactive-methodology" plays-out or 'works' is important because knowing will immediately improve everyone's aptitude for tapping into its many remarkable capabilities.

Although implications are thoroughly discussed in Book-three, **Way Better** Your L.I.F.E$^2$.: **Tactics** a few highlights seem appropriate for continuity at this point.

Following questions will be familiar: they form a short 'capabilities-list', if you like. To uncover and explain what is at work making these possible is the task at hand.

- How does one pick-up from where they left off?
- How do similar events get tied together?
- How does a seemingly new event inspire recollection and resolution of a decades old issue?
- What compels the statement: "It's like a huge weight was lifted off my shoulders".
- If something is uninteresting, what can I do to get interested?
- Why do I excel at some things but find others painfully difficult?
- Why does taking a break from a problem assist in its resolution and why isn't that counter-productive?
- How does one remember to "pick up milk": and why does one forget?
- How does Deja-vu work?
- How do viewpoints and attitudes morph?

So completely do most take for granted the competencies needed to accomplish any of the above, your inner-voice (Devise-Mulling) may have already chimed in with a 'so what'?

It is expected, after examination of the intrinsic methodologies deployed to accomplish these and other amazing comparable feats, explanations will catapult everyone onto the pathway of understanding 'How-We-Work': and therefore to more usefully choosing and fulfilling personal aspirations.

There is a commonality inherent in the above list: they require a comparator and a comparatee.

Notably these are the two fundamental components of substantially-similar recall as well. In other words, Bombardment and/or Devise-Mulling delving events provide the 'comparator' trigger: data-archive reference sites housing frequency experiences provide the 'comparatee'.

> Clearly then, recall has an absolute reliance on the long-term stability or 'persistence-capability' of data-resources.

At a granular structural level, broad range neural-plasticity provisions the Figure-It-Out environment within which fulfillment of the 'capabilities-list' relies.

Globally speaking, two broad data-resource classifications exist, which demand different neural-structures with dissimilar plasticity: unresolved and concluded. P-Cluster neural real-estate is by far the most malleable, as its unresolved data-elements are being continually referenced, updated and resolved: whereas concluded Data-Matrix, E-Clusters and C-Clusters are variously less flexible by design.

CP-Sets therefore command the most flexible P-Cluster neural-resources as access to their data-sets is unrelenting. However, requirement for extended data-archiving durations (potentially decades) is also mandatory.

> Perhaps most notable though, data-archives endure primarily because Figure-It-Out simply does not provide a delete tool for either P-Cluster or any other data-resource: For instance once created (health issues aside) CP-Sets can only be morphed by 'Solutioning': from P-Cluster into higher constructs.

Now understood are the two fundamental CP-Set 'facets' created and retained during both Deluge acquisition and/or selected Devise-Mulling activities: 'questions' (E-Puzzles) and individually associated 'answer' details (F-Puzzles).

> Resultantly, at the forefront of 'capabilities-list' fulfillment is CP-Sets: They provide the primary targeting 'fodder': whereas Figure-It-Out, the mechanism enabling 'answer' fulfillment for all 'questions'.

There are other players though. Additionally assisting CP-Set with 'unresolved' data-storehousing is DM-Assembly 'Key-Groups' and possibly PT-Assembly Key-Groups depending on timing. Note 'Key-Groups' and their 'Details' will remain unresolved when not only outbound Test-It deployment is postponed by Devise-Mulling 'mulling' activities (i.e., searching data-archives) but also inbound Deluge intensity is extreme as during Cognitive-Pathway One events.

---

**How does one pick-up from where they 'left-off'?**

The purpose of examining this 'capabilities-list' item is to enhance understanding of Cognition-Complex 'workings' by detailing the physical and processing resources involved in its fulfillment: it will be the only one detailed as the fundamental principles are similar for the others as well. To set the scenario stage, several underlying assumptions require disclosure.

> The primary circumstance presupposes an associated 'new-event' is underway. Secondly, this 'new-event' in some way is similar to and able to be matched to an unresolved one: therefore by default, significantly-similar 'unresolved-event' or events exist. Thirdly, the unresolved-event must have somehow, been stored somewhere: because it is ipso facto retrievable. Fourthly, this scenario dictates time has elapsed since one 'left-off' from the last 'Solutioning' attempt: perhaps a day, a week or longer.

The 'new-event' has two possible origins: derived either from random Bombardment; or from Devise-Mulling 'silent-delving' activities, which includes day or night dreaming.

A third option also normally exists of course: Delving-Trio and/or Devise-Mulling can be creating Test-Its from current Deluge parameters. However, as this condition does not fit our 'elapsed-time' scenario, it will be excluded.

The stage is set then: the 'left-off' event has been triggered by either the 'drop-in' of significantly-similar (frequency-matched) "random-Deluge" or Devise-Mulling Test-Its designed to inspire "requested-feedback" or 'tailored-bombardment' (also therefore corresponding CP-Sets and DM-Assemblies).

In the 'drop-in' scenario 'Match' locates a P-Cluster resident frequency-similar CP-Set E-Har. Recognition thereby inspired Targeted and Ranged-Delving to grab other significantly-similar CP-Sets and create a larger reference pool (DM-Assembly).

> Ample quantities of unresolved F-Puzzles are assumed available to sufficiently increment intensity to inspire Delving-Trios Ranged-Delving attention. Recall, Devise-Mulling cues off the delivery of a P-package to RD-IN.

Once Devise-Mulling retrieves the P-package, it goes about locating all DM-Assembly groups associated with all recovered CP-Set E-Hars.

For scenario purposes, this activity is sufficiently intense to cause some awareness of a target previous similar-event, which was of course retrieved from DM-Assembly.

> Devise-Mulling resultantly reinitiates delving processors responsible for incorporating 'drop-in' information with associated archived experiences. These activities also populate DM-Assembly, potentially initiate Test-Its and most likely raise awareness (gradient) as well.

Additional Test-Its resultantly set-up 'requested-bombardment' cyclical feedback processes. Feedback can result in two outcomes: either revelation and resolution; or putting DM-Assembly on hold once again, which thereby effectively forces postponement until future sensory-feedback reinitiates recognition.

> Random event triggering is resultantly less robust in terms of archive retrieval because initially Devise-Mulling has not participated as fully to either create additional CP-Sets or augment DM-Assembly. Ultimately though after much cycling, the outcome is the same even though the 'drop-in' event required more Test-Its to catch-up.

Here then is a straightforward answer to the restated posed question; "How does one pick-up from where they 'left-off'"? Both because 'group' event pointers and associated SLID details can be reliably storehoused and processes are available to 'Match', retrieve and recognize significantly-similar events.

> These capabilities enable redefinition from 'just physical survival' with limited options to proactive environment management, which thereby permits choosing lifestyle from an almost unlimited range of possibilities.

---


**Template-Components Overview**

Template-Component interfaces Figure-It-Out and Cognitive-Self modules by acquiring two inbound data-streams, "The-Flows", from the former and compiling a substantially enhanced outbound data-stream for the latter's Response-Component. Its transitioning role can thus be restated: Cognitive-to---**TEMPLATE**---to-Response.

> Recall both contain Somatic Tags or physical Sensor Location ID's (SLIDs) indicating originating bombardment acceptance sites. For Template mandate fulfillment the importance of this immutable signature will once again prove essential.

Although both inbound data-streams originate within Figure-It-Out they have different origins, uses, consequences and therefore labels. Continually streaming "DE-Flow", named due to its data-members being shaped by Data-Matrix during the second phase process of Distinct-Episode Bracketing, provides unbroken 'raw' data-stream contiguity.

> Even during resting and deep-sleep states when data-flow is far less saturated, DE-Flow continuously inspires micro-responses, such as, eye movements, breathing, tossing-and-turning, etc.

TI-Flow on the other hand, comprised of finely tuned Cognition-Complex Test-Its, is only available when Cognition-Complex has an insertable condition.

Notably, even during lower volume and intensity states when Cognitive-Alerts are minimal, Figure-It-Out's perpetually active neural-network crawling activities can populate CC-Pend-OUT when Data-Matrix and P-Cluster data-element realignments inspire CP-Set creation. Resulting TI-Flow will be evidenced as dreams or nightmares, which can additionally instigate Soma-Self responses: such as restlessness, and/or more pronounced actions: such as sleep-walking.

> Most have probably experienced being startled awake when Cognitive reconnections are sufficiently intense: Sometimes in a sweat and other times with an image which is hard to shake or perhaps with a startling revelation, which one is compelled to write down.

Cognitive-Filter is charged with maintaining interactive data-resources and rapid Pattern determination. Specifically, Template-Component realigns The-Flows data-elements to not only augment its dynamic data-storehouses but also determine an optimal outbound (to Response-Component) Pattern or "T-Patt".

Foundationally, Response-Component relies on the accuracy of inbound T-Patt harmonic configurations as the basis for sending successful physical or somatic instructions. Template-Component therefore has a critical responsibility as a compromised T-Patt will invariably result in erroneous responses.

> Think of an outbound T-Patt as a pulse of sensory-integrated continually varying instructions upon which Response-Component relies to deploy accurate physical interface

Response-Component output is fluid and continuous: not jerky or strobing. This is so even though data-flow can massively fluctuate in terms of volume and/or intensity.

Ones sense of resulting continuity is a marvel. Perceived continuousness is provided by an adept Mind-Self integrator. It hoppers throughput then continuously flows extreme quantities of 'routine-to-extreme' responses into a seamless "Movie-of-Your-Life" presentation. In depth discussion of this topic will be saved for last.

---

## Inter-related Selves

Purposed to attain granular recognition of new Deluge events, when alerted by Body-Self via Cognitive-Alert, Figure-It-Out is the master at utilizing both random and requested (Deluge and Test-It) inbound data-elements to solve E-Puzzles. Mind-Self data-archives are thus created in every case; even though Body-Self gradually recognizes repetition and thereby ultimately copes with repetitive Deluge itself, without sending Cognitive-Alerts.

Somewhat comparatively, Template-Component has mastered incoming DE-Flow and TI-Flow. It utilizes them to devise Pattern solutions (T-Patt's) to benefit Mind-Self's Response-Component. Relying on its own data-resources, Template-Component also comes to recognize new and repeating data-structures.

Although Body-Self epitomizes sameness and Mind-Self welcomes exception, unbreakable cyclical symmetry and connectivity exists between the two "Selves". Body-Self employs Cognitive-Alert to interact new Deluge with Mind-Self; whereas Mind-Self deploys Response-Component to cause physical interaction within ones Bombardment-Sphere thus providing new fodder for Soma-Self sensors.

One Mind-Self methodology purposed to impact Deluge via physical-responses was deployed utilizing Figure-It-Out Test-Its (TI-Flow): specifically calculated to trigger Template-Components to create or enhance a T-Patt. These provide Response-Component fodder for the creation of outbound packages purposed to adjust our macro and micro positions within our Bombardment-Sphere: thus affecting specific aspects of the external environment.

>   Of course, once "newness" abates and Body-Self recognizes sensory-data, Deluge is channeled to Soma-Response (Soma-Habit).

As the diagram below provides the lay of the Template-Component processing landscape, it will be utilized throughout this section.

# *WayBetter* Your L.I.F.E$^2$.: **Mind-Self** 243

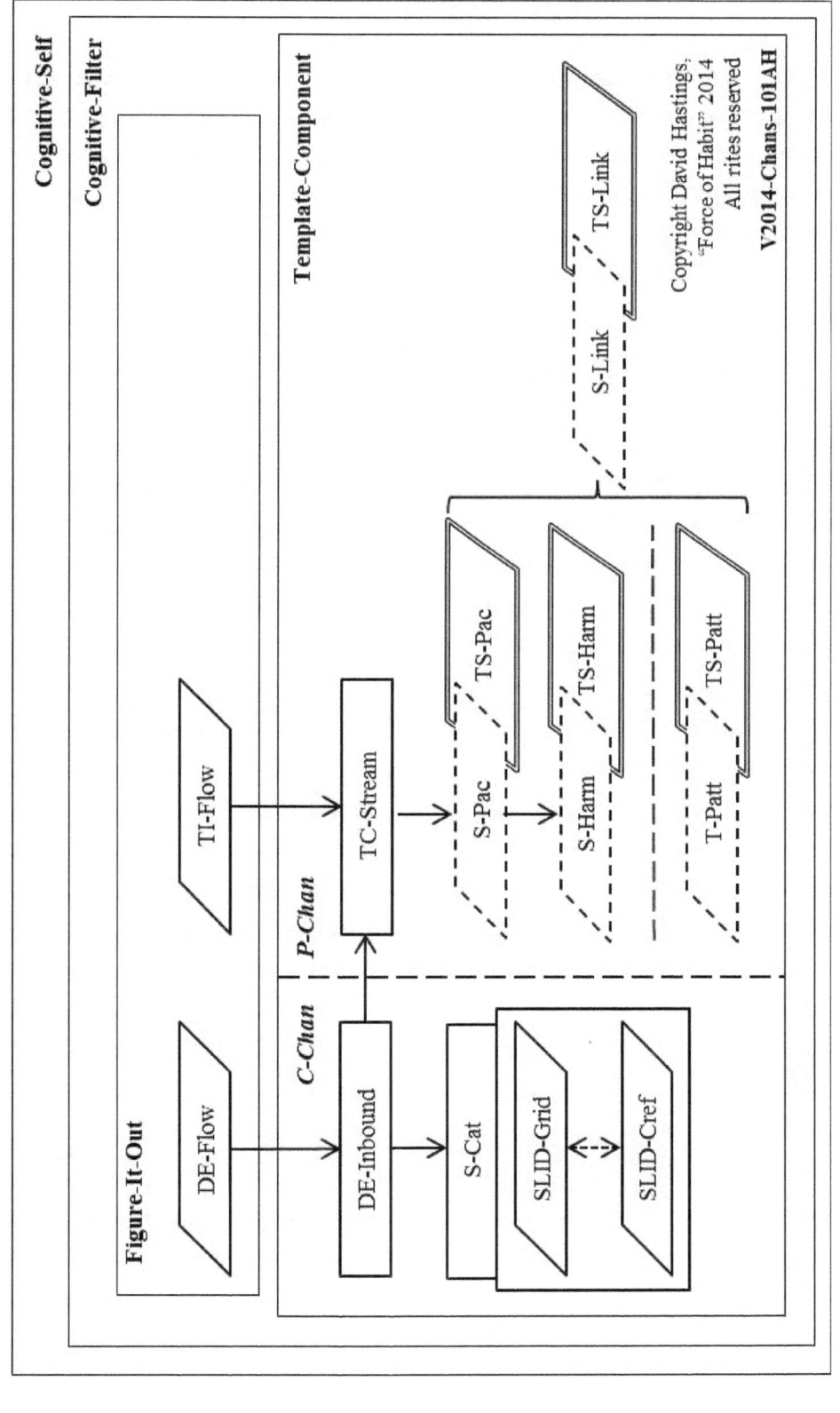

## Template-Component Facets

The-Flows are pivotal for exacting an optimal T-Patt. Additionally, any provisioned T-Patt must appropriately represent (to Response-Component) not only bombardment (DE-Flow) but also any appropriate and/or corresponding Test-It (TI-Flow) conditions. If it didn't, inaccurate responses will result, which could significantly compromise survival efforts.

> It would not be useful for instance, if when hot fat spit onto your arm, T-Patt's suggested you wait for a second or two to watch the event dissolve your flesh and then move slowly toward rather than quickly away from the source

To accomplish incredibly complex feats of "Flow-Integration" and T-Patt selection, many inter-reliant Template-Component processes require effective and efficient handling. This section is organized to track the data-flow and detail all processes as encountered: Soma-Catalogue first.

### C-Chan

This event signals transition of the DE-Flow data-stream from Figure-It-Out Data-Matrix to Cognitive-Filter Template-Component. Although this section will explain "Catalogue-Channel" or "C-Chan" functionality, it will leave the majority of integration discussions until presentation of the second channel: "Pattern-Channel" or "P-Chan".

C-Chan responsibilities initiate when DE-Flow is injected by Data-Matrix into its "DE-Inbound" neural arena; "S-Cat" or "Soma-Catalogue". Two of ten Template-Component data-resources are located within its purview.

As stated previously, DE-Flow never ceases. There is always soma activity flowing through the Pathways: even if only minimally on CP-5.

> For effective discussion of functional principles (creation, maintenance, access and use of target data-resources) simplification of the massive volume of DE-Flow will be useful. Therefore to minimize complication the strategy is to isolate a few representative data-elements with associated events.

---

Immediately upon arrival at DE-Inbound, a DE-Flow package ("DE-package") is cloned: the original is held for diverse integration into "SLID-Grid" and "SLID-Cref", the two S-Cat data-resources; whereas its clone is fired to "TC-Stream" for assimilation with any retrieved TI-Flow (following section).

## SLID-Grid

The primary C-Chan data-repository is labeled SLID-Grid; for its not only SLID (Sensory-Location-IDentifier) contents but also grid-like data-configuration. SLID-Grid thus provides a referenceable primary grid-resource, whose unique SLID reference frequencies are employed to define permanent resident grid locations. Resultantly, each SLID is housed in the grid-resource by a distinguishing "Grid-Identifier" or "SG-ID" (SLID-Grid IDentifier) equal to its immutable SLID frequency.

> Conceptualize SLID-Grid as a huge honeycomb, where individual 'cells' define single SG-ID permanent locations

Moreover, SG-ID's are not randomly assigned to cells within the framework but permanently and symmetrically organized by frequency. This makes sense as the global range, into which all SLID frequencies fit, is genetically pre-designated and fixed.

> In this way every possible Soma-Self Location ID (sensory uptake frequency) is comprehensively and unalterably genetically mapped in SLID-Grid neural real-estate

SLID-Grid structure thereby ensures constant orientation, which is imperative for all T-Patt processes to come.

## SLID-Cref

This data-resource is aptly termed SLID-Cref, because it provides extensive SLID-to-SLID cross-referencing (Cref) information: i.e., not only what SLIDs have interacted with what other SLIDs up to any current point in time but also a definitive measure of interaction magnitude.

The following discussion is presented to assist in conceptualizing SLID-Cref structure and data inter-relationships. Although to simplify explanations, only touch skin sensor SLIDs will be utilized, the principles can be extrapolated to all Soma-Sensors.

If we could lay skin sensors flat, something like a Mercator map (let's call it the "Location ID Map" or "LIM" for short), it would display SLIDs within close proximity and others increasingly remote. Even so, their relative locations one-to-the-other, would remain physically constant. Notably, this SLID-Grid permanent juxtaposition is emulated within a Template-Component neural-array.

Furthermore, as we zoomed in and perused the "skin-scape" an additional characteristic would become evident: same-sized areas would be variably dense with SLIDs. In other words, some have hundreds of SLIDs per same-sized area whereas others much fewer.

For discussion purposes, let's take a representative sample area of the LIM representing the pad on the end of the left index finger. As we scrutinize, hundreds is SLIDs are evidenced.

Comparatively, observation of SLID quantity in a same-sized LIM area on the back of the hand is only dozens. This is important because it exposes the two criteria, proximity and denseness, which potentially determine whether and which SLIDs might directly inter-relate or fire simultaneously.

> Let's do a hands-on (excuse the pun) experiment to discover how closely SLIDs are packed. You will be aware of each one because the position, the feeling of the prod on your skin, will cognitively seem different one from the other, even if only slightly.

While prodding, be careful not to cause yourself any injury. Take a small-sized paperclip and straighten the outside ravel. Seat yourself comfortably and lay your left hand on a table; relaxed and palm up. While your eyes are closed, very gently (keeping a tight grouping) prod the end pad of the left index finger twelve times with the unravelled tip of the paperclip.

Next, also perform 'the prodding' in the middle of the back of the left hand, with your eyes closed, and note the less closely packed SLIDs. Three different nerve branches provide the receptors: Median Nerve for the index finger; and depending on the location chosen, the Radial and/or Ulnar Nerve on the back of the hand.

> Does not only a huge quantity of information come in through our fingertips delivered by the extensive neural-networks of our Soma-Selves but also the vast dedicated neural-resources of our Cognitive-Selves process in miniscule portions

My finding is this end-to-end multi-branch capacity, much more than the opposable thumb theory, is one critical enabler distinguishing Humans from the apes and other species.

This capability provisions our seemingly unlimited competency to perfect tools, which in turn enables ever more precise bombardment interaction and therefore control of noxious external inbounds.

Now, using a flat surface (table-top), gently press the left finger pad you previously prodded onto it. Try and include the entire area in one go if you can. If not, don't worry as there will be no reduction in outcome. We will get to the reason for this a little later.

These three experiments expose some remarkable absolutes: we definitely have the ability to finely sense very small distance increments on the surface of the skin; we do not confuse one SLID with another; SLID density is definitely different depending on location or LIM choice; LIM's certainly work together in groupings due to proximity.

These absolutes are only possible because each location has an immutable frequency which identifies it-and-it-alone to the cognitive apparatus: the very definition of a SLID.

> There may be several questions (E-Puzzles) sliding into awareness. Such as, how are the multitudes of inter-relationships (especially relating to which SLID activated with which SLID when the pad of the finger was pushed onto the table top) maintained? Also, why does saving this inter-relationship matter? How is it used to maximize survival potential and many more, no doubt? Answers will be forthcoming.

As a fundamental then, Soma Location ID (SLID) is immutability carried forward into Template-Component. Template-Component must be able to resource the interrelationship of these incontrovertible markers or there would be no use for senses.

In order to provide translation from sensors to cognitive and then to response, it must of necessity be possible to embed best location information into a T-Patt. After all, Response-Components actually utilize an iteration of the same identifiers (Tag-Clusters) to enact appropriate response scenarios.

> Integrated system competencies keep us surviving in each of our perpetually morphing Bombardment-Spheres

The SG-ID inter-relationships in the situations above are maintained in SLID-Cref. Each Tag-Cluster (SLID) within a single DE-Flow is cross-referenced to each of the other Tag-Cluster's by incrementing the SLID-Cref data-resource quantity or "Q-value" marker by one. This process is detailed below.

> The structure of this grid-resource is built for fast access. SLID-Cref has a primary identifier, pointer or index called "SG-Prime-ID", which is frequency equal to its SLID counterpart, as previously indicated.

SLID-Cref also contains a secondary identifier, called "SG-Secon-ID". It represents Tag-Clusters which arrived in DE-Flows with an SG-Prime-ID. Resultantly, each Tag-Cluster is cross-referenced: each to each other.

> This forms a one-to-many relationship: i.e., "one-(SG-Prime-ID)-to-many-(SG-Secon-ID's)". Rounding-out SG-Secon-ID information retention is a quantity usage record called "SG-Secon-Q" or "Q-value". Q-value discussions will follow shortly.

Let's construct an example, a very simple (impossibly small) scenario, of only four SLIDs located on the finger pad you were just poking. Each will share a border with the other and cover the entire finger pad area.

> Let's augment the configuration by having one SLID in the middle, identified as S-1, and three surrounding concentric touching SLIDs, identified as S-2 to S-4. One final condition assumes (for convenience) there has not been any previous activity: SLID-Cref is a blank slate, so-to-speak.

The first case scenario will use the touch of your left finger pad onto a table-top event: Assume in so doing S-1 through S-4 were simultaneously activated only once and therefore form part of the same DE-Flow.

> Resultantly then, each DE-Flow Tag-Cluster (S-1 through S-4) would cross-reference each to the other and the data added to SLID-Cref.

In other words S-1 would be identified as SG-Prime-ID first, with S-2 through S-4 being cross-referenced as its three associated SG-Secon-ID's; then S-2 would be identified as SG-Prime-ID with S-1, S-3 and S-4 being cross-referenced as its three associated SG-Secon-ID's; and so on.

**WayBetter** Your L.I.F.E$^2$.: **Mind-Self**

As each is being processed their corresponding "Q-values" (SG-Secon-Q) would be incremented by one (per presented configuration conditions).

On this first occasion, the SLID-Cref data-resource interrelationship would display as below.

| SG-Prime-ID | S-1 | | | | SG-Prime-ID | S-2 | | | |
|---|---|---|---|---|---|---|---|---|---|
| SG-Secon-ID | S-2 | S-3 | S-4 | | SG-Secon-ID | S-1 | S-3 | S-4 | |
| SG-Secon-Q | 1 | 1 | 1 | | SG-Secon-Q | 1 | 1 | 1 | |
| **SG-Prime-ID** | S-3 | | | | **SG-Prime-ID** | S-4 | | | |
| SG-Secon-ID | S-1 | S-2 | S-4 | | SG-Secon-ID | S-1 | S-2 | S-3 | |
| SG-Secon-Q | 1 | 1 | 1 | | SG-Secon-Q | 1 | 1 | 1 | |

In the next scenario assume three subsequent pushes with your eyes closed, which correspondingly activated and therefore created cross-referencing for only S1 and S-4. SLID-Cref data-resource would look as follows: (note for S-1, only the S-4 Q-value is "4"; and for S-4, only the S-1 Q-value is "4").

| SG-Prime-ID | S-1 | | | | SG-Prime-ID | S-2 | | | |
|---|---|---|---|---|---|---|---|---|---|
| SG-Secon-ID | S-2 | S-3 | S-4 | | SG-Secon-ID | S-1 | S-3 | S-4 | |
| SG-Secon-Q | 1 | 1 | 4 | | SG-Secon-Q | 1 | 1 | 1 | |
| **SG-Prime-ID** | S-3 | | | | **SG-Prime-ID** | S-4 | | | |
| SG-Secon-ID | S-1 | S-2 | S-4 | | SG-Secon-ID | S-1 | S-2 | S-3 | |
| SG-Secon-Q | 1 | 1 | 1 | | SG-Secon-Q | 4 | 1 | 1 | |

If pushes were sustained, SLIDs would continue to be variously activated and therefore counterparts incremented, depending on the focal point of the touch. Notably there is a potential for broad variance of both bombardment and SLID activation depending on a person's orientation and activity.

> Activities create personalized inter-dependencies determining not only what SLIDs interact with what SLIDs but also the quantity of these interactions: thus individualization is enabled

Suffice it to say for now activity variability's have huge repercussions for T-Patt determination and therefore for bombardment interface. Additional details will be provided during discussions of P-Chan (C-Chan's companion channel), where S-Cat grid-resources will be utilized.

**P-Chan**

> T-Patt's play a vital role: They are the source of rapidly deployable patterns. As such, T-Patt's strongly influence physical-world action responses or behaviour and therefore, survival success

Pattern-Channel or P-Chan is directly responsible to serve the correct T-Patt to Response-Component. While questing to accomplish its task however, an appropriate T-Patt may not exist. When this is the case, P-Chan must be ready and able to create and then preserve the new T-Patt.

T-Patt creation is not a simple task. This Template-Component mandate requires interacting substantial Cognitive-Filter processing capabilities with C-Chan's S-Cat and P-Chan's eight diverse data-resources. Fulfillment will necessitate much Filtering-and-Slotting as P-Chan processors strive to provide best-information via a T-Patt to Resource-Component.

DE-Flow and TI-Flow both contain Tag-Clusters, albeit derived from different sources: DE-Flow from bombardment; TI-Flow from Figure-It-Out. To represent the complete current "data-picture" appropriate amalgamation is key. In other words, contiguously 'zippering' The-Flows together ensure an outbound T-Patt is co-ordinated with associated inbound-data from both Deluge and Test-It sources.

---

## TC-Stream

The "TC-Stream" data-resource on P-Chan is the starting point for the many process, which dedicate either selecting an existing T-Patt or creating a new one.

> When the DE-Flow clone is loaded by C-Chan, P-Chan processing initializes by immediately loading a concurrent TI-Flow into TC-Stream as well.

The purpose of the next tasks is to create a "Stream-Package" or "S-Pac". S-Pac formation is accomplished by first merging the two sources into a dedicated virtual-resource: first by combining 'same' Tag-Clusters; then hierarchically arranging the resulting expanded Tag-Cluster population by descending SLID (Tag-Cluster) frequency; and finally instilling the 'assemblage' as an S-Pac into the "TS-Pac" holding data-resource for later retrieval.

Although 'S-Pac' now contains the core trigger Tag-Cluster information destined to somehow inspire selection or creation of a T-Patt, there is a significant snag.

> For S-Pac to inspire 'either selection or creation' of a T-Patt, comparison of something-to-something will have to occur to determine T-Patt recognition.

In other words, recognition of an existing T-Patt match would spawn one kind of process whereas non-recognition, another.

> Two difficulties with direct comparison emerge at this point though.

The first hitch has been encountered before. Due to the dissimilarity between S-Pac (populated with multitudes of individual frequency defined members) and a singular Harmonic T-Patt comparison is not possible.

> As discussed in other sections, Harmonic configuration is common in Brackets because a singular structure not only supports rapid comparison but also requires minimal neural real-estate; i.e., its resulting footprint is substantially smaller than the individual data-parts which originated it.

The solution for the first issue is elegant in its clarity: keep the newly formed S-Pac intact in TS-Pac and create the needed harmonic from it: then store the result in another data-resource.

P-Chan expedites this strategy by harmonizing the S-Pac into an "S-Harm" or "Stream-Harmonic". Critically, the S-Harm still truly represents The-Flows but in the needed format.

> Unfortunately, the second problem now rears up.

S-Harm is currently in the correct format for harmonic-to-harmonic comparison (S-Harm to T-Patt) but unfortunately S-Harm only represents a miniscule portion of the information, which is incorporated to form a T-Patt harmonic. Thus, it is still not directly comparable to the "TS-Patt" data-repository.

The solution to the second problem is also direct and robust: maintain two additional referencing data-resources; "TS-Harm" and "TS-Link". The first to storehouse S-Harm's (also as a holding data-resource destined for later retrieval), the other to sustain the 'S-Harm to T-Patt' or "S-Link' relationship.

> Maintaining the relationship between the source S-Pac and blended S-Harm is critical for following process.

To capture connection, Cognitive-Filter cross-references three associated data-elements. These are utilized to create an "S-Link" data-element, which it stores in "TS-Link" link-resource: the target S-Harm is the primary key; the source S-Pac is the secondary key; and a third data-pointer (T-Patt) is explained below as a tertiary key.

> The primary task of quickly recognizing if a matching pattern (T-Patt) already exists can resultantly be accomplished in two stages. S-Pac is saved in TS-Pac and then additionally morphed to its S-Harm harmonic representation.

Once accomplished, the new S-Harm is matched (utilizing the now familiar harmonic matching protocols) to the TS-Harm data-resource.

> If the S-Harm exists TS-Link is accessed, the corresponding T-Patt seized and deployed. However, if there is no S-Harm match, S-Harm is saved in its dedicated TS-Harm data-resource: and the process of formatting a new T-Patt initiates.

---

The diagram below unveils "Assemblage-Processor" ("A-Pro"), which scopes following discussions.

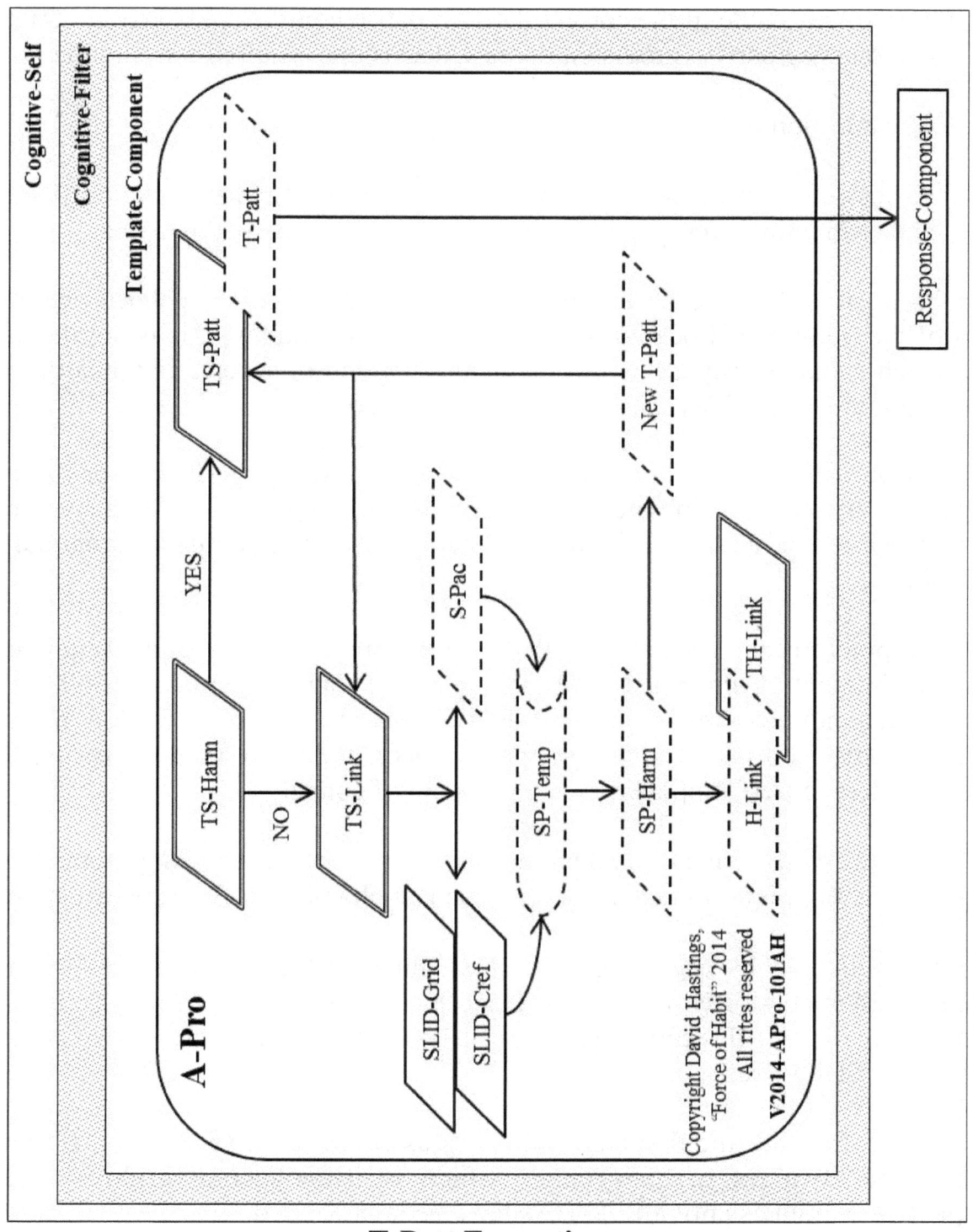

**T-Patt Formation**

The launch point for the formation of a new pattern (T-Patt) must be The-Flows as its two data-streams are the only data-sources available to Template-Component. Although S-Pac is already available in the correct data-format, it contains only a small fraction of the information necessary to provision the raw-data scope required for pattern creation.

So the question is, "from where does the balance of the content derive?"

The quick answer is from S-Cat. However, the compilation has exacting parameters keyed to the originating events as represented by Tag-Clusters within S-Pac.

Reflect back on SLID-Grid structure and recall its 'honeycomb' echoes one-hundred percent of the Soma-Self Location IDentifiers (SLIDs). Notably, this is not the case for S-Pac, which contains only a few milliseconds sampling of accepted bombardment and depending on the time of day, possibly Test-It injections.

Regardless, to incorporate current data, the C-Chan Assemblage-Processor must begin at S-Pac. A-Pro therefore initiates the process of building a new T-Patt by a reverse location process: i.e., it utilizes the unmatched S-Harm to locate the appropriate S-Pac via TS-Link.

To create a precisely representative T-Patt, several processing stages are required. As a pivotal requirement, A-Pro must only include S-Pac Tag-Clusters (or "SP-TC's") and their connected counterparts, in a new T-Patt. If this was not the case then information flow would manifest as sporadic and disconnected due to random content being suggested to Response-Component: which it is not of course.

> As with other critical evaluators in many other processing venues so far encountered, highest intensity signals the launch point: A-Pro is no exception.

A-Pro thus initializes by accessing the highest intensity SP-TC within S-Pac (already organised highest-to -lowest intensity). Once located, the target SP-TC is first cross-referenced to its SG-ID counterpart in SLID-Grid and then to its SG-Prime-ID companion in SLID-Cref.

> Next, A-Pro adds the first target SP-TC plus all associated SG-Secon-ID and their specific Q-values to "SP-Temp", which is its collection grid-resource: The process continues until all SP-TC's have been processed.

The diagram below will form the focal point for discussions. Explanations will elucidate the utilization of SP-Temp data-resource for both Tag-Cluster accumulation and determining intensity. Although simplified for clarity, there is no compromise to the integrity of underlying principles.

| SP-TC ID | Orig Int | SP-Temp | | | | | | | | |
|---|---|---|---|---|---|---|---|---|---|---|
| | | Associated SG-Secon-ID's | | | | | | | | |
| | | | from "Sampling" | | | | not from "Sampling" | | | |
| | | | S-1 | S-2 | S-3 | S-4 | S-5 | S-6 | S-7 | S-8 |
| S-1 | 9 | Q-Value | --- | 10 | 30 | 60 | 10 | 300 | 90 | 110 |
| S-2 | 6 | Q-Value | 40 | --- | 20 | 40 | 45 | --- | --- | 60 |
| S-3 | 3 | Q-Value | 50 | 20 | --- | 30 | --- | 90 | 50 | --- |
| S-4 | 5 | Q-Value | 60 | 30 | 10 | --- | 90 | --- | 20 | 80 |
| S-1 | | I-Ratio | --- | 0.9 | 2.7 | 5.4 | 0.9 | 27.0 | 8.1 | 9.9 |
| S-2 | | I-Ratio | 2.4 | --- | 1.2 | 2.4 | 2.7 | --- | --- | 3.6 |
| S-3 | | I-Ratio | 1.5 | 6.0 | --- | 0.9 | --- | 2.7 | 1.5 | --- |
| S-4 | | I-Ratio | 3.0 | 1.5 | 0.3 | --- | 4.5 | --- | 4.0 | 4.0 |
| **Accumulated I-Ratio** | | | 6.9 | 8.4 | 4.2 | 8.7 | 8.1 | 29.7 | 13.6 | 17.5 |
| **Original Intensity** | | | 9.0 | 6.0 | 3.0 | 5.0 | 0.0 | 0.0 | 0.0 | 0.0 |
| **Intensity Total** | | | 16 | 14 | 7 | 13.7 | 8.1 | 29.7 | 13.6 | 17.5 |

In the provided example, S-Pac houses four SP-TC (Tag-Clusters), identified in the "ID" column as S-1 through S-4 (for convenience): these are equivalent to SG-Prime-ID's aggregated by A-Pro. In reality there would probably be thousands in an S-Pac; certainly many hundreds.

As an additional condition, because there are only four represented SLIDs, each SP-TC has a relationship to the other. This convergent inter-relationship means there are also only four SG-Secon-ID's Tag-Clusters as noted (also as S-1 through S-4) within the "from Sampling" column on the diagram.

Also, four addendum SG-Secon-ID's, S-5 through S-8 are located under the "not from Sampling" column: these represent events outside of (or think of them as prior to) the current sampling. These have been contrived for example purposes to indicate prior activity.

Look along the first or upper 'S-1' row (comparable to SG-Prime-ID in SLID-Cref): Notice some of the intersections of columns S-1 through S-8 (equivalent to SG-Secon-ID in SLID-Cref) contain numeric Q-Values. In other words, again perusing row S-1: (S-1 is blank as it cannot interact with itself); S-2 has interacted 10 times with S-1; S-3, 30 times with S-1; S-4, 60 times; and so on.

Note rows and columns in the diagram were the focus of discussions from above: namely, SG-Prime-ID cross-matching and corresponding Q-value fetching, respectively.

Intensity-Ratios are represented in the lower S-1 through S-4 'ID' grouping: the result of A-Pro's calculation stage. By viewing the lower S-1 row there are ratio values in each of the intersections for each of the corresponding Q-Values in the upper section.

> Recall for T-Patt to be effective, it must represent three conditions: current activity as represented by S-Pac (The-Flows); historical information of what has interactively occurred between each S-Pac Tag-Cluster; and in what proportion (I-Ratio) current conditions (S-Pac Tag Cluster intensities) impact historical (S-Cat) interactions

Without the above, Response-Component would only be able to respond to current conditions, which would mean previous pattern experience would count for naught…which is simply not the case. Conversely if current conditions were denied credence, there would only be the past; rudimentary at best without cross-integration, which would garner inappropriate Body-Self action.

> Human survival would have been impossible in either extreme: fortunately The-Flows integration strategy manifested as the enabler of much higher functioning.

Therefore, it is the mixture of current and archive which provides rapid pattern deployment success for our species. Mixture must be based on what-occurred-with-what (S-Cat) coupled with intensity (archive) referenced in proportion to what just occurred (S-Pac).

I-Ratio is that mixture. It enables experience to not only modify current content but also provide the broad range of interaction between cross-implicated participants.

This enables not only applicable current response but also preparation for a possible broad range of follow-on responses. It is this preparation which enables our actions to smoothly transition one-to-the-next without the jerkiness of re-initializing somatic responses for each millisecond acceptance cycle.

I-Ratios are evaluated (as a ratio) by taking the SP-TC (current) intensity and multiplying it by the Q-Value of the associated SG-Secon-ID (divide result by 100 for ratio).

This ratio is then utilized by A-Pro to determine how many additional Tag-Clusters must be replicated for each SP-Temp SG-Secon-ID in order to represent the calculated ratio. For example purposes use a one to one relationship; a ratio of one will result in one replicated Tag-Cluster for each whole number ratio value (round up to the nearest whole number).

As Tag-Clusters are replicated, they are inserted into the "SP-Harm" data-resource, which is appropriately configured and capable of being morphed into a harmonic. SP-Harm is then Filtered-and-Slotted by SLID-Grid ascending frequency in order to conform to and be insertable as a whole into its new T-Patt format.

It may help to conceptualize the pre-T-Patt format as a bar graph platform, say 100 wide and 100 deep, where information content is represented by each of the 'bars', which are in immutable frequency order.

Remember, the only information individual 'bars' can contain is limited to a single SLID frequency (corresponding to a Tag-Cluster frequency).

Even if only thirty percent of the possible range of SLID frequencies (all possible bar locations) was represented within an SP-Harm, the zero values would still contribute to overall pattern configuration. In other words, although some 'bars' would remain nominal, populated 'bars' would be variably higher than the less unpopulated 'bars'.

Now, conceptualize vacuum sealing a thin layer of transparent material over the entire surface of this 100-by-100 grid and then rotating the 'platform' into a three-dimensional view.

The resulting three-dimensional rolling surface would actually be formed of multitudes of 'spires', which would thus create a very specific and unique terrain-like "Shape-Complex". This T-Patt is the desired end result of the unique contributions of Template-Component processes, which systematically populated the 'bars'.

> Each Shape-Complex thereby fulfills Template-Components primary goal: formation of a new T-Patt. It is a complex harmonic representation of not only The-Flows but also applicable S-Cat historical inter-relationships to the Tag-Clusters as originally delivered by DE-Flow and TI-Flow

Once accomplished, Assemblage-Processor completes three final tasks: deploys T-Patt to Response-Component; adds the new T-Patt to TS-Patt data-resource for referenceability; and updates TS-Link, thereby linking this new T-Patt to its S-Harm inspirator.

**Response-Component**

Although Response-Component will be dealt with more fully when Cognitive-Pathway Three (CP-3) is presented, a brief overview will round out CP-4 discussions.

Recall, each spire of the T-Patt harmonic 'Shape-Complex' represents a frequency with specific intensity. Additionally, every 'spire' was defined by Template-Components SLID-Grid frequency matrix and as such was exactingly designed to emulate a Response-Component receptor configuration as well.

> T-Patt is designed for actioning not just archiving.

Consequently, as T-Patt is propagated through the Response-Component matrix it is aligned to a pre-determined Response-Component receptor grid to ensure exact orientation to each frequency specific, multiple-receptor network or "MR-Net". Then, as T-Patt pulses through Response-Component, it simultaneously activates all MR-Net's for which there is a corresponding T-Patt spire.

Receptors are not just on and off but provide vast combinations micro to MACRO reactivity, originally inspired by the predominance of various T-Patt spires.

> Notably then, 'higher' spires (greater potential) simultaneously enable (have their potential transferred to) more neurons within each corresponding MR-Net.

Finally, once MR-Nets are activated, Response-Component engages neural and endocrine systems to fulfill an appropriately coordinated symphony of outbound responses, thereby enabling interaction within individual Bombardment-Spheres.

This concert is possible because Response-Component Soma connections were built from the ground up. In other words, from the time proliferating cells were too few to be easily seen, connections were being made. As the body grew, every miniscule connection applicable was being genetically wired to Response-Component: each link fixed in relation to the next.

Not only singular connections but also, as development continued, relational groups were determined by feeder neural-tissue. For example, the brachial plexus provides five neural branches to the arm: the axillary, median, musculocutaneous, radial and ulnar nerves which each serve their own grouping of connected outbound responders (and inbound sensors). Therefore, these neural trunks refine a series of sub categories ultimately defining each tiny responder (muscle and tendon).

In the CP-4 'Tepid' scenario, "Standard-Response" might incorporate physical responses or "Mild-DO's" such as a slight posture change, a slight realignment of sensory contributors toward the causal event, a marginally heightened hormonal delivery in preparation for potential dramatic activity, etc.

In that all possible connections are available in adulthood, it is T-Patt's which turn-on the connections by interaction or experience with the Deluge.

> In other words, the more you "DO", the more detailed the pattern and therefore the more accurate the response. This is why practice works. It is a significant enabler of ingenuity and all we consider as human capability.

---

## CP-4 Implications

Visual information remains unremarkable as intensity is insufficient to trigger CP-3 and therefore Visual-Sensors. Therefore, it continues to flow flowing through to Nominal-Response.

> However, minor Body-Self intensity increases resulted in a major upgrade to processing as intensity escalation created 'request-alerts', which notified Mind-Self via Cognitive-Alert of a 'problematic' issue.

Assistance-requests were instrumental for documenting the Bombardment event by creating cognitive data-repositories such as Data-Matrix.

Request-alerts additionally inspired the first stage of cognitive evaluation by not only 'puzzle' creation but also engaging Parameter-Processor.

Parameter-Processor, for the first time, engaged both 'Template' and more poignant mild-action responses. Also, low-level Test-Its, purposed to seek additional Deluge information or pertinent feedback, were created: thus initializing a feedback-loop designed to solution created 'puzzles'.

Resulting 'mild-responses', additionally escalated physical world interaction, by enhancing 'response-directives'. So augmented they not only sent level appropriate outbound 'Neural-Packages' to muscles and organs but also appropriately solicited the Endocrine System as the cooperative supporting instigator.

> Even though visual information continued to lacks any specific alerting content or 'Remarkable-Feature', it still silently provided positional and associated sensor information, which Nominal-Response utilized to ensure granular physical orientation and other survival necessities are not being eroded.

Constantly integrating all information, the Mind-Self presentation center is forever at work. It continuously and innocuously morphs and fills blank pockets to ensure no breaks are perceptible in ones seemingly continuous visual 'reality' experience I call the "Movie-of-Your-Life".

---

**Characteristics Summary: Cognitive-Pathway 3**

### Something is definitely clawing

**Mind-Self** inbound
    Cognitive-Alerts: 4 to 6 out of 9: 'Warm' mid- range intensity
    Cognitive-Sensors: casually engage

----------

**Cognitive-Filter** inbound
    Cluster-Works: active; mid-intensity Pooled-Assemblies
    Visual-Works: VLID-travelers brought on-line
    Cross-Sensory-Bundling: progressively
    Channel: PRIORITY
    Continuity-Controller: Yes

----------

**Figure-It-Out**
    Pathway: CP-3
    Experiential-Accrual: Brackets and Links
    Information-Assembly: Brackets
    Visual: Links
    DE-Notify: Yes
    TI-IN:
      Parameter-Processor: Yes
      Delving-Trio: Targeted-Delving
      Devise-Mulling: not directly
    TI-OUT:
      Test-Its: Delving-Trio escalation

----------

**Cognitive-Filter** outbound
    Template-Component: activity escalation

----------

**Mind-Self** outbound
    Considered-Response: Modestly-DO
    Movie-of-Your-Life Presentation center: some remarkable

**Transition to CP-3**

## Recap

In the CP-4 scenario, no Cluster-Works // Visual-Works integration occurs as 'Tepid' mid-range intensity is in no way indicative of threat: i.e., Tepid-status precludes CP-4s responder-mechanism from engaging Cognitive-Sensors to search-out pertinent 'remarkable-features'.

> Stated differently, 'Standard-Response' simply does not induce Visual-Sensors into action because no design for Cognitive-Sensor involvement has been patterned into its response-mechanism as a consequence of its 'NORM' designation.

In other words, although visual-sensors did continue to provide visual-background VLID-Traveler data-packets, no association of Cluster-Works to Visual-Works data-packets occurred in 'Cross-Sensory-Bundling'.

> Consequently, Cluster-Works 'Pooled-Assemblies', due to both configuration and slightly elevated intensity were passed to 'NORM-Filter', while VLID-Travelers were utilized as normal by Mind-Self for presentation of the 'Movie-of-Your-Life'.

---

CP-3 not only dramatically changes the way data-flows are handled but also is the first Cognitive-Pathway where awareness is possible. Within its scope (and CP-2 following) manifest all capabilities, which typically inspire choice and conscious activity.

> Situated between 'unaware' CP-4 and 'totally-aware' CP-2, CP-3 is a transitional Cognitive-Pathway. It accommodates the broadest array of mid-range intensities.

To initiate CP-3, inbound request-alert intensities must be in the 'Warm (4 to 6) range. This is fundamental because Cross-Sensory-Bundling, although it can escalate 'Cool' or 'Tepid' request-alerts when certain 'matches' between Cluster-Works and Visual-Works are determined, cannot bring Cognitive-Sensors on-line in the first place without engaging CP-3s Considered-Response.

> CP-3 is thereby reserved for initial engagement of originating Bombardment conditions, which are at least 'Warm' mid-intensity.

However, in the instance where a sustained event is delivering lowest request-alert intensities (4), both Cross-Sensory-Bundling (because Considered-Response is being engaged) and Continuity-Controller (because CC-Match is being populated) can not only increment CP-3 intensity to five or six but also redirect to CP-2 when intensities exceed CP-3 tolerance range.

> Cognitive-Pathway 3 intensity grading is important because awareness is symmetrical with CP-3s intensity: i.e., it also ranges from embryonic at lowest (4) to substantial at highest (6) mid-intensity.

Additionally, CP-3 builds upon CP-4s foundation by continuing creation and enhancement of data-archives responsible for beliefs, future vision, hopes, dreams, aspirations and all that we hold precious as indicators of our uniqueness as individuals.

## CP-3 State-of-Affairs

A definite strongly unsettling apprehension is evident: something significant but as yet undefined is occurring.

> Post-event, it was obvious: milliseconds previous, the first few drops of hot fat had struck a small group of SLID receptor-neurons on the back of your hand.

Although preliminary SLID grouping was small, intensity was markedly escalated: SLID receptor-neurons were firing expanded quantities of Tags to Inception-Filter.

Although the first few initial drops of hot fat were still too sparse to alarm Body-Self into MACRO Survival-Threat, Tag-Clusters were 'large' enough for Threat-Check to create mid-intensity request-alerts.

> In other words, due to mid-intensity determination by Recognition-Assessment, Threat-Check sent the first of many Cognitive-Alerts to Mind-Self.

Consequently, its request-alerts resulted in forming Cluster-Works Pooled-Assemblies, which contained mid-intensity Tag-Clusters pertaining to the SLID areas of insult.

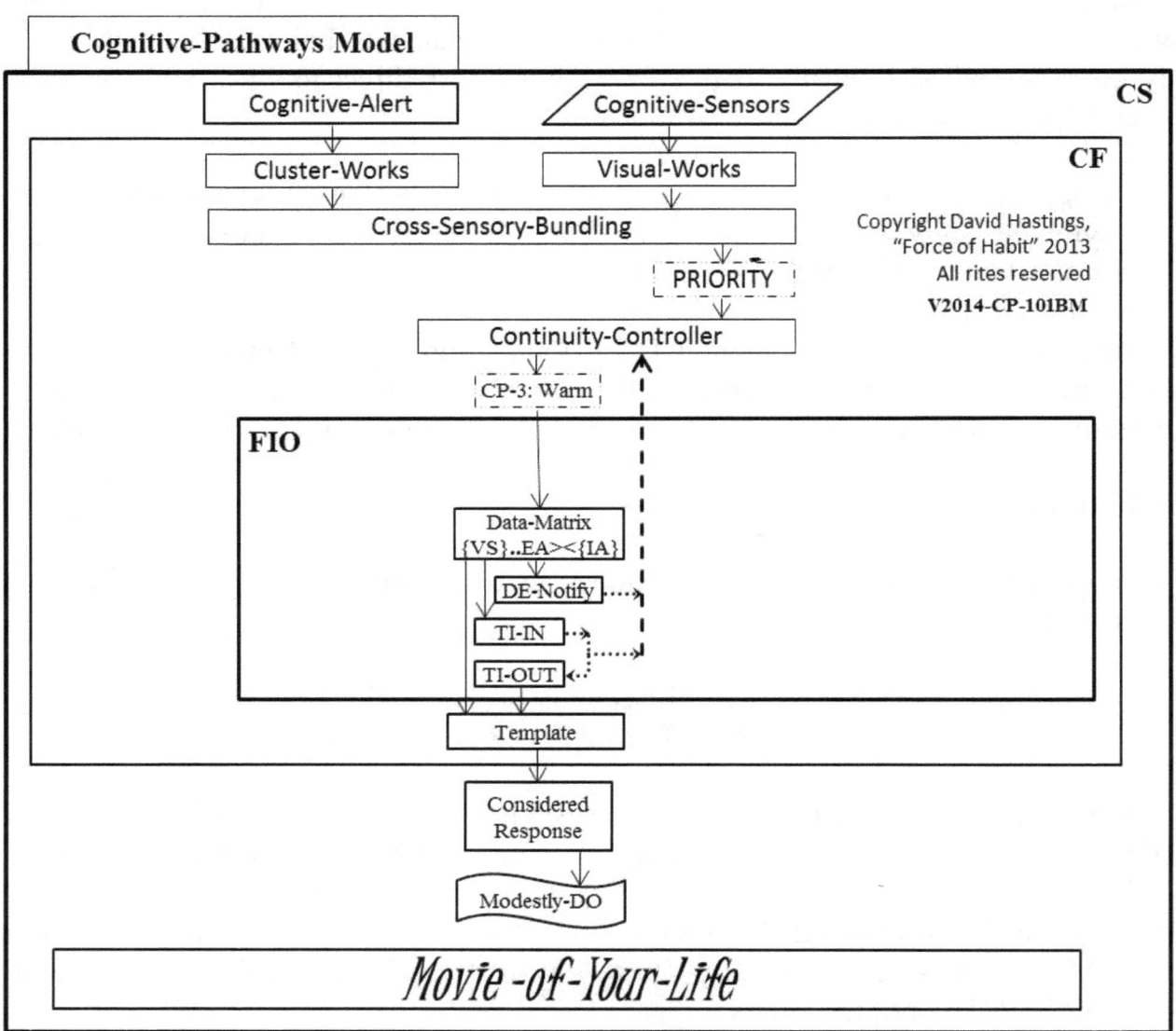

The sense of mounting uneasiness was the result of event escalation from 'Tepid' to 'Warm' as the first mid-intensity data-flows hit Cognitive-Pathway 3.

Visual-Sensors were not initially activated because original mid-intensity Pooled-Assemblies had not yet engaged CP-3 "Considered-Response": however, when CP-3's responder mechanism does deploy, this situation will soon change.

> Initially Pooled-Assemblies being received by Cross-Sensory-Bundling were also not yet matchable as there was no cross-comparable Cognitive-Sensor VLID-Traveler data.

Regardless of matching, Cross-Sensory-Bundling, due to mid-intensity, pushed Tag-Clusters to PRIORITY channel and thus Continuity-Controller, which upon finding no similar Tag-Clusters within its CC-Match hopper-resource, sent the data-flow to CP-3.

> Although initial 'request-alerts' were mid-intensity, they could soon be replaced by 'imperative-alerts' as Threat-Check and Trend-Analysis flag incrementing conditions as survival-critical.

In this eventuality, Continuity-Controller would also exacerbate escalation due to CC-Match containing significantly-similar 'just-previous' data-elements.

> Resultantly it could engage CP-2 and possibly CP-1 if "Intensity-Resolution" determines Deluge is sufficiently extreme and beyond CP-2 handling capabilities.

## Continuity-Controller

Massive quantities of Bombardment Tag-Clusters are continually flowing, not in isolation one event from the next, but instead with mild-to-strong connection to sequential events occurring within a few seconds previous.

> Identification of similar, not just identical interrelationships (new to just previous) is a must because correct assessment of an inbound-event as either new or ongoing provides key 'fodder' so Figure-It-Out can design applicably tuned Test-It outbounds.

Additionally, must not only similarity but also "intensity-variance" between the "current-inbound" and the previous few seconds of matched events be assessed.

Regardless, revision of Cognitive-Pathway will be needed if the intensity of a current-inbound changes significantly in comparison to its matched previous event (whether decreasing or increasing).

Earliest possible detection of "related-sequential-conditions" posing threat is critical as their identification enables avoidance: which is after all a primary "cognitive-survival" strategy. Without such capability all "inbound-events" would seem new and/or disconnected: without hope of interlacing connections between Deluge events.

Actually, the inability to formulate related-sequential-conditions, due to lack of sufficient neural-mass complexity is a major limiting circumstance for most of 'lower' creatures.

Continuity-Controller is thus charged with not only evaluating "current-to-previous-event" coinciding but also managing intensity escalation or de-escalation (i.e., incrementing or decrementing).

Stating the twofold related-sequential-conditions evaluation as a compound question helps clarify: is an inbound Tag-Cluster 'matched' (similar or same) to Tag-Clusters, which exist in the CC-Match hopper-resource, which retains a few seconds of previous events: and if so, which of the two has the highest intensity?

When the inbound Tag-Cluster is both matched and higher intensity, Bombardment is potentially escalating to dangerous or survival-critical. In such a situation Continuity-Controller will effect escalation by amalgamating 'inbound' and 'matched' CC-Match Tag-Clusters, which thereby ensures correct Cognitive-Pathway choice and thus allocation of appropriately tuned resources.

Resultantly, depending on merged intensity, escalation to 'Hot' may result: thereby allocating resources more aligned for quick resolution of this type of event.

When the inbound Tag-Cluster exhibits less intensity than 'matched' counterparts, de-escalation will naturally result: thereby releasing resources for either more pressing conditions or neural-recovery.

Recall the CC-Match data-resource is comprised of limited and 'volatile' short-term neural real-estate, which only preserves Tag-Clusters for a few seconds. In this way all unmatched CC-Match events simply dissipate, which ensures cross-matching will not occur between a current and an hour old event.

> As higher-intensity is always handled before lower-intensity, CC-Match 'volatility' is especially effective in extreme Deluge situations because only the most intense events will be addressed.

In other words, in ongoing intense bombardment, lesser intensities will simply not be addressed and therefore dissipate: effectively allocating neural-resources for imperatives.

---

However, for CP-3 discussion purposes, Continuity-Controller originally allocates the data-stream to 'Warm', even though Cross-Sensory-Bundling 'matches' do not initially exist, due to initial lower-range mid-intensity evaluation.

## CP-3 Data-Matrix Notation

The rectangle below represents Data-Matrix. Both the grey background and the non-bolded standard typefaces on the 'Cognitive-Pathways Model' illustration are intended to indicate CP-3 'Warm' intensity conditions.

$$\boxed{\text{VS..EA><\{IA\}}}$$

This notation is additionally upgraded from CP-4 to include a new symbol to the left of 'EA'. Although 'VS..' is not active until Cross-Sensory-Bundling's 'matching' of a Pooled-Assembly and VLID-Traveler, a short explanation of symbology will be useful at this point.

'VS' is the abbreviation utilized to indicate Visual-Scape data-repositories. The two dots following are intended to indicate a 'Link' between Experiential-Accrual and Cognitive-Sensor data being retained within several visual neural-arrays.

> Keep in mind 'EA' is pivotal: inspiring retrieval of not only 'VS' but also joined '{IA{DE}}' data-elements as well.

## CP-3 Data-Matrix Role

### EA-Harmonic

As previously explained Pooled-Assembly provisions not only variable intensity Tag-Clusters, which were propagated from a range of SLIDs but also once 'harmonized', forms an EA-Harmonic signature, which comprehensively represents an 'impression' of a few milliseconds of Deluge.

> Resultantly, EA-Harmonic energy-potential specifically embodies not only the intensity of all its Pooled-Assembly Tag-Cluster participants but also their diversity.

Critically, therefore, a Pooled-Assembly created in extreme Deluge conditions will have a total energy-potential substantially higher than one formed while at rest: because is not only the Tag-Cluster range broader but also the overall intensity of participants much higher.

> This makes sense as one definitely has variable impressions, mild through repulsed, of things and events to which one has been re-exposed.

So it is with our sample scenario, where the 'Tepid' EA-Harmonic created in CP-4, provides far less energy-potential than the one for CP-3. This energy-potential variance is a major factor which activates awareness in balance with unfolding Bombardment conditions.

> As one interacts within ones Bombardment-Sphere, an "impression-gradient", negligible through strong, guides ones day: i.e., one avoids negative impressions and approaches positive ones

As a consequence of Continuity-Controllers determining CP-3 (in this initial scenario), 'Warm' data is thus creating more intense (greater energy-potential) EA-Harmonics than did CP-4.

As Cognitive-Pathway Three is designed to handle higher mid-intensities, one additional EA-Harmonic data-archive facet requires explanation: No neural facility is provided to retain EA-Harmonic sub-sets of significantly-similar occurrences.

Consequently, when an inbound EA-Harmonics exhibits greater energy-potential than its significantly-similar or 'matched' data-archived counterpart; Data-Matrix processors merge them.

> In other words, a higher energy-potential EA-Harmonic will add to the intensity (energy-potential) of its 'matched' harmonic mate.

The data-archived EA-Harmonic is thus effectively supplanted with one of greater action-potential than even the inbound mid-intensity EA-Harmonic because the replacement is composed of combined action-potentials.

> This also makes sense as the resident emotion of an occurrence will always be the most intense one.

Although no neural facility is available to retain EA-Harmonic sub-sets of significantly-similar occurrences, Distinct-Episodes exist for the very purpose of detailed recall of similar events. For a 'recall' refresher please feel free to review the sections called 'Recall-Cascading', 'Retrieval-Bundles' and 'Cognitive-Impetus-Equation' above.

### Information-Assembly

> CP-3 Distinct-Episodes also have a larger footprint than CP-4 due to increased Tag-Cluster intensity.

As a natural consequence of not only Distinct-Episode's 'bigger footprint' but also the greater EA-Harmonic 'driver' action-potential, stronger 'Joins' are established.

> This is important because 'stronger-joins' have direct significance for recall.

In that higher intensity always gets addressed first, so will these be the first acquired as Figure-It-Out strives to resolve E-Puzzles.

> An old adage goes something like: "Your first guess or instinct is usually on the right track". This is so because a higher-intensity EA-Harmonic will grab the biggest associated Information-Assembly 'Distinct-Episode' array first: such is our design.

## DE-Notify

As stated, CP-3 Data-Matrix 'Distinct-Episodes' have a higher energy-potential than those created by CP-4. Intensity is also a critical factor to Continuity-Controller as discussed above: higher intensity means preferential treatment. Therefore, when replicated, DE-Notify ensures Distinct-Episodes are contiguously represented before transmitting them to CC-Match.

## TI-IN

### Test-It creation

Recall, regardless of 'intensity-value', Parameter-Processor will always expedite creation of a basic configuration Test-It: please review the Parameter-Processor section if needed. This strategy ensures not only data-flow remains ostensibly uninterrupted but also action-responders are not jerky but fluid. However, due to its rapid deployment mandate, its Test-It configuration source must be restricted to a single CP-Set.

> For convenience the strategic data-flow events, which brought us to this point are reiterated as follows: Figure-It-Out was initiated by a TEA-Dat; TEA-Dat was subsequently transformed into an unresolved CP-Set; P-package was created; and Parameter-Processor has acquired the P-package from P-Pend.

Parameter-Processor besides apprehending and utilizing a 'P-package' to create a Test-It has another immediately deployable parallel duty: to determine P-package intensity. Computation is vital as it dictates the creation of either both a Test-It and a CC-Pend-IN, if 'sufficiently-intense' is ascertained or just a Parameter-Processor Test-It, if not.

> Parameter-Processor is simply not equipped to design more complex Test-It requests, especially when intensity escalates to sufficiently-intense.

'Sufficiently-intense' thus inspires an incredible set of specialized Cognition-Complex capabilities, which earmark transition to 'proactive' capabilities.

Additionally, as 'sufficient-intensity' is not a single point but a range stretching from 'just-sufficient' to 'extreme-threatening', Cognition-Complex's Delving-Trio is outfitted with three scalable 'escalation-layers': Targeted-Delving; Ranged-Delving and

Extensive-Delving, respectively. Please review Cognition-Complex, Delving-Trio and Targeted-Delving sections as necessary.

As Cognitive-Pathway Three will always present 'sufficiently-intense', populating of CC-Pend-IN and therefore engaging Targeted-Delving are givens.

## TI-OUT

One additional task-set, regardless of Test-It origins, is performed by Delving-Trio and/or Devise-Mulling: Tag-Clusters from the retrieved F-Freqs, once replicated, are hierarchically arranged by descending frequency to form a "TI-Package", which is then inserted into Continuity-Controller's CC-Match 'in-box'.

This connection is indicated on the 'Cognitive-Pathways Model' illustration as dotted lines from the TI-IN // TI-OUT conglomerate, which encompasses Parameter-Processor and Cognition-Complex on 'The-Ways: Proactive' illustration.

'Proactive' notification is a critical step enabling Continuity-Controller to assess the intensity of incoming Deluge by incorporating Cognition-Complex Test-It assessments.

TI-Parameter (refer to 'The-Ways: Proactive' illustration) resultantly will receive two types of Test-Its: one a Parameter-Processor 'Test-It'; and one a Targeted-Delving '**Test-It**'.

Where 'Test-Its' have provided huge 'fodder' to action-responders and Deluge is still significant, escalation can thus be gauged appropriately. Without feedback from Cognition-Complex at this level early warning escalation would not be so easily possible.

Resultantly, augmented CP-3 intensity provides 'Test-Its' with greater impetus, which is one factor underpinning the sense of being present, conscious or aware.

## Implications: Template-Component

As 'fodder' intensity has been escalated, thus engaging CP-3, so too does Template-Component provide more robust T-Patt's, which will causally involve not only broader-range but also more dramatic responses than CP-4: including the engagement of Cognitive-Sensors.

Recall from previous discussions 'Template-Component' interfaces two inbound data-streams, 'The-Flows': namely, DE-Flow from Data-Matrix and TI-Flow from tuned Cognition-Complex Test-Its.

The 'Cognitive-Pathways Model' indicates 'The-Flows' with arrows from both Data-Matrix and TI-OUT. Please review Template-Component if required.

Similarly, both DE-Flows, propagated from Data-Matrix and TI-Flows created by Cognition-Complex contain Body-Self Tags or Soma-Sensor Location ID's (SLIDs), which mark multitudes of Bombardment sensory-acceptance sites.

Differently, continually streaming DE-Flows provide an unbroken 'raw' data-stream from Data-Matrix: whereas TI-Flows are only produced when a Cognition-Complex member has an intricately formulated Test-It to insert.

Template-Component utilizes DE-Flow and TI-Flow to devise Pattern solutions (T-Patt's) to benefit Mind-Self's Response-Component.

Think of an outbound T-Patt as a pulse of sensory-integrated continually varying instructions upon which Response-Component relies to deploy not only appropriate Endocrine-response but also accurate physical interface.

Relying on its own data-resources, Template-Component also comes to recognize data-structures as new or repeating.

Although Body-Self epitomizes sameness and Mind-Self welcomes exception, unbreakable cyclical symmetry and connectivity exists between the 'Self-Duo'.

Body-Self employs Cognitive-Alert to interact new Deluge with Mind-Self; whereas Mind-Self deploys Response-Component to cause physical interaction within ones

Bombardment-Sphere: Thus providing not only new 'fodder' for Soma-Self sensors but also unique visual-sensor 'fodder' when CP-3 is engaged.

> DE-Flow and TI-Flow interactions form a significant portion of one's feedback-loop.

Test-It configurations are of paramount significance because they are first decoded by Template-Component and then enable Cognitive-Response.

Cognitive-Response instructions in turn instigate solicited sensory feedback through activating physical interaction with the 'Out-There', which thereby provides the additional sensory-data (TEA-Dats). TEA-Dats are utilized for resolving unresolved F-Puzzle F-Freq's and therefore potentially E-Hars. The cycle continues until target 'Puzzles' are 'Solutioned'.

> Even during resting and deep-sleep states when data-flow is far less saturated, DE-Flow continuously inspires micro-responses, such as, eye movements, breathing, tossing-and-turning, etc.

Notably, even during lower volume and intensity states, when Cognitive-Alerts are minimal, Devise-Mullings perpetually active neural-network crawling activities can populate CC-Pend-OUT and therefore **Test-IT**s.

Resulting TI-Flow can be evidenced as dreams or nightmares, which can additionally instigate Soma-Self responses: such as restlessness and/or more pronounced Soma-Actions: such as, sleep-walking.

> Immutable SLID signatures also prove indispensable for Template-Component mandate fulfillment because its outbound patterns or T-Patts contain the pertinent Bombardment SLID markers, which thus 'fodder' appropriate Response-Component "action-drivers".

Essentially then, Response-Component relies on the accuracy of inbound T-Patt harmonic configurations as the foundation for its three responsibilities: sending physical-responder or somatic "action-instructions" to appropriately regulate proportional sensory-reception based Soma-Actions; alerting Endocrine System (hormonal) instigators; and initiating visual-sensors for CP-3, CP-2 and CP-1 higher-intensity events. Please review the 'Cognitive-Sensor' section if needed.

Alignment between occurrence and response is obviously indispensable

Template-Component therefore has a critical responsibility because a compromised T-Patt will invariably result in erroneous responses.

Template-Component transitioning role can thus be indicated as: Cognitive-to---**TEMPLATE**---to-Response.

## CP-3 Implications

Recall the CP-4 'Tepid' scenario where 'Standard-Response' incorporated Mild-DO physical responses: such as a slight posture change; a slight realignment of Body-Self sensory-receptors toward the causal event; a marginally heightened hormonal delivery in preparation for potential dramatic activity; etc.

Differently, CP-3 'Warm' outcomes are more pronounced. CP-3 intensities not only couple 'Modestly-DO' broader 'Considered-Response' soma-actions as a consequence of the engagement of Cognition-Complex 's Targeted-Delving '**Test-It** with greater Endocrine involvement but also alert Cognitive-Sensors to target areas of intrusion.

Although initially visual information was unremarkable, the CP-3 response-mechanism quickly triggered visual-sensors.

Resultantly, within about 500 milliseconds Cross-Sensory-Bundling was able to begin to associate Body-Self provided Cluster-Works data with Visual-Works data and therefore direct the data-stream to Continuity-Controller via PRIORITY channel.

In initial 'request-alert' stages Continuity-Controller's CC-Match contained only remnants from DE-Notify and Cognition-Complex: i.e., not sufficient to cause escalation.

Resultantly, data-flow was directed to 'CP-3: Warm'. Figure-It-Out CP-3 processors thus appropriately, 'Modestly', engaged both Template-Component and Response-Component.

However, 'Modestly-DO' was sufficient for Considered-Response to enact more muscle-groups, more quickly: including head motions to direct the visual-sensors toward the infringement.

Resulting posture changes thereby not only realigned both Soma-Self sensory-receptors and Cognitive-Sensors toward the causal event but also appropriately incremented hormonal delivery in preparation for potential grander activity.

Constantly integrating all information as always, the Mind-Self presentation center was characteristically at work, continuously and innocuously ensuring no blank pockets or breaks are perceptible in ones seemingly continuous visual 'reality' experience I call the "Movie-of-Your-Life".

**Characteristics Summary: Cognitive-Pathway 2**

**Intrusion is evident and Bombardment-Sphere positional changes essential**

**Mind-Self** inbound
    Cognitive-Alerts: 7 or 8 out of 9: 'Hot' mid-range intensity
    Cognitive-Sensors: fully engaged

    ---------
    **Cognitive-Filter** inbound
        Cluster-Works: active; high-intensity Pooled-Assemblies
        Visual-Works: VLID-Travelers come on-line
        Cross-Sensory-Bundling: cross-match 'foddering'
        Channel: PRIORITY
        Continuity-Controller: CC-Matches escalate
        ---------
    **Figure-It-Out**
        Pathway: CP-2
        Experiential-Accrual: Brackets and Links
        Information-Assembly: Brackets
        Visual: multitudes of Links
        DE-Notify: Yes
        TI-IN:
          Parameter-Processor: Yes
          Delving-Trio: Targeted-Delving and Ranged-Delving
          Devise-Mulling: activated
        TI-OUT:
          Test-Its: Delving-Trio escalation to Ranged-Delving
    ---------
**Cognitive-Filter** outbound
    Template-Component: high-intensity escalation
---------

**Mind-Self** outbound
    Considered-Response: Boldly-DO
    Movie-of-Your-Life Presentation center: remarkable

**Transition to CP-2**

## Recap

At the initialization of the CP-3 scenario, request-alerts 'Warm' mid-range intensity did not indicate the full seriousness of the threat until later, about 500 milliseconds, when CP-3's maximum intensity handling range was exceeded.

Although mid-intensity (4 to 6) did inspire allocation of 'Pooled-Assemblies' to PRIORITY-channel, Cluster-Works // Visual-Works integration by Cross-Sensory-Bundling was also not initially possible because Cognitive-Sensors had not yet been prompted by CP-3's responder-mechanism.

> Subsequently though, due to ongoing mid-intensity Bombardment, 'Considered-Response' engaged, thereby inducing visual-sensor involvement. Consequently, Cognitive-Sensors began to hone-in on areas-of-intrusion by searching-out pertinent 'remarkable-features'.

As Bombardment continued and visual-sensors provided their initial unique perspectives, so too did DE-Notify and Cognition-Complex continue to populate CC-Match. As Cross-Sensory-Bundling combined contributions and Continuity-Controller assessed and incremented mid-range intensity from 4 through 6, awareness and therefore focus on the intruding event also escalated.

> In other words, when mid-intensity reached 'six', one was both not only aware of the Body-Self location of the hot fat infringement and visually tuned to or looking at its origins but also primed to adjust Bombardment-Sphere position.

Additionally, CP-3 Endocrine System prepared muscle-systems for small body movements to get a better view, which contrasts with CP-2's bold movements to get out of the way.

---

Cognitive-Pathway Two (CP-2) continues to not only enhance the way data-flows are handled but also engage additional processing-resources, which serve to maximize one's awareness and thereby conscious assessments, which resultantly express individual choice.

CP-2 continues to expand Data-Matrix data-repositories, which upon recall and remixing by Devise-Mulling are responsible for beliefs, hopes, dreams, aspirations, future vision and all one holds precious as indicators of one's uniqueness as an individual.

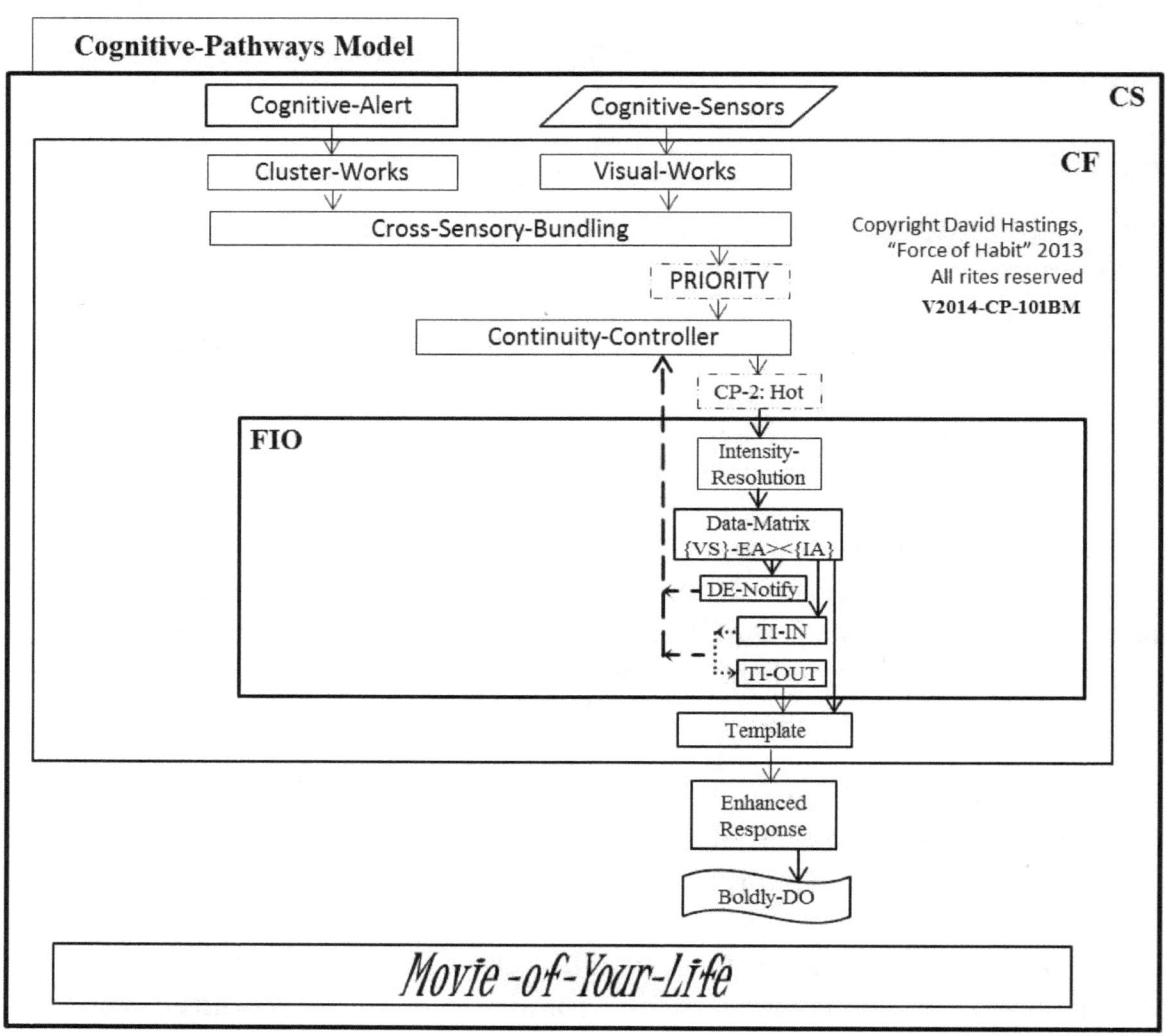

## CP-2 State-of-Affairs

Initial 'something not good is underway' diffuse CP-3 awareness has rapidly escalated in less than a second into total awareness the now significant pain on the back of your hand is quickly getting worse.

Post-event you could Figure-It-Out: within about 500 milliseconds (one-half second) the many additional drops of hot fat were inundating a much larger array of SLID receptor-neurons. This was pushing the extents of Threat-Checks mid-range 'request-alerts' toward maximum.

Intensity is now (at about the 750 millisecond mark) markedly escalated for one or both of the following reasons, which force the CP-2 allocation. Either highest (7 and 8) mid-intensity request-alerts are being generated directly by Threat-Check or (4 to 6) mid-intensity request-alerts are being escalated by 'Continuity-Controller' to CP-2 as a consequence of CC-Matching.

> Threat-Check is responsible for request-alert content as a consequence of Bombardment.

Resultantly, request-alert intensity is due to not only the quantity of Tags from a single SLID receptor-neuron but also the overall quantity of Tags being simultaneously generated at neighboring SLID sites.

> Therefore a request-alert can present a broad-range of mid-intensities from 1 to 8. To become a CP-3 issue though, already understood is mid-intensity must be at least '4'.

Once CP-3 engages however a new set of Continuity-Controller evaluators kicks-in due to the CP-3 Response-Component being the first response-mechanism able to alert Cognitive-Sensors, thereby ensuring PRIORIY-channel designation.

> Additionally, when CP-3 is active both physical actions and therefore DE-Notifies increase, which thus prompts Continuity-Controller engagement.

Continuity-Controllers task is to utilize 'just-previous' data-elements as comparatives against current data-elements to locate related-sequential-conditions.

When a CC-Match data-element (Tag-Cluster) is assessed as significantly-similar, it is melded with its current data-element companion thereby incrementing intensity. Importantly, "melded-intensity" from this point forward will be utilized to allocate the appropriate Cognitive-Pathway.

In other words, much of the rapidly increasing quantities of current Bombardment are being 'matched' by Continuity-Controller because CC-Match, as a consequence of DE-Notify, also contains ample just previous significantly-similar data-elements.

Consequently, even the less 'splattered' SLID locations, which might have remained in CC-Match as 'Tepid' CP-4 or 'Warm' CP-3, are being upgraded to 'Hot' by Continuity-Controller.

Continuity-Controllers mandate is to determine if intensity is sufficient to engage either CP-3 or more robust CP-2 resources: it does not evaluate if intensities are at Survival extreme however. This function is reserved for CP-2s Intensity-Resolution Component.

Its assessment determines whether inbound data-element intensity is beyond CP-2 handling capabilities. If so the most extreme data-elements will be directed to CP-1. However, as CP-2 is designed to handle level-8 intensities, it remains fully engaged handling higher survival-intensities when capacity permits.

---

> Soon both responder-mechanism and resultantly Cognitive-Sensors are in full swing. Additionally the endocrine-system, which was prepping in CP-4 and incrementing due to CP-3 responder-mechanism, now pulls out most of the stops to **Boldly-DO**.

Cognitively Figure-It-Out during CP-3 evolutions created multitudes of symmetrical Puzzles and fired hundreds of Parameter-Processor Test-Its and Targeted-delving **Test-Its**.

CP-2 processors however leap evaluation to another level by engaging both Ranged-Delving and Devise-Mulling. Each substantially intensify awareness, data-archive retrieval and processing speed as well as create pronounced and directed Test-Its.

> Resulting 'Hot' solutioning endeavors thus usurp most resources and one feels focused on the issue at hand: or should I say 'on-hand': again excuse the pun.

Cognition searches for solutions to its puzzles by injecting action-requests through Template and Response Components, while Soma-Response is initiating 'flight' reactions. Huge neural activity has been instigated: for Body-Self by Deluge and for Mind-Self initially by Cognitive-Alert and subsequently by Devise-Mulling. Cross-

Sensory-Bundling is matching Cognitive-Sensor VLID-Traveler data while Continuity-Controller is processing related-sequential-condition CC-matches.

> Unfortunately while you were pondering way back 1000 milliseconds (one-second) ago someone blocked your escape route from the stove with a table. Escalation to MACRO Survival-Threat is just milliseconds away.

Earliest possible detection of posing threat is critical as its identification enables avoidance: which is after all a primary "cognitive-survival" strategy. Without such capability all "inbound-events" would seem new and/or disconnected: without hope of interlacing connections between Deluge events.

## CP-2 Data-Matrix Implications

### EA-Harmonic

As previously explained Pooled-Assembly provisions not only variable intensity Tag-Clusters, which were propagated from a range of SLIDs but also once 'harmonized', forms an EA-Harmonic signature, which comprehensively represents an 'impression' of a few milliseconds of Deluge.

> Resultantly, EA-Harmonic energy-potential specifically embodies not only the intensity of all its Pooled-Assembly Tag-Cluster participants but also their diversity.

Critically, therefore, a Pooled-Assembly created in more extreme Deluge conditions will have a total energy-potential substantially higher than one formed while at rest: because is not only the Tag-Cluster range broader but also the overall intensity of participants much higher.

> This makes sense as one definitely has variable impressions, mild through wild, of things and events to which one has been re-exposed.

So it is with the CP-2 scenario, where the 'Warm' EA-Harmonic created in CP-3, provides far less energy-potential than the one for CP-2. Critical to remember is this energy-potential variance is a major factor which activates awareness in balance with unfolding Bombardment conditions.

As one interacts within ones Bombardment-Sphere, an "impression-gradient", negligible through strong, guides ones day: i.e., one avoids negative impressions and approaches positive ones

As a consequence of Continuity-Controllers determining CP-2 (in this initial scenario), 'Hot' data is thus creating more intense (greater energy-potential) EA-Harmonics than did CP-3. Unlikely this event will be forgotten: although the surrounding less-intense ones might.

Recall from CP-3 discussions, when an inbound EA-Harmonics exhibits greater energy-potential than its significantly-similar or 'matched' data-archived counterpart, Data-Matrix processors merge them. In other words, a higher energy-potential EA-Harmonic will add to the intensity (energy-potential) of its 'matched' harmonic mate.

The data-archived CP-2 EA-Harmonic is thus effectively supplanted with one of greater action-potential than even the inbound mid-intensity CP-4 or CP-3 EA-Harmonic because the replacement is composed of combined action-potentials.

This also makes sense as the resident emotion of an occurrence will always be the most intense one.

## Information-Assembly

CP-2 Distinct-Episodes also have a larger footprint than CP-3 due to increased individual Tag-Cluster intensities.

As a natural consequence of not only Distinct-Episode's 'bigger footprint' but also the greater EA-Harmonic 'driver' action-potential, stronger 'Joins' are thus established: crucially important because 'stronger-joins' have direct significance for recall.

As higher-intensity always gets addressed first, they will be the first acquired as Figure-It-Out strives to resolve E-Puzzles.

In other words, a higher-intensity EA-Harmonic will grab the biggest associated Information-Assembly 'Distinct-Episode' array first: such is our design.

## TI-IN

### Test-It creation

Parameter-Processor always quickly expedites creation of a basic configuration (i.e., restricted to a single CP-Set) Test-It: to ensure not only data-flow remains ostensibly uninterrupted but also action-responders are not jerky but fluid. Please review the Parameter-Processor section if needed.

Besides apprehending and utilizing a 'P-package' to create a Parameter-Processor Test-It, it must additionally determine P-package intensity. Assessment is vital because if 'sufficiently-intense' is ascertained CC-Pend-IN is also appropriately populated, which launches an incredible set of specialized Cognition-Complex capabilities, which earmark transition to 'proactive' capabilities.

Recall, as 'sufficient-intensity' is not a single point but a range stretching from 'just-sufficient' to 'extreme-threatening', Cognition-Complex's Delving-Trio is outfitted with three scalable 'escalation-layers': Targeted-Delving; Ranged-Delving and Extensive-Delving, respectively. Please review Cognition-Complex, Delving-Trio and Targeted-Delving sections as necessary.

> As Cognitive-Pathway Two will always present 'sufficiently-intense' toward the extreme-threatening end of the range, populating of CC-Pend-IN and therefore engaging Targeted-Delving and subsequently Ranged-Delving and thus Devise-Mulling are givens.

## TI-OUT

One additional task-set, regardless of Test-It origins, is performed by Delving-Trio and/or Devise-Mulling: Tag-Clusters from the retrieved F-Freqs, once replicated, are hierarchically arranged by descending frequency to form a 'TI-Package', which is then inserted into Continuity-Controller's CC-Match 'in-box'.

> This connection is indicated on the 'Cognitive-Pathways Model' illustration as dotted lines from the TI-IN // TI-OUT conglomerate, which encompasses Parameter-Processor and Cognition-Complex on 'The-Ways: Proactive' illustration.

'Proactive' notification is a critical step enabling Continuity-Controller to assess the intensity of incoming Deluge by incorporating Cognition-Complex Test-It assessments. Parameter-Processor (refer to 'The-Ways: Proactive' illustration) will ultimately receive three types of Bombardment inspired Test-Its: a Parameter-Processor 'Test-It'; a Targeted-Delving '**Test-It**'; a Ranged-Delving **TEST**-it; and at some point an internally inspired Devise-Mulling **Test-IT**.

For this scenario-event not only is ongoing Deluge still significant but also 'Test-Its' are providing huge 'fodder' to action-responders: thus escalation can be gauged appropriately. Without feedback from Cognition-Complex at this escalated level neither proactive capabilities nor the sense of being present, conscious or aware be possible.

## Implications: Template-Component

As 'fodder' intensity has been escalated, thus engaging CP-2, so too does Template-Component provide more robust T-Patt's, which will causally involve not only broader-range but also more dramatic responses than CP-4 or CP-3: including the ongoing engagement of Cognitive-Sensors.

Recall from previous discussions 'Template-Component' interfaces two inbound data-streams, 'The-Flows': namely, DE-Flow from Data-Matrix and TI-Flow from tuned Cognition-Complex Test-Its. Please review if needed.

## Recap

As previously stated, Body-Self employs Cognitive-Alert to interact new Deluge with Cognitive-Self; whereas Mind-Self deploys Response-Component to cause physical interaction within ones Bombardment-Sphere: Thus providing not only new 'fodder' for Soma-Self sensors but also unique visual-sensor 'fodder' when CP-2 is engaged. Therefore, DE-Flow and TI-Flow interactions form a significant portion of one's feedback-loop.

Test-It configurations are of paramount significance because they are first decoded by Template-Component and then enable Cognitive-Response.

Cognitive-Response instructions in turn instigate solicited sensory feedback through activating physical interaction with the 'Out-There', which thereby provides the additional sensory-data (TEA-Dats). TEA-Dats are utilized for resolving unresolved F-Puzzle F-Freq's and therefore potentially E-Hars. The cycle continues until target 'Puzzles' are 'Solutioned'.

> Even during resting and deep-sleep states when data-flow is far less saturated, DE-Flow continuously inspires micro-responses, such as, eye movements, breathing, tossing-and-turning, etc.

Notably, even during lower volume and intensity states, when Cognitive-Alerts are minimal, Devise-Mullings perpetually active neural-network crawling activities can populate CC-Pend-OUT and therefore **Test-IT**s. However, with RD-IN population Devise-Mulling is also triggered.

> Immutable SLID signatures also prove indispensable for Template-Component mandate fulfillment because its outbound patterns or T-Patts contain the pertinent Bombardment SLID markers, which thus 'fodder' appropriate Response-Component "action-drivers".

Essentially then, Response-Component relies on the accuracy of inbound T-Patt harmonic configurations as the foundation for its three responsibilities: sending physical-responder or somatic 'action-instructions' to appropriately regulate proportional sensory-reception based soma-actions; alerting Endocrine System (hormonal) instigators; and initiating visual-sensors for CP-3, CP-2 and CP-1 higher-intensity events. Please review the 'Cognitive-Sensor' section if needed.

> Alignment between occurrence and response is obviously indispensable

Template-Component therefore has a critical responsibility because a compromised T-Patt will invariably result in erroneous responses.

## CP-2 Implications

>Recall the CP-3 'Warm' scenario where 'Considered-Response' incorporated Modestly-DO physical responses: such as a posture change; a realignment of Soma-Self sensory-receptors toward the causal event; a heightened hormonal delivery in preparation for potential accelerated activity; etc.

Differently, CP-2 'Hot' outcomes are more pronounced than CP-3. CP-2 intensities not only manifests 'Boldly-DO' broader 'Enhanced-Response' Soma-Actions, as a consequence of the engagement of several Cognition-Complex Test-Its from Targeted-Delving, Ranged-Delving and Devise-Mulling with much bolder Endocrine involvement, but also alert Cognitive-Sensors to substantially and proactively broaden scope to additionally target associated ranges well beyond the intrusion.

Resultantly, within about 750 milliseconds, Cross-Sensory-Bundling began to associate Body-Self provided Cluster-Works data with Visual-Works data and therefore direct the data-stream to Continuity-Controller via PRIORITY channel.

>However, 'Boldly-DO' is sufficient for Template-Component to devise T-Patts (from ongoing feedback from Test-It action-suggestions) to accommodate Enhanced-Responses requirement to enact many more muscle-groups, more quickly and continuously: including head motions to direct visual-sensors outward beyond the infringement.

Resulting positional changes thereby serve several functions: realigned both Body-Self sensory-receptors and Cognitive-Sensors toward the causal event; appropriately increment hormonal delivery in preparation for potential grander activity; and initialize appropriate movements designated by Template-Response to maximize survival-potential.

Constantly integrating all information as always, the Cognitive-Self presentation center was actively at work, continuously and innocuously ensuring no blank pockets or breaks are perceptible in ones seemingly continuous "Movie-of-Your-Life" 'reality' experience.

---

**Characteristics Summary: Cognitive-Pathway 1**

### Intrusion is Survival-Critical

**Cognitive-Self** inbound
    Cognitive-Alerts: 9 out of 9: 'Survival' extreme-intensity
    Cognitive-Sensors: fully engaged

    ---------
    **Cognitive-Filter** inbound
        Cluster-Works: active; imperative-alerts
        Visual-Works: VLID-Travelers maximized
        Cross-Sensory-Bundling: cross-match maximized
        Channel: PRIORITY
        Continuity-Controller: CC-Matches maximized
        ---------
        **Figure-It-Out**
            Intensity-Resolution: Yes
            Pathway: CP-1
            Experiential-Accrual: Brackets and Links
            Information-Assembly: Brackets
            Visual: copious Links
            DE-Notify: Yes
            TI-IN:
              Parameter-Processor: Yes
              Delving-Trio: Targeted, Ranged and Extensive-Delving
              Devise-Mulling: maximized
            TI-OUT:
              Test-Its: Delving-Trio escalation to Extensive-Delving as well
        ---------
    **Cognitive-Filter** outbound
        Template-Component: extreme-intensity escalation
    ---------

**Cognitive-Self** outbound
    Considered-Response: Survival-DO
    Movie-of-Your-Life Presentation center: maximized
**Transition to CP-1**

Unfortunately while you were pondering way back 1000 milliseconds (one-second) ago, someone blocked you in with a table.

A survival-critical situation is now in full-swing as the realization of the seriousness of the 'hot-fat' event hits home.

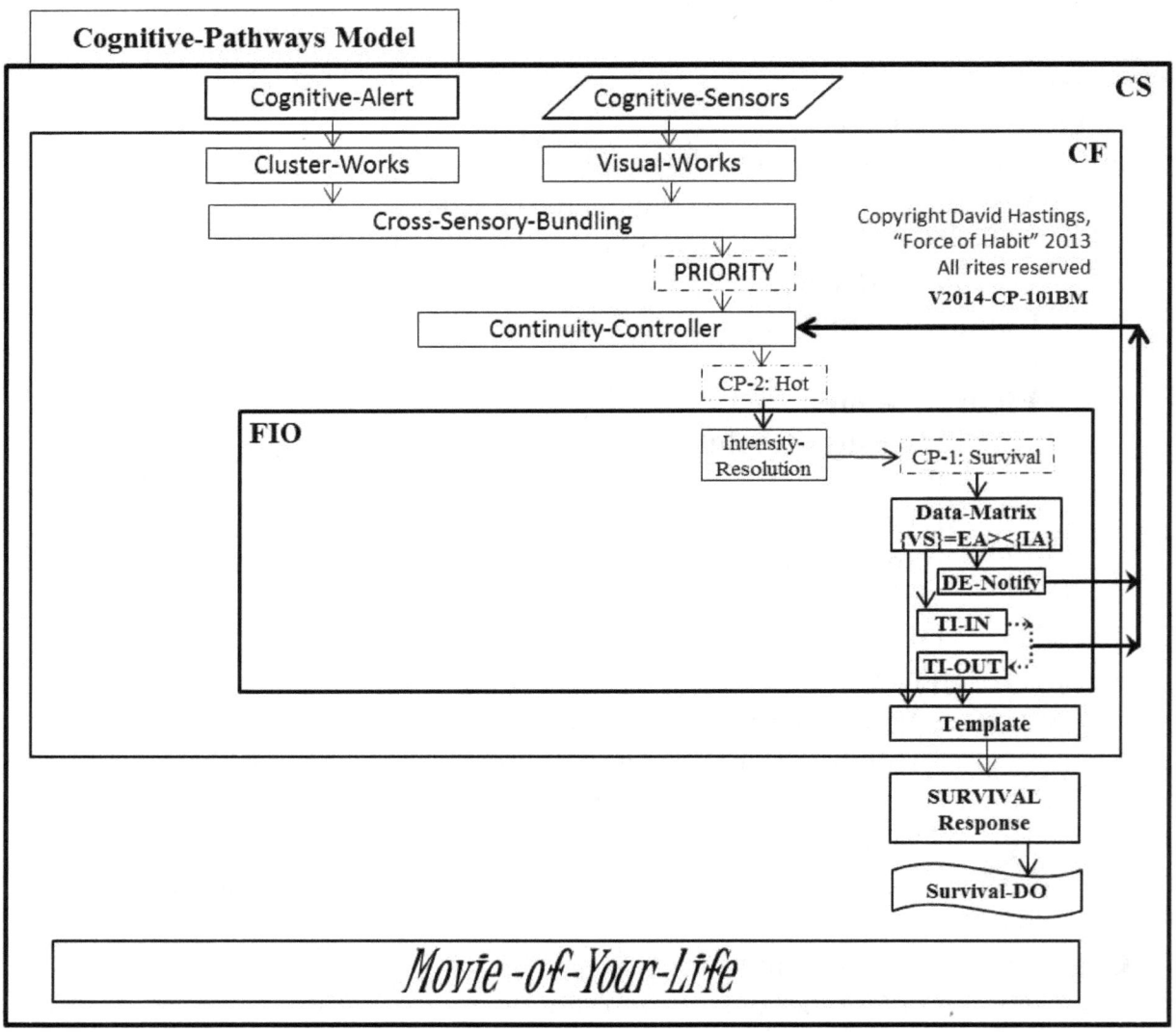

Survival-situational impetus is being maximally driven due to not only creation of copious 'Puzzles' requiring 'Solution' as a consequence of imperative-alerts from Body-Self plus Delving-Trio and Devise-Mulling extensive activities but also because visual-sensor VLID-Travelers are providing information to CP-1 Figure-It-Out confirming your optimal escape route is blocked.

Notably, escalation through other Cognitive-Pathways from CP-5 to CP-2 has not resulted in ameliorating the Bombardment situation. Early resolution was not accomplished as a consequence of two factors: the critical onslaught was occurring too quickly; and/or cognitive or physical resources to this point were insufficient to migrate ones Bombardment-Sphere to a less intrusive venue.

> When CP-1 becomes the go-to pathway, no other alternates or possible escalations are available to maximize survival-potential. CP-1 is the last stop: survive or be terminated: that's it as far as the 'Self-Duo' is concerned.

Immediate actions for extraction from the Bombardment-Sphere intrusion arena are necessary to avoid certain disaster: 'DO' something dramatic is the only option. All resources must fully engage to solve the survival-issue: regardless of whether concurrent lesser events are lost.

> As random movement does not serve the survival-mandate, alternate strategies are needed to Figure-It-Out. Question is what resources are available?

Advantageously, an integrated arsenal of cooperative 'Puzzle-solving' mechanisms is available, which provide superlative methodologies: for 'Out-There' data-gathering (soma and cognitive sensors); data-assessment (neural real-estate mechanisms); action-suggestions (Test-Its); action-suggestion feedback evaluation (E-Puzzles, Cognition and Reference-Complex); and cyclic readjustment until 'The-Ways' solution is achieved.

> Of course the methodologies arsenal would be useless if the multitudes of Test-It action-suggestions were not rapidly deployable to one's mobile-framework.

Favorably, a different genre of cooperative mechanical implementation systems, each providing a broad range-of-acceptable activity, is in place to 'DO' the Test-Its: such as, delivery (neurological); movement (skeletal; muscles); supporting (tendons; ligaments); chemical preparatory (endocrine; circulatory); and sustaining (breathing; cellular maintenance; lymphatic).

> Post-event you could Figure-It-Out: within about 1000 milliseconds (one-second) extreme quantities of 'hot-fat' were inundating a vast array of SLID receptor-neurons on the back of your hand and up your arm. Maximizing Threat-Check

MACRO-range, its mandate was clear: send survival 'imperative-alerts' to Mind-Self to get help while Soma-Survival responding as best as possible.

During survival conditions extreme-intensity (9) imperative-alerts are being generated directly by Threat-Check.

However, compounding the situation is not only Cross-Sensory-Bundling escalating 'Warm' and 'Hot' mid-intensity request-alerts due to VLID-Traveler coordination but also 'Continuity-Controller' due to "intensity-melding" of significantly-similar CC-Match data-elements.

Much of the rapidly increasing quantities of current Bombardment are being 'matched' by Continuity-Controller because CC-Match, as a consequence of DE-Notify, also contains ample just previous significantly-similar data-elements.

When received by the Intensity-Resolution some of the slightly lesser intensity data-events will be handled by CP-2 when CP-1 is "capacity-maximized". If not they will simply dissipate and be lost.

Both responder-mechanism and consequently Cognitive-Sensors are in full swing. Additionally the Endocrine System, which was "boldly-active" in CP-2 due in part to Responder-Component endocrine-alerts, is now maximized as well.

CP-1 processors contribute to the maximized state-of-affairs. They not only engage both Delving-Trios Extensive-Delving and Devise-Mulling but also provision maximum resources for incrementing both processing speed and data-archive retrieval: both critically necessary to create CP-1 extensively tailored Test-Its and intensify "focused-awareness".

Consequently, CP-1 'Survival' solutioning endeavors usurp all resources: cognitive focus on the survival issue is so intense all else is excluded: i.e., no other coinciding events can be recalled.

Cognition searches for solutions to its puzzles by injecting action-requests through Template and Response Components, while Soma-Response is initiating 'flight' reactions.
Maximum neural activity is pulsing: for Body-Self due to Deluge; for Mind-Self due to Delving-Trio and Devise-Mulling. Cross-Sensory-Bundling is matching copious

Cognitive-Sensor VLID-Traveler data while Continuity-Controller is processing masses of related-sequential-condition CC-matches.

As a consequence of Continuity-Controllers determining 'Survival' intensity, CP-1's Data-Matrix is creating maximized energy-potential EA-Harmonics and associated Information-Assemblies and Distinct-Episodes.

> This event will absolutely not be forgotten: although surrounding less-intense events will.

## TI-IN

Besides apprehending and utilizing a 'P-package' to create a Parameter-Processor Test-It, Parameter-Processor must additionally determine P-package intensity.

As CP-1 'extreme-threatening' is definitely 'sufficient-intensity', all three Delving-Trio 'escalation-layers', Targeted-Delving, Ranged-Delving and Extensive-Delving, will not only engage almost simultaneously but also stay 'on' until resolution is accomplished. Devise-Mulling will also rapidly engage as RD-IN populating alerts it into action.

As ongoing Deluge is CP-1 extreme, Parameter-Processor will receive, additional to its 'Test-Its', four other maximized Test-It varieties (refer to 'The-Ways: Proactive' illustration): three Bombardment-inspired 'Test-Its'; Targeted-Delving '**Test-It**s', Ranged-Delving **TEST**-its and Extensive-Delving **TEST-Its:** and one internally inspired Devise-Mulling **Test-IT**.

---

> Alignment between occurrence and response is obviously indispensable

Template-Component therefore has a critical responsibility because a compromised T-Patt will invariably result in erroneous responses.

Immutable SLID signatures prove indispensable for Template-Component mandate fulfillment because its outbound patterns or T-Patts contain the pertinent Bombardment SLID markers, which thus fodder 'appropriate-to-sensory-acceptance' Response-Component 'action-drivers'.

Response-Component, particularly for CP-1 events, relies on the accuracy of inbound T-Patt harmonic configurations as the foundation for its three obligations.

It must send physical-responder or somatic 'survival-action-instructions', which have been specifically designed to appropriately and proportionally regulate Soma-Actions based on original sensory-acceptance benchmarks, maximally alert the Endocrine System (hormonal) and direct visual-sensors toward the CP-1 extreme-intensity event.

**CP-1 Implications**

> Recall the CP-3 'Warm' scenario where 'Considered-Response' incorporated Modestly-DO physical responses: such as, slight posture changes, casual realignment of Soma-Self sensory-receptors toward the causal event and slightly incremented hormonal delivery in preparation for potential accelerated activity, etc.

Escalating CP-3, CP-2 'Hot' outcomes were more pronounced. CP-2 not only manifested 'Boldly-DO' broader 'Enhanced-Response' Soma-Actions (as a consequence of the engagement of several Cognition-Complex Test-Its from Targeted-Delving, Ranged-Delving and Devise-Mulling with much bolder Endocrine involvement) but also alerted Cognitive-Sensors to substantially and proactively broaden their scope to additionally target associated ranges well beyond the intrusion.

> 'Survival-DOs' however capitalize on CP-1s extensive Test-It feedback-cycle to enable Template-Component to devise T-Patts, which maximize Survival-Responses very demanding make-or-break requirements.

In other words, Survival based T-Patts maximize not only both single muscle bundles and muscle-group arrays with extreme quickness and accuracy but also Endocrine contribution. Of course, response-actions include rapid head and body motions to direct visual-sensors to proactively survey beyond the infringement as well.

> Fatigue is a natural consequence of 'survival-activity': mental and/or physical.

Neither biological nor neurological systems are designed for continuous extreme-intensity: if sustained, one can experience burnout where 'Experience-Sense' attempts to filter-out all but the most essential sensory-data.

In such a situation, the outside world would describe a person suffering burnout as un-receptive and/or un-responsive. The assessment is actually accurate because we now know minimal sensory-reception, even when restricted by internal mechanisms, allocates everything to CP-5.

Clearly, to maximize preservation, the higher the danger gradient, the greater is the need for a "Cognitive Survival-Response". Flight is normal in new CP-1 dangerous situations because Template-Component has minimal basis to instruct response-mechanisms and therefore Body-Self pervasive genetic memory rules: i.e., run first, evaluate second.

However, as firefighter, police and Special-Forces are exposed to controlled dangerous conditions during training, Figure-It-Out in concert with 'Experience-Sense', T-Patts and response-mechanisms are able to redirect, due to Devise-Mulling control, CP-1 to CP-2 thus giving the opportunity to execute Enhanced-Responses, which can be retailored to occurrences due to recognition.

---

## Movie-of-Your-Life

Initializing an incredible sequence of data-management processing, which culminates in awareness of what is going on 'Out-There' are arrays of Soma-Self sensory-neurons. These bio-mechanical marvels convert random Bombardment into specifically identifiable sensory-accepted action-potential 'signals' or Tags.

> Subsequently transported to applicable neural real-estate via shared neural conduits, Tags are gathered into like-kind Tag-Clusters to additionally disclose impact location intensity. If determined as sufficiently-intense to be 'problematic', Mind-Self is notified by transmission by Body-Self of an explicitly designed Cognitive-Alert information packet, which discloses the issue at hand.

When received, Mind-Self's mandate to Figure-It-Out is clear. A 'problematic' issue is utilized to establish Solutioning foundations by not only creating distinguishable 'Brackets' within multiple different kinds of data-archives but also create a 'Puzzle', which thereby characterizes the Cognitive-Alert requiring resolution.

Puzzle Solutioning is purposed to enhance survival-potential by honing interactions with the 'Out-There'. Resolution is accomplished by a three-fold cyclical strategy: retrieve pertinent 'Brackets' within data-archives to not only compare 'current-data' to 'previous-data' but also utilize appropriate data-elements to resolve the target Puzzle(s); engage Cognitive-Sensors to provide additional perspective; and send positional modifying Test-It action-requests to Body-Self from Cognition-Complex to gather tailored feedback.

> Subsequently transformed by Cognitive-Pathway Components, sensory-signals ultimately establish retrievable and distinguishable Mind-Self C-Cluster Experience-Senses, which form the 'guiding-platforms' from where all aspects of one's "Movie-of-Your-Life" reality is launched.

To render a continuous and contiguous Movie-of-Your-Life comprehensible reality or "devised-view" of what is going on 'Out-There', Mind-Self utilizes Visual pass-through and Cognitive-Pathway 5 as background against which is overlaid not only visual-sensor 'remarkable-features' but also various outbounds from Cognitive-Pathways 4-through-1 via Cognition-Complex renderings.

Not surprisingly 'devised-views', which articulately provision ones reality, imitate Mind-Self's sensor-array by presenting "cognitive-visions".

However, if either data-stream flow is interrupted even briefly by sensory-deprivation or disease or Mind-Self processing is compromised by pharmaceuticals or anger, 'reality' will quickly change to "false-ality".

> When one turns on a faucet, water-flow is expected to be stable: whether throttled up to high or diminished to a trickle. Contrast favorable 'steady-flow' to another condition where plumber error lets air into the pipe resulting in sporadic 'sputter-and-spit'.

> No question: sputter-and-spit would be a terrible way to experience living.

Incredibly then, by constantly integrating several data-stream layers and tapping into data-archives as necessary, Mind-Self presentation center processors are consistently, continuously and innocuously interweaving compiled presentation-data to ensure no blank-pockets or breaks are perceptible in ones combined "reality-construct" or seemingly continuous Movie-of-Your-Life "reality-experience".

### Interestingly though, one's 'current-reality' actually transpired in the 'past'

Decidedly, all events one believes they are currently experiencing happened in the past. Let me explain why, in absolute terms, no such thing as 'the present' exists.

No doubt so called 'current-events' initiated with sensory-acceptance at event-horizons at least 250 milliseconds (1/4 second) or perhaps even minutes prior. This is true because neither transmission from SLID origins nor processing through multiple stages is instantaneous.

> Therefore, any consequent awareness of flowing-events is definitively due to many sophisticated processors manipulating, coalescing and rendering 'past' sensory-events into a flow of current reality-construct's, which are being presented at the rate of sixty Movie-of-Your-Life frames-per-second.

Mind-Self however, regardless of duration between sensory-acquisition and Movie-of-Your-Life presentation, is unequivocally going to use its most recent compiled 'frame' as a current-event benchmark of so-called 'present' goings-on. Notably therefore, one's true 'frame-of-reference' is not absolute but malleable.

> Additionally, as Experience-Sense is not only utilized extensively in 'presentation' data-manipulations but also substantially variable between people and cultures, Movie-of-Your-Life renderings will depict a 'current-event' a-little-to-a-lot differently between observers.

Proofing of the gap between 'actual' and 'presented' occurrence is difficult as one cannot simultaneously both observe 'Out-There' Bombardment and experience it directly. In other words, one cannot 'stand' outside oneself to verify event-stream timing because one's observation is the direct result of event-stream acceptance and morphing: this is inescapable. Consequently, one is always a 100% biased observer for the following reasons.

> **One:** one can never actually 'see' the 'present' as data-handling steps take time: at least from the Movie-of-Your-Life perspective
>
> **Two:** one's "sense-of-elapsed-time" and "sense-of-condition-change", whether initiating from 'current' unfolding events (i.e., duration and proximity) and/or delivered by Devise-Mulling processors (from recall or intuition) into Movie-of-Your-Life renderings, rely solely on comparison of a Movie-of-Your-Life 'current-frame' snippet to a Movie-of-Your-Life 'previous-frame' snippet.
>
>> Notably, two capabilities make possible elapsed-time and condition-change evaluations: comparable 'frames' for 'current' events; and time-stamped and re-constitutable memories, Brackets or data-archives for recall.
>
> **Three** – one has no way of knowing, due to one's 'observances' being a 'devised-view', whether the Movie-of-Your-Life was propagated by originating information hundreds of our years previous
>
> **Four:** "cognitive-fill" from data-archives is necessary for the Movie-of-Your-Life to continuously and contiguously present its renderings: manipulation thereby introduces morphed past events into the presentation caldron

Although one must trust the current Movie-of-Your-Life 'reality' presentation, it is absolutely possible to modify your 'Movie' by "DOing". Incredibly, the more exciting the 'DOing' experiences the greater the adjustment: both short and long term.

After all, this is 'How-We-Work'. 'DOing' works in absolute terms because it changes sensory-input, which is the baseplate of who we are and who we can become, by shifting ones Bombardment-Sphere position and therefore perspective: and thereby the acquisition of different sensory-data.

> By deploying "The-DO" will not only the Movie-of-Your-Life radically morph but also "Living-In-Full-Excitement-and-Experience" or "L.I.F.E$^2$." as this author coins it, be yours for the taking.

'The-DO' will hugely enhance life experiences. "Choice-fully" deployed, it will automatically recreate positive and plentiful 'realities' because will not only new broader-scope 'Experience-Senses' filter-and-slot more usefully but also new Cognitive-Habits be created: working tirelessly in the background to secure what you truly want.

---

The contiguous Movie-of-Your-Life presentation occurs similarly for everyone because collaboration between interactive-systems is genetically provided within one symbiotic organism: from sensory-acceptance through data-archive creation, retrieval, comparison and Puzzle-Solving capabilities.

> Stated differently, cooperative bio-systems provision not only immutable impact location and intensity defined sensory-data, near speed-of-light action-potential transmission and extensive data-archiving but also incredible data-retrieval, new-to-old data-comparison and Puzzle-Solving capabilities.

However, a different tried and true system is utilized by multitudes of species without our vast neural real-estate resources: Although effective, it is much slower, scope-limited and mostly volition compromised.

> Stated differently, although the human 'How-We-Work' all-in-one model is very efficient, effective and enables sentience, awareness, choice and volition, a much older system exists, which rivals ours for success: however, significant limits (from our perspective) pervade for all but perhaps a few of its members.

As deeper understanding is accomplished by not only accumulation of new data-elements but also comparison of existing paradigms to broader-scope, information gathering is a requisite. Therefore, presenting an alternate and much older and functioning system, which I have defined as "Layer-Intelligence Theory", will serve nicely to solidify previously presented 'How-We-Work' constructs.

Although methodologies are quite different; outcomes are incredibly similar. Serving as a representative population for "Layer-Intelligence" Theory, which also rebuts 'Frequency-Based-Intelligence' and other similar inaccurate theories, are five caste Ant colonies: (outward to inward) "DC-caste"; "S1-caste"; "S2-caste"; and "H-caste".

---

## Layer-Intelligence Theory

Ant societies form a useful basis for comparison between the two model systems because they house several groups or castes, which hierarchically fulfill specific cooperative "caste-roles" to produce seemingly 'intelligent' outcomes to condition-gatherings from the Deluge.

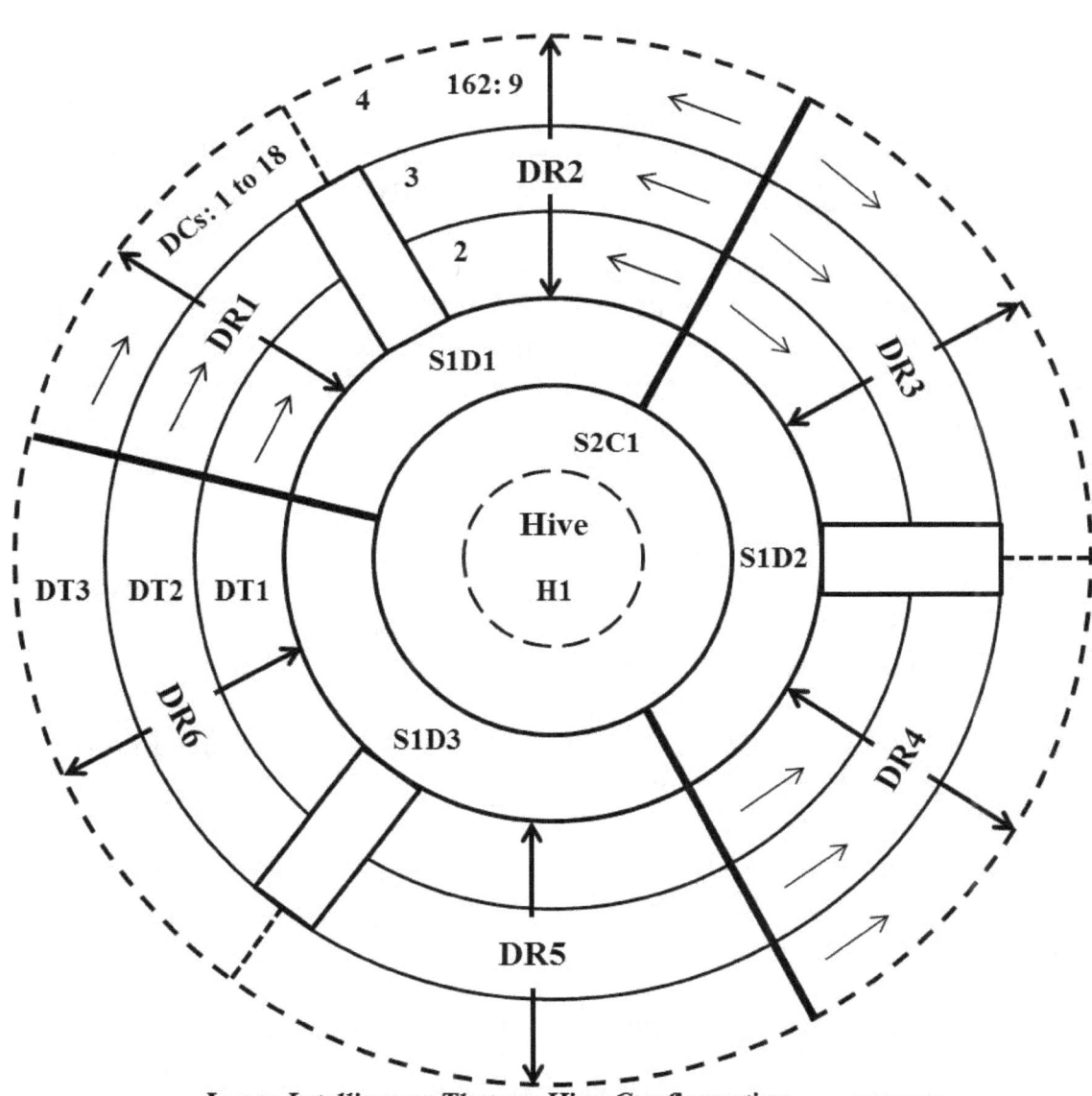

*Layer-Intelligence Theory: Hive Configuration*   V201512A
Copyright 2015 David J. Hastings 'Force-of-Habit'

Caste structure, detailed in the "Hive-Configuration" illustration above, compels comparison because its chemoreceptor-systems like our neural-systems perform to both assess the repercussions of Deluge and respond appropriately.

Literally surrounding and encompassing the central hive-core (H1), much like the layers of an onion slice, are five specific purpose zones or Deluge-territories: outward to inward, DT3; DT2; DT1; (DT stands for Deluge-Territories) S1; and S2 ('S' is for Service).

Circular territories are additionally partitioned into six regions, BR1 through BR6 ('B' is for Bombardment), which enable comprehensible integration of inbound-to-S2 chemo and specific dissemination of outbound-from-S2 directives.

Although a detailed explanation of each structure and strategy is beyond the scope of this book the following should provide enough detail to understand both the differences and similarities of neural vs chemo communication systems and their features and benefits. Most importantly, cross-comparison will better equip one to better understand 'How-We-Work'.

## DC-castes

Patrolling the outer three territories of each region are eighteen "DC-castes" ('D' is for Deluge; 'C' for condition), which provide all direct Bombardment interface. Each DC-caste is sensitive to or is genetically designed with a chemo-receptor for one of eighteen Bombardment-Sphere conditions: such as, various vibrations; heat; light; sound; light; movement; food; intrusion; etc. Keep in mind some descriptors are a convenience as many Ant sensors are 'tuned' differently than ours.

> In other words, much like human sensory-neuron specific mandates (tastes; hearing; etc.), each DC-caste provides chemo-gathering for a single Deluge event-type.

Additionally, the nine members of each DC-caste are specifically disseminated within each of six regions (note the 4; 3; 2 in the BR2 region on the illustration) to accommodate larger outward coverage areas. As there are 18 DC-castes, which provide 162 members (9 members x 18 DC-castes) per region (note the 162:9 in BR2), their total population of 972 is by far the largest of all castes.

Resultantly, configuration provisions regions with not only a complete cross-section of condition-sensitivities but also needed redundancy to ameliorate chemo-gathering in extreme-conditions.

## S1-Castes

Notably, without exception, all castes inter-communicate via chemoreceptors: i.e., not by neural link. Fortunately, short-term chemo-retention capabilities significantly increase as caste member populations dramatically diminish outward to inward.

> Generally, "up-link" provisions chemo-acquisition by an "inward-caste" from an adjoining "outward-caste"; whereas "down-link" provides chemo-delivery from an inward-caste to an adjoining outward-caste.

Both event-intensity and occurrence-proximity are essential to convey as a mild something far away in DT3 is substantially less threatening than an extremely noxious event occurring in DT1.

'Captured' by a DC-caste member's chemoreceptor, the monitored-condition and its intensity are communicated by the potency of its endocrine-morphed essence or "chemo-gist" via its outbound chemo-pad. In other words, to appropriately 'Tag' the intensity of a Deluge condition, genetics has provided a range of chemo-potencies, which are interpretable by up-link layers: the first being S1.

> Think of a "chemo-gist" like the concentration of salt in water: one grain would be barely perceptible but a thousand, potent indeed.

Up-link will be discussed first: followed by down-link handling protocols.

As each of the six regions is homogeneously populated by 162 DC-caste members, S1D1 ('D1' is for district one) from the 'S1' fourth layer can be used as a model for the other two districts: i.e., S1D2 and S1D3.

S1D1 members are responsible for not only acquiring information from designated DC-caste members within its two regions (BR1 and BR2) and transferring it upward to S2 but also disseminating directives downward to them from the S2-caste.

Auspiciously, while S1D1-caste members are actively pursuing chemo-gathering BR1 and BR2 DC-caste members are cooperatively assisting S1D1 chemo-gathering by similarly striving to make their outward-caste 'findings' available by hustling to their designated S1D1-corridor every 30 seconds or so (note DT-territory arrows).

Championing up-link from DC-caste are 144 S1D1 members, who under 'normal' conditions are segregated into two region-groups (S1BR1 and S1BR2) of seventy-two members: i.e., one group responsible for BR1 and one for BR2. Additionally, a region-group of 72 members is comprised of three sub-groups each responsible for a particular function: chemo-gathering; chemo-reception; and chemo-transfer.

## S1 Chemo-gathering

Chemo-gathering as accomplished by fifty-four runner-members. Charged with actively and continuously traversing the corridor (the shaded rectangles) between designated regions, they physically encounter as many diligently patrolling DC-caste members as situationally feasible within a 30 second window to acquire their 'S1' capacity of three DC-caste "chemo-packets".

> Takeaway: if being touched isn't your thing; don't be reincarnated as a DC-caste ant.

In extreme Bombardment conditions region-groups can perform double duty depending on the region under stress. Regardless, to ensure up-link and down-link continuity chemo-gathering is not random because runner-members are relegated to specific retrieval regions and territories; and thereby DC-caste members.

> In other words, each designated runner-group chemo-gathers only from its assigned region-territory and no other.

Unless a threat is encountered or food cache located, 'S1BR1' runner-members are assigned to their three region-territories as follows: nine for DT1; fifteen for DT2; and twenty-four for DT3.

This strategy effectively not only compensates for expanding territory boundaries but also as will shortly be disclosed maintains territory chemo-integrity. Each 'S1BR' workload thereby calculates to a reasonably comfortable but busy 3-to-1 ratio (162 DC members / 54 S1BR runner-members).

## S1 Chemo-reception

The eighteen remaining S1D1 members for each "BR-group" form three coordinated 'rotating' squads of three members each for: up-link chemo-reception from S1D1 runner-members; chemo-transfer to comparably structured S2C1 chemo-reception squads (discussed below); and acceptance of down-link chemo-directives (discussed below).

Specifically, S1 chemo-reception squads 'rotate' from chemo-acceptance receiving-position; to chemo-acceptance transfer-position; to chemo-acceptance downlink-acquisition position; to chemo-acceptance receiving-position once again.

> Three rotating chemo-reception squads not only reduce workload by a factor of three but also allow for chemo-acceptance buffering while the similarly configured activated chemo-transfer trio is divesting its chemo-array to an aligned S2C1 chemo-reception squad.

Furthermore, each enhanced member of the chemo-acceptance receiving-position squad is enabled to capture one instance of each of the 18 possible conditions from only its designated region and territory: thereby ensuring region-territory information integrity.

> In that 324 DC-caste members are ferreting to gather Deluge information for only eighteen Bombardment-Sphere conditions within the six territories of their two regions (BR1 and BR2) many duplicates are bound to occur within an S1D1 chemo-reception squad.

Therefore, only the most intense chemo-gist for each condition is preserved by an S1D1 chemo-reception member. This is so for two reasons: each of chemo-receptors can only accommodate a single chemo-gist; and as high-intensity always supersedes lower-intensity in this universe, highest-intensity will be favored, which effectively replaces any less-intense occupant thereby providing best information to up-layer inward-castes.

## S1 Chemo-transfer

Chemo-transfer is similarly accomplished by three different 'rotating' squads of three members each. The chemo-transfer chemo-reception squad receives from the three member 'S1' chemo-acceptance transfer-position squad. In other words, chemo-transfer squads 'rotate' from chemo-transfer acceptance-position; to chemo-transfer transfer-position (to S2C1); to chemo-transfer downlink-acquisition position; to chemo-transfer acceptance-position once again.

> Effectively then an 'S1-Caste' member rejects significantly-similar DC-caste information of the 'foddering' DC-caste squad members in favor of best information, which is defined as most-intense at the time of gathering in a particular situation.

In other words, this squad repositions itself to come in contact with a primed S1 transfer-reception squad before moving to the down-link acceptance position. Subsequently the transfer-reception squad repositions itself to come in contact with a primed S2C1-reception squad before moving to the downlink-acquisition position.

## S2-Caste

As the S2C1-reception squad chemo-accepts from all regions and is responsible for balanced responses via chemo-directives to region-territory condition-intensity, its population is highly specialized. Although detailing specific functionalities are well beyond the scope of this book it a few capabilities are worthy of mention to round-out Layer-Intelligence discussions.

In order to respond quickly to threat, intensity is concurrently captured in three different ways: by region; by condition; and by territory. Region intensity capture is accomplished by allocating one S2-squad member for each region: six in this model. Condition intensity capture is accomplished by allocating eighteen S2-squad members one for each condition. Territory intensity capture is accomplished by also allocating eighteen S2-squad members one for each regions territory.

> Once acquired each S2-squad can independently send a directive based on its intensity trigger via a down-link S2-squad. However, resultant chemo-gist is dictated by genetics, much like human autonomic functionality: not by decision.

The down-link S2-squad is utilized to ensure downward information arrives at the correct territory and region. In this way, regardless of intensity origin directives are correctly sent to inspire appropriate condition-action in the appropriate region and territory.

> Notably, this type of response capability was utilized somewhat similarly by Body-Self except Body-Self had a rudimentary capability to compare and recognize whereas Ants are only utilize current information to trigger genetic responses.

Critically, each DC-caste member boasts a single chemo-receptor by which it accepts inbound-directives or down-links requests from its managing S1-caste members: i.e., S1-caste runner-members perform chemo-delivery of a single down-link action-message directive to its designated DC-caste members.

Layer-Intelligence maximizes hive survival-potential because inward-castes, although each also embraces a specialized purpose, provision not only buffering between the outermost external-caste and the innermost "hive-core" where species viability is maintained but also protocols for handling up-link chemo-acquisition and down-link chemo-delivery between adjacent castes.

> Strategic symmetry is evident between Layer-Intelligence chemoreceptor deployment and our sensory-neuron data-acquisition strategies. Sensory-neurons are neither always in ready-state nor designed to gather 100% but only a representative Bombardment-Sphere sampling. Likewise, even though an S1-caste may not physically contact all DC-caste members, their diligence assures a representative Deluge sampling is acquired.

Inbound up-link and outbound down-link in Layer-Intelligence are achieved by physical contact with chemoreceptors rather than by inbound sensory-receptor mechanical energy being converter to electrical energy. Additionally divergent is transmission to specific cephalic neural-arrays, cerebral processing by data-comparison to retained data-archives and outbound Test-It requests via neural-transmitters to physical-expediters in order to adjust position within ones Bombardment-Sphere.

Neural-processors approach the speed-of-light, so almost instantaneous, as is access by Modules. As you might recall Modules are both cooperative and hierarchical.

Inbound summary: Mind-Self initializes 'Puzzle' Solutioning by receiving not only reconfigured soma-sensor accepted Bombardment-Events as data-alerts from Body-Self but also providing Cognitive-Sensor data-elements. Mind-Self then performs "data-morphing", which it forwards to inbound Cognitive-Filter processors, which also perform data-morphing, which it forwards to Figure-It-Out, which also performs data-morphing.

**Outbound summary**: Figure-It-Out sends its "data-morphs" to Cognitive-Filter outbound processors, which again perform data-morphing. Renderings are subsequently forwarded to Mind-Self, which not only performs additional data-morphing but also directs proportionate 'DO' activity while it integrally presents a continuous, contiguous and sometimes very interesting movie of 'what is going on Out-There'.

Although speed and transmission type are radically different,
Parallels are uncanny!

# Index

# A

Acceptably-similar, 153, 159
Accumulated closely-similar, 228
action-drivers, 273, 285, 291
action-instructions, 273, 285, 292
action-potential, 5, 6, 36, 44, 269, 282, 294, 297
action-suggestions, 19, 34, 36, 58, 138, 286, 289
Active-puzzle, 179
**Acuity**, 49
Amplified-drivers, 177
android robot, 4
A-Pro, 253, 254, 255, 256, 257
Archive-resource, 168
Assemblage-Processor, 253, 254, 258
ata-resource, 165

# B

Background-Processor, 158, 163, 176, 177
band, 5, 58, 59
Blended-harmonic, 229, 230
Bombardment, 5, 6, 7, 8, 16, 19, 33, 38, 39, 40, 41, 46, 51, 57, 60, 61, 66, 70, 71, 72, 77, 91, 96, 106, 110, 112, 114, 117, 122, 123, 129, 131, 132, 133, 134, 138, 140, 143, 144, 146, 150, 157, 160, 161, 163, 166, 169, 178, 179, 181, 187, 194, 195, 196, 197, 198, 199, 200, 201, 202, 207, 209, 210, 211, 212, 213, 214, 215, 216, 218, 219, 221, 225, 226, 229, 232, 237, 238, 239, 240, 242, 244, 247, 249, 250, 254, 260, 263, 265, 266, 267, 268, 272, 273, 277, 279, 280, 281, 284, 285, 289, 290, 291, 294, 296, 300, 302, 303, 305, 306
**Bombardment-Sphere**, 13, 197, 199, 207, 215, 228, 235, 247, 259, 268, 273, 277, 282, 289, 297, 300
Boundary-leaping, 224
Bracket, 6, 16, 29, 51, 63, 67, 68, 69, 73, 74, 75, 98, 118, 119, 120, 124, 150, 217
Bracketing, 6, 16, 51, 63, 68, 73, 74, 75, 111, 116, 118, 119, 143, 151, 194, 240
Bracketing-Principle, 228
brain-mass, 8, 40, 44, 59, 69, 73
Breakout-facility, 200
broader-scope, 29, 35, 58, 117, 163, 164, 165, 166, 167, 177, 297, 298
bundling, 39, 91

# C

Catalogue-Channel, 244
CC-Bundle, 228
CC-Group, 230
**C-Chan**, 244, 245, 250, 251, 254
CC-Har, 187, 188, 189, 190, 191, 192, 227, 228, 229, 230, 232
CC-Harmonic, 187
C-Cluster, 151, 154, 179, 187, 191, 209, 228, 229, 230, 232, 237, 294
CC-Match, 128, 129, 130, 212, 263, 265, 266, 267, 270, 271, 274, 277, 279, 280, 281, 283, 287, 290, 291
CC-Pend-IN, 197, 198, 201, 203, 204, 209, 214, 225, 270, 271, 283
CC-Pend-OUT, 208, 210, 218, 221, 223, 230, 234, 241, 273, 285
CE-Link, 191, 192
Characteristics Summary, 93, 94, 98, 261, 276, 287
Circadian rhythm, 113, 118
Cluster-packets, 56, 57
Cluster-Works, 25, 26, 27, 37, 38, 39, 55, 56, 57, 58, 60, 62, 70, 71, 72, 94, 98, 99, 261, 262, 263, 274, 276, 277, 286, 287
Cognition, 93, 104, 150, 154, 163, 166, 178, 194, 195, 271, 280, 289, 290
Cognition-Complex, 284, 286, 292, 294
Cognition-Complex, 7, 179, 188, 189, 192, 193, 194, 195, 197, 199, 200, 201, 202, 203, 204, 210, 211, 212, 213, 225, 226, 228, 230, 231, 234, 235, 238, 240, 270, 271, 272, 274, 277, 283, 284
Cognition-Complex, 294
Cognitive Pathways Model, 128
Cognitive Survival-Response, 293
**Cognitive-Alert**, 4, 6, 7, 9, 10, 15, 17, 25, 26, 28, 29, 33, 34, 35, 36, 38, 39, 46, 56, 61, 62, 69, 70, 71, 72, 75, 76, 94, 98, 99, 111, 117, 120, 123, 124, 132, 134, 149, 150, 153, 157, 172, 197, 201, 240, 242, 260, 261, 263, 272, 273, 276, 280, 284, 285, 287, 294
cognitive-assessment, 36, 37
Cognitive-Edge, 179
Cognitive-expectation, 187
Cognitive-facilities, 177
Cognitive-Filter, 7, 25, 26, 27, 39, 55, 60, 62, 71, 72, 77, 82, 83, 90, 91, 94, 98, 234, 241, 244, 250, 252, 261, 276, 287, 306
Cognitive-Habit, 75, 82, 187, 188, 189, 190, 227, 228, 297
**Cognitive-Impetus**, 126
Cognitive-Impetus-Equation, 269
Cognitive-Pathway, 27, 71, 77, 84, 90, 91, 92, 93, 94, 95, 97, 98, 100, 102, 121, 122, 124, 128, 129, 138, 178, 194, 198, 204, 210, 212, 219, 222, 225, 238, 258, 261, 262, 263, 264, 266, 268, 271, 276, 277, 279, 283, 287, 294
Cognitive-Pathways, 7, 25, 26, 27, 63, 75, 81, 82, 83, 90, 91, 92, 97, 102, 104, 114, 128, 135, 289, 294
Cognitive-Pathways Model, 24, 25, 26, 34, 55, 63, 77, 81, 90, 102, 138, 145, 212, 216, 267, 271, 272, 283
Cognitive-puzzle, 167
Cognitive-Response, 75, 234, 235, 273, 284
Cognitive-Self, 4, 7, 9, 10, 13, 14, 15, 16, 17, 19, 23, 25, 26, 27, 28, 29, 34, 35, 36, 37, 38, 39, 40, 42, 43, 46, 51, 58, 59, 60, 61, 62, 63, 68, 69, 70, 71, 72, 74, 75, 76, 77, 82, 83, 90, 91, 94, 95, 96, 98, 99, 116, 120, 123, 134, 135, 149, 150, 153, 166, 179, 188, 190, 191, 199, 221, 225, 240, 241, 242, 260, 261, 262, 263, 272, 275, 276, 280, 284, 286, 287, 290, 294, 295, 296, 306
Cognitive-Sense, 230
Cognitive-Sensor, 7, 19, 39, 63, 94, 99, 135, 150, 157, 262, 265, 267, 273, 281, 285, 291, 306
Cognitive-Sensors, 7, 19, 25, 26, 29, 34, 38, 39, 62, 65, 70, 94, 98, 133, 151, 261, 262, 272, 274, 275, 276, 277, 279, 280, 284, 286, 287, 290, 292, 294
Cognitive-survival, 266, 281
Cognitive-Survival-Response, 62

Cognitive-to---**TEMPLATE**---to-Response, 240, 274
Cognitive-Values, 180
cognitive-visions, 295
Comparatee, 142, 149, 150, 237
Comparator, 142, 143, 149, 150, 237
Component, 23, 25, 26, 27, 33, 39, 63, 71, 77, 82, 84, 90, 91, 92, 93, 94, 96, 97, 98, 100, 102, 103, 124, 128, 129, 132, 134, 135, 136, 138, 140, 149, 192, 197, 215, 217, 234, 235, 240, 241, 242, 244, 247, 250, 254, 256, 258, 259, 261, 272, 273, 274, 276, 279, 280, 284, 285, 286, 287, 290, 291, 292, 293, 294
Concept-Cluster, 82, 179, 187, 190, 192, 226, 235
**Cones**, 45
Considered-Response, 261, 262, 263, 265, 274, 275, 276, 277, 286, 287, 292
Continuity-Controller, 25, 77, 94, 98, 128, 129, 212, 261, 263, 265, 266, 267, 268, 270, 271, 274, 276, 277, 279, 280, 281, 282, 283, 284, 286, 287, 290, 291
Conveyor-resource, 129
Cool, 7, 71, 91, 92, 94, 95, 97, 99, 124, 262
Core-Puzzle-Set, 142
CP-1, 26, 71, 77, 91, 97, 102, 114, 138, 198, 201, 222, 225, 265, 273, 280, 285, 287, 288, 289, 290, 291, 292, 293
CP-1: Survival, 26
CP-2, 26, 114, 198, 201, 216, 262, 263, 265, 273, 276, 277, 278, 279, 280, 281, 282, 284, 285, 286, 289, 290, 292, 293
CP-2: Hot, 26
CP-3, 26, 106, 114, 121, 128, 198, 201, 258, 260, 261, 262, 263, 265, 267, 268, 269, 270, 271, 272, 273, 274, 277, 278, 279, 280, 281, 282, 284, 285, 286, 292
CP-3: Warm, 26
CP-4, 26, 91, 92, 96, 97, 98, 99, 100, 102, 114, 115, 122, 124, 128, 138, 142, 145, 201, 224, 258, 259, 260, 262, 267, 268, 269, 270, 272, 274, 280, 282, 284
CP-4: Tepid, 26
CP-5, 26, 77, 91, 92, 94, 95, 96, 97, 100, 123, 124, 198, 244, 289, 293
CP-5: Cool, 26
C-Pend, 190
CP-Sets, 142, 143, 144, 146, 147, 149, 156, 157, 158, 159, 160, 162, 163, 164, 166, 167, 168, 172, 173, 175, 176, 177, 195, 196, 197, 199, 203, 204, 205, 206, 207, 208, 209, 210, 211, 212, 213, 214, 215, 218, 219, 221, 222, 223, 224, 226, 228, 231, 236, 237, 238, 239, 241, 270, 283
CP-Work, 159
Create Your Own Habits, 189
Cross-Sensory, 7, 25, 26, 27, 39, 43, 55, 56, 60, 62, 64, 70, 71, 72, 76, 77, 94, 95, 98, 99, 261, 267
Cross-Sensory-Bundling, 27, 76, 262, 263, 265, 267, 274, 276, 277, 281, 286, 287, 290
Current-inbound, 265, 266
Current-Processing, 158
Cyclical-Phase, 231, 232

# D

Data-acquisition, 122, 181, 190, 305
Data-and-link resource, 141, 142, 219

Data-archive, 5, 6, 29, 116, 117, 122, 132, 236, 237, 268, 280, 290, 297
data-archives, 7, 14, 17, 19, 29, 56, 83, 111, 112, 115, 117, 124, 135, 166, 179, 192, 215, 237, 238, 242, 263, 294, 295, 296, 305
data-archiving, 6, 7, 8, 122, 199, 237, 297
data-band, 9, 56, 57, 59, 60, 61
Data-bundle, 196
**data-elements**, 27, 29, 62, 71, 81, 82, 90, 92, 97, 103, 106, 116, 117, 121, 122, 124, 127, 129, 132, 134, 139, 140, 144, 145, 146, 147, 153, 156, 167, 176, 181, 182, 183, 184, 202, 203, 206, 208, 209, 210, 212, 218, 223, 224, 229, 234, 236, 237, 241, 242, 244, 252, 265, 267, 279, 280, 290, 294, 298, 306
Data-hopper, 201
Data-Matrix, 7, 25, 27, 81, 90, 97, 100, 102, 103, 106, 107, 111, 112, 114, 117, 122, 123, 124, 128, 135, 138, 139, 142, 144, 145, 150, 154, 159, 163, 166, 167, 168, 176, 179, 188, 189, 192, 214, 215, 216, 217, 220, 223, 224, 228, 232, 237, 240, 241, 244, 260, 267, 268, 269, 270, 272, 278, 281, 282, 284, 291
Data-members, 103, 104, 240
data-package, 9, 139, 153, 213
data-packages, 9, 35, 77, 138, 194
**data-packet**, 26, 27, 71, 96
Data-packets, 7, 58, 77, 96, 97, 262
**data-reconfigure**, 26
data-repository, 16, 74, 102, 106, 118, 122, 164, 169, 188, 219, 226, 228, 229, 245, 252
Data-resolution, 132
data-resource, 62, 82, 91, 102, 103, 104, 107, 108, 116, 118, 119, 120, 122, 123, 124, 129, 135, 138, 139, 140, 142, 143, 144, 146, 147, 156, 159, 165, 169, 173, 176, 177, 179, 182, 183, 186, 188, 190, 191, 192, 194, 200, 201, 202, 204, 206, 208, 217, 218, 220, 221, 224, 237, 241, 242, 244, 245, 248, 249, 250, 251, 252, 255, 257, 258, 266, 272
Data-retrieval, 103, 115, 122, 179, 228, 297
Data-storehousing, 238
data-stream, 8, 9, 33, 35, 61, 90, 92, 93, 94, 95, 97, 102, 132, 135, 138, 139, 149, 158, 225, 234, 240, 244, 254, 267, 272, 274, 284, 286, 295
Deeper-reach, 218, 220
DE-Event, 103, 107, 108, 114, 117, 118, 119, 120
DE-Flow, 240, 242, 244, 245, 248, 250, 251, 258, 272, 273, 284, 285
Deluge, 4, 8, 9, 19, 28, 33, 35, 37, 38, 41, 43, 44, 49, 57, 58, 67, 70, 83, 94, 96, 110, 113, 116, 122, 123, 124, 129, 131, 132, 133, 134, 138, 168, 179, 187, 194, 195, 197, 198, 202, 204, 209, 210, 212, 213, 215, 216, 217, 219, 222, 225, 226, 229, 230, 231, 232, 235, 236, 238, 239, 242, 250, 259, 260, 265, 266, 267, 268, 271, 272, 280, 281, 284, 290, 291, 299, 300, 301, 303, 305
Delving, 7, 98, 197, 201, 202, 203, 204, 205, 206, 207, 208, 209, 211, 212, 213, 214, 215, 216, 217, 218, 219, 220, 221, 222, 223, 224, 225, 226, 229, 230, 231, 235, 239, 261, 270, 271, 274, 276, 280, 283, 284, 286, 287, 288, 290, 291, 292
Delving-intensity, 202, 203

Delving-Trio, 7, 98, 201, 202, 203, 204, 205, 206, 209, 211, 212, 213, 214, 215, 221, 222, 223, 225, 226, 229, 235, 239, 261, 270, 271, 276, 283, 287, 288, 290, 291
DE-Notify, 25, 27, 81, 90, 98, 101, 128, 129, 138, 212, 218, 221, 226, 261, 270, 274, 276, 277, 280, 287, 290
Devised-conditions, 226
devised-view, 294, 295, 296
Devise-Intensity, 203, 213
Devise-Mulling, 7, 98, 203, 204, 208, 211, 212, 218, 221, 223, 225, 226, 228, 229, 230, 231, 232, 235, 236, 237, 238, 239, 261, 271, 273, 276, 278, 280, 283, 284, 285, 286, 287, 288, 290, 291, 292, 293, 296
Distinct-Episodes, 103, 104, 107, 108, 112, 114, 117, 118, 119, 120, 121, 124, 125, 126, 127, 128, 139, 140, 144, 145, 154, 176, 213, 215, 216, 217, 218, 220, 221, 223, 224, 232, 240, 269, 270, 282, 291
DM-Alert, 138, 139, 140, 142, 149, 150
DM-Assembly, 221, 222, 223, 224, 226, 230, 231, 232, 233, 236, 238, 239
DM-Key-Group, 233
DO, 7, 26, 98, 132, 133, 259, 261, 274, 275, 276, 280, 286, 287, 289, 292, 306
DOing, 297
Down-link, 169, 183, 189, 230, 231, 232, 301, 302, 303, 304, 305
**Dreaming**, 121
Driver-sense, 187

# E

EA-Harmonics, 103, 104, 106, 107, 108, 109, 110, 111, 112, 113, 114, 115, 117, 118, 120, 121, 124, 125, 126, 127, 128, 135, 139, 140, 144, 145, 154, 159, 176, 216, 217, 220, 223, 224, 232, 268, 269, 281, 282, 291
Early-warning-system, 168
EC-Har, 182, 183, 190, 191, 192
E-Cluster, 151, 176, 179, 182, 183, 184, 186, 190, 191, 232, 237
EC-pool, 190
E-DHar, 206, 217, 220, 229, 230, 232
EDH-Pool, 230, 233
EF-Dat, 141, 158, 159, 164
E-Har, 144, 145, 146, 147, 148, 149, 150, 152, 154, 156, 158, 159, 162, 164, 168, 169, 170, 176, 177, 195, 196, 197, 198, 204, 205, 206, 207, 208, 209, 211, 212, 213, 214, 215, 217, 219, 220, 223, 229, 232, 235, 239, 273, 285
E-Har // EA, 220
EI-and-IE joins, 124
EI-Join, 103, 113, 139, 144
Elapsed-time, 239, 296
Elasticity, 60
Electromagnetic Spectrum, 41, 42, 151, 152
Elevated-intensity, 6
E-Link, 147, 148, 164
Emotional-driver, 187
EM-Work, 182, 183
Endocrine System, 9, 82, 96, 260, 273, 277, 285, 290, 292
Enhanced-Response, 286, 292, 293
E-Pend, 176, 182, 190, 192
EP-Link, 165
E-Puzzle, 141, 142, 143, 144, 146, 147, 149, 150, 151, 152, 153, 154, 156, 159, 160, 161, 164, 168, 170, 173, 175, 176, 177, 181, 206, 207, 208, 209, 211, 213, 238, 242, 247, 269, 282, 289
**E-Puzzle Formation**, 144
E-Puzzles, 147
Equivalency-Processor, 138, 140, 141, 142, 143, 149, 150, 152, 156, 175, 195, 210, 211
Escalation, 29, 92, 99, 108, 124, 129, 130, 178, 198, 201, 202, 203, 206, 207, 209, 212, 213, 214, 224, 260, 261, 264, 265, 266, 270, 271, 274, 276, 283, 284, 287, 289, 291
ES-Pool, 221, 233
Event-Cluster, 179, 181, 182, 235
Event-Condition, 133, 135, 139, 140, 141, 144, 145, 150, 151, 153, 154, 155, 164, 168, 178
Event-fusion, 166
Event-horizon, 5, 8, 15, 28, 29, 36, 39, 42, 44, 48, 50, 73, 117, 131, 132, 145, 295
event-intensity, 8, 9, 301
Event-streams, 202
Expansive-scope, 177
Expectation-yardstick, 226
Experience-archives, 225
Experience-Sense, 186, 187, 188, 189, 192, 221, 226, 227, 228, 229, 230, 231, 232, 292, 293, 294, 296, 297
Experiential-Accrual, 81, 98, 101, 103, 104, 106, 107, 111, 121, 124, 128, 261, 267, 276, 287
Experiential-expectation, 231
Extended-reach, 207
Extensive-Delving, 201, 203, 209, 218, 220, 235, 271, 283, 287, 290, 291
External-condition proactive management, 225

# F

Facet-element, 159
Facet-Resolution, 160
false-ality, 295
Familiarity-sense, 124
FD-Freq, 145, 146, 147, 148, 159, 160, 161, 162, 163, 168, 169, 170, 171, 173, 175, 176, 177, 196, 208, 222
feedback-loop, 15, 235, 260, 273, 284
FEP-Har, 163, 168, 169, 170, 173, 174, 177, 178, 183, 186, 188, 191
FEP-KID, 162, 168, 169, 170
FEP-Link, 169, 170, 173
FEP-Pend, 161, 162, 163, 168, 169, 170, 173
FEP-Processor, 168, 169, 170
FEP-Set, 168, 169, 170
F-Freq, 145, 146, 147, 148, 149, 154, 159, 160, 161, 164, 175, 176, 177, 196, 206, 207, 208, 209, 211, 213, 214, 217, 220, 222, 223, 229, 235, 271, 273, 283, 285
Field-of-Vision, 50
Fields-of-Vision, 49, 51
Fifth-Tier, 179
Figure-It-O, 131

Figure-It-Out, 7, 9, 25, 26, 27, 28, 29, 43, 47, 48, 62, 68, 73, 76, 77, 81, 82, 83, 84, 85, 86, 87, 88, 90, 91, 92, 97, 98, 99, 100, 102, 106, 107, 111, 113, 114, 115, 116, 117, 118, 119, 120, 121, 123, 124, 126, 127, 131, 133, 135, 138, 139, 140, 141, 142, 143, 149, 150, 152, 153, 154, 157, 163, 164, 166, 170, 172, 173, 174, 176, 177, 179, 181, 182, 187, 188, 189, 190, 192, 193, 194, 195, 198, 200, 210, 224, 225, 234, 235, 237, 238, 240, 242, 244, 250, 261, 265, 269, 270, 274, 276, 279, 280, 282, 287, 288, 289, 293, 294, 306
Figuring-It-Out, 14, 127, 199, 225
Filter-and-Slot, 9, 15, 35, 70, 90, 134, 138, 181, 187, 195, 199, 200, 208, 225, 227, 229, 234, 250, 257
Finding-the-Ways, 195
F-KID, 145, 146, 147
F-Link, 147, 149, 164
Flow-Integration, 244
Flow-Packet, 60, 61
Flow-Regulator, 34, 35, 36, 37, 38, 61
Fodder, 34, 38, 66, 110, 122, 128, 140, 142, 143, 159, 163, 168, 172, 177, 191, 194, 196, 200, 202, 207, 212, 214, 215, 217, 220, 223, 225, 226, 228, 230, 231, 232, 238, 242, 265, 271, 272, 273, 284, 285, 291
Force-of-Habit, 10, 19, 36, 83, 89, 122, 141, 189
Fourth-Tier, 179
F-Puzzle, 141, 142, 143, 144, 145, 146, 147, 148, 149, 154, 158, 159, 160, 161, 164, 168, 175, 176, 181, 186, 190, 195, 196, 197, 198, 203, 204, 208, 211, 213, 217, 220, 235, 238, 239, 273, 285
F-Puzzle Formation, 144
F-Puzzle Key-IDentifier, 146
F-Puzzles, 149
Frame-Assembly, 55, 60, 62
frame-band, 58, 59, 60
frame-rate, 58, 59
Frame-snippets, 133
Frames-per-second, 55, 57, 58, 59, 295
Frequency-match, 150, 176
Frequency-matching, 159, 209
Frequency-signature, 107, 149, 154

## G

Game-changer, 225
Go-To-Habit, 189, 190
Gradient-of-Acceptability, 152
Grid-Identifier, 245
Grid-resource, 245, 248, 250, 254

## H

Habitual-Actions, 13
Habitual-Reactive, 223
Hans Lippershey, 88
Hardened, 163, 179, 188, 189
Harmonic configuration, 251
Harmonically-blended, 230
Harmonic-archive, 167
Harmonic-drivers, 179
Harmonic-frequency, 167
Harmonic-signature, 107, 110, 112, 144
Harmonic-template, 230
Higher-level, 62, 69, 167
Hive-Configuration, 300
Hopper-resource, 56, 128, 156, 194, 203, 204, 265, 266
Hot, 7, 71, 93, 106, 107, 112, 139, 167, 170, 198, 266, 276, 280, 282, 286, 290, 292
Hot-Fat scenario, 93, 106
How-We-Cognitively-Work, 91, 96
**How-We-Work**, 3, 4, 5, 7, 8, 9, 4, 10, 151, 237, 297, 298, 300
**Hypnosis**, 121

## I

I.D.E.A.S., 226
IA bracket, 217, 220
IA-Facets, 103, 104, 106, 107, 108, 109, 112, 113, 114, 117, 118, 119, 120, 124, 125, 126, 127, 129, 139, 140, 144, 145, 154, 159, 160
IE-Join, 103, 113, 118, 125, 126, 139, 140, 144
impact-data, 8
**imperative-alert**, 17, 33, 35, 36, 37, 38, 61, 71, 265, 287, 288, 290
Implications Section, 93
impression-gradient, 268, 282
Inbound, 25, 48, 55, 63, 65, 66, 77, 136, 138, 142, 149, 190, 192, 194, 196, 244, 245, 305, 306
Inbound-buffer, 234
inbound-data, 29, 250
in-box, 26, 27, 35, 37, 38, 39, 56, 57, 60, 143, 271, 283
Inception-Filter, 9, 29, 33, 263
Inception-Filtering, 61
Information-Assembly, 81, 98, 101, 103, 104, 106, 107, 116, 117, 119, 120, 121, 124, 125, 126, 127, 128, 140, 215, 216, 217, 220, 223, 224, 232, 261, 269, 276, 282, 287, 291
Ingenuity, 14, 25, 82, 84, 85, 87, 88, 89, 90, 153, 154, 179, 218, 259
Ingenuity-Journey, 85
Initialization-Processor, 143, 144, 149, 157, 175, 204, 211
Initial-phase, 229
intensity, 5, 6, 7, 9, 10, 16, 17, 27, 29, 33, 35, 36, 37, 38, 51, 61, 62, 69, 70, 71, 72, 74, 76, 83, 91, 92, 94, 97, 98, 99, 100, 102, 108, 110, 111, 112, 113, 117, 120, 121, 123, 124, 128, 129, 132, 134, 140, 144, 150, 159, 160, 161, 163, 170, 172, 175, 176, 177, 178, 195, 196, 197, 198, 201, 202, 203, 204, 207, 209, 210, 212, 213, 214, 218, 219, 228, 229, 230, 231, 235, 238, 239, 240, 241, 254, 255, 256, 257, 258, 260, 261, 262, 263, 264, 265, 266, 267, 268, 269, 270, 271, 272, 273, 276, 277, 279, 280, 281, 282, 283, 284, 285, 287, 290, 291, 292, 294, 297, 301, 303, 304, 305
Intensity-Assessment, 6, 9
Intensity-Check, 35
Intensity-Grading, 76
intensity-melding, 290
Intensity-Ratio, 256
Intensity-Resolution, 265, 280, 287, 290
Internally-driven, 210, 225, 226, 235

**I**ntuition **D**rives **E**xperiences, **A**wareness and **S**entience, 226
Intuition-scenarios, 226
I-Pend, 143, 144
I-Ratio, 256, 257

# J

Join-resources, 102, 103, 113, 144

# K

Key-DHar, 206, 212, 230, 232
Key-GHar, 205, 206, 211, 229, 230, 233
Key-Group, 238
Key-identifier, 156, 159, 162, 174, 182, 195, 205, 208
Key-set, 206

# L

L.I.F.E$^2$., 297
landing-zones, 5, 45
Layer-Intelligence, 298, 299, 304, 305
Layer-Intelligence Theory, 298, 299
lesser-intensity, 37
LID-Links, 73, 74
LIM, 246, 247
Link-resource, 147, 154, 164, 165, 169, 173, 183, 225, 232, 252
Living-In-Full-Excitement-and-Experience, 297
Living-story, 226
Locus-Match, 71, 76
Locus-Matching, 55, 72, 76

# M

MACRO, 17, 36, 50, 51, 52, 59, 61, 72, 76, 99, 259, 263, 281, 290
Macro puzzles, 235
Macro-Bundles, 165
Macro-Sense, 167, 171, 172, 173, 174, 175, 177
**Major game-changer**, 197
Master-Frequency-Array, 151
**Match-Condition**, 149, 156
Matched-Base-Frequency, 16, 17
MB-Har, 172, 173, 174, 175, 176, 177, 178, 179, 182, 183, 186, 190
MB-Har // PG-Har, 173
M-Bundle, 168, 172, 173, 174, 175, 176, 178, 179, 181, 182, 190, 231
M-Bundles, 151, 163, 165, 168, 172, 176, 177, 182, 235
mechanisms, 6, 7, 9, 13, 19, 23, 28, 35, 36, 37, 38, 40, 43, 49, 56, 61, 62, 70, 82, 84, 89, 113, 116, 122, 124, 126, 133, 149, 164, 177, 179, 190, 195, 196, 199, 200, 202, 221, 224, 225, 235, 289, 293
M-Group, 168
ML-Har, 174, 175
M-Link, 151, 165, 173, 174, 175, 183
Module, 23, 26, 56, 63, 76, 77, 82, 83, 90, 91, 93, 99, 135, 305

**morphed-package**, 27
Mosaic-Grouping, 72
Motion-focus, 68
Movie-of-Your-Life, 7, 25, 26, 43, 57, 59, 94, 96, 98, 241, 260, 261, 262, 275, 276, 286, 287, 294, 295, 296, 297
MP-Link, 186
MP-Work, 182, 183
MR-Net, 258, 259
Mulling, 176, 177, 188, 190, 200, 210, 221, 222, 223, 224, 225, 232, 236, 238
Mulling-processors, 177
Multiple Fields-of-Vision, 34, 49
Multitudes-of-data-at-a-time, 213

# N

Neural real-estate, 36, 58, 61, 62, 83, 91, 163, 176, 179, 188, 237, 245, 251, 266, 289, 294, 297
Neural-Packages, 96, 260
neural-pathways, 14, 58
neural-resources, 13, 83, 122, 186, 237, 246, 267
neuron-array, 8
Neuron-receptor, 58
No-Match, 142, 143, 144, 149, 150, 159, 163, 175, 181, 198, 210
nominal, 6, 9, 46, 72, 94, 99, 123, 150, 201, 257
nominal-intensity, 9
Nominal-Response, 94, 96, 260
NORM, 7, 25, 27, 71, 76, 77, 92, 94, 95, 97, 98, 99, 262

# O

**Observability**, 42
Out-There, 7, 8, 13, 43, 59, 73, 223, 235, 273, 284, 289, 294, 296, 306
**Overt-Mode**, 222, 224, 225, 226, 229

# P

Package-set, 158
Parameter-Processor, 98, 99, 193, 194, 195, 196, 197, 198, 200, 201, 202, 203, 204, 208, 210, 212, 213, 214, 224, 234, 260, 261, 270, 271, 276, 280, 283, 284, 287, 291
Passion-Sense, 178
Passive-Mode, 224, 225
Passive-puzzle, 179
Pattern-Channel, 244, 250
Patterns-of-similarity, 167
**P-Bundle**, 163, 168, 169
P-Chan, 244, 250, 251, 252
PC-Har, 172
P-Cluster, 141, 142, 143, 149, 150, 158, 164, 168, 175, 176, 177, 178, 181, 182, 183, 186, 190, 192, 195, 196, 204, 206, 207, 209, 212, 214, 237, 239, 241
PE-Link, 184, 186
Persistence-capability, 237
PE-Work, 182, 183
PG-Dat, 186

PG-Har, 169, 170, 171, 172, 173, 174, 175, 177, 178, 183, 184, 186
P-Group, 151, 164, 168, 169, 172, 173, 174, 176, 178, 179, 181, 182, 190, 235
Phase puzzles, 235
Phase-Sense, 167, 169, 170, 173, 177
PL-Har, 169, 170, 173
P-Link, 169, 170, 173, 183
P-Links, 151, 165
PM-Link, 165, 173, 174
Polling-Phase, 158
Pooled-Assembly, 39, 55, 62, 70, 71, 72, 76, 94, 98, 99, 106, 107, 110, 112, 119, 125, 135, 140, 144, 145, 153, 154, 261, 262, 263, 265, 267, 268, 276, 277, 281
P-package, 194, 195, 196, 197, 198, 201, 202, 203, 204, 205, 206, 207, 208, 209, 212, 213, 214, 215, 218, 219, 222, 223, 225, 229, 234, 239, 270, 283, 291
P-Pend, 149, 192, 194, 195, 196, 200, 270
PRIORITY, 7, 25, 27, 71, 76, 261, 265, 274, 276, 277, 286, 287
Proactive-centric, 200
Proactive-methodology, 236
Problematic, 6, 9, 16, 17, 33, 38, 260, 294
PT-Assembly, 201, 202, 203, 204, 205, 206, 208, 209, 211, 212, 213, 214, 215, 217, 218, 219, 220, 221, 223, 224, 229, 231, 238
PT-Freq, 206, 207, 211, 212, 217, 220, 229, 232
PT-Group-Detail, 206, 208, 232
PT-Key-Group, 205, 206, 208, 214, 229
Puzzle-Package, 182
Puzzles, 7, 131, 141, 149, 161, 167, 170, 172, 173, 175, 177, 178, 179, 181, 182, 186, 206, 273, 280, 285, 288, 289, 294, 306
Puzzle-solving, 82, 141, 177, 297
Puzzle-status, 172

# Q

**Questioning**, 120
Q-value, 248, 249, 254, 256, 257

# R

Ranged-Delving, 201, 203, 207, 209, 212, 214, 218, 219, 225, 229, 239, 270, 276, 283, 284, 286, 291, 292
range-of-acceptance, 5, 6, 68
RD-IN, 209, 214, 222, 225, 229, 239, 285, 291
Reactive-cycle, 196
Really big deal, 194
recall, 8, 47, 72, 81, 82, 83, 91, 97, 113, 114, 115, 116, 117, 118, 120, 121, 124, 127, 128, 139, 141, 144, 180, 186, 187, 188, 189, 196, 215, 235, 237, 254, 269, 278, 282, 296, 305
Recall-Bundle, 223
**Recall-Cascading**, 124, 223, 269
Recall-Package, 188, 217, 220
receptor-neuron, 8, 279
recognition, 8, 13, 16, 17, 19, 33, 46, 49, 50, 51, 73, 74, 111, 112, 113, 116, 117, 118, 122, 124, 126, 129, 146, 166, 167, 168, 169, 186, 187, 205, 206, 207, 214, 239, 242, 251, 293

Recognition-Assessment, 6, 9, 17, 33, 263
Recognition-sense, 168
recognized, 6, 9, 10, 13, 16, 17, 29, 33, 35, 38, 47, 70, 75, 95, 99, 112, 118, 122, 123, 132, 150, 170, 208
Reference-Complex, 176, 179, 187, 188, 192, 289
Reference-Resources, 181
Refresh-rates, 42
refresh-state, 8
Related-sequential-conditions, 266, 279
Remarkable-feature, 67, 73, 96, 150, 157, 260, 262, 277, 294
Replicate, 35, 128, 129, 138, 139, 140, 145, 159, 170, 176, 196, 197, 202, 206, 209, 213, 218, 221, 230, 257, 270, 271, 283
request-alert, 17, 33, 34, 35, 36, 37, 38, 61, 99, 260, 262, 263, 265, 274, 277, 279, 290
Resolution, 38, 69, 71, 129, 135, 141, 144, 154, 158, 160, 171, 175, 176, 177, 190, 195, 196, 198, 203, 207, 209, 210, 222, 224, 231, 233, 236, 239, 266, 289, 291, 294
Resolution-Phase, 159
Resolution-Processor, 156, 158, 159, 161, 175, 176, 192
Response-Component, 82, 217, 240, 241, 242, 258, 259, 272, 273, 285, 291
Response-directives, 260
**Retinal Ganglion**, 46
Retrieval-Bundle, 126, 127, 269
Revelation, 87, 154, 239, 241
**Rods**, 45
R-package, 156
R-Pend, 156, 158, 159
RP-package, 158

# S

S-Cat, 244, 245, 250, 254, 256, 258
Selective-Harvesting, 66
Self-Duo, 17, 19, 23, 272, 289
sense-of-condition-change, 296
sensory-acceptance, 9, 17, 29, 39, 272, 291, 292, 295, 297
sensory-data, 9, 13, 16, 17, 19, 26, 33, 56, 90, 133, 235, 242, 273, 285, 297
Sensory-event, 106, 107, 112, 135
Sensory-Location-ID, 198
sensory-receptor, 8, 305
sensory-type, 8
SG-ID, 245, 248, 254
SG-Prime-ID, 248, 254, 255, 256
SG-Secon-ID, 248, 254, 255, 256, 257
Shape-Complex, 258
S-Harm, 252, 254, 258
Significantly-similar, 108, 111, 112, 117, 124, 126, 128, 159, 160, 161, 166, 167, 170, 172, 174, 175, 178, 181, 188, 189, 191, 196, 206, 207, 208, 209, 210, 213, 214, 219, 220, 223, 228, 229, 230, 231, 238, 239, 240, 265, 268, 269, 279, 280, 282, 290, 304
Significant-similarity, 111, 159, 190
Similarity-compounding, 207
Similarity-matching, 151
SLID, 5, 6, 8, 9, 35, 36, 38, 50, 58, 60, 74, 75, 99, 110, 111, 112, 117, 129, 132, 134, 145, 146, 147, 150, 153, 196, 208, 213,

214, 217, 228, 234, 240, 245, 246, 247, 248, 249, 251, 254, 257, 263, 273, 279, 280, 285, 289, 291, 295
SLID-Cref, 245, 248, 249, 254, 256
SLID-Grid, 245, 246, 254, 257, 258
SLIDs, 8, 35, 36, 61, 62, 72, 73, 107, 125, 129, 134, 145, 146, 147, 154, 196, 198, 208, 216, 228, 234, 240, 245, 246, 248, 249, 250, 254, 255, 268, 272, 281
S-Link, 252
Solution, 135, 167, 168, 170, 172, 173, 186, 225, 231, 288
**Solutioning**, 19, 25, 82, 127, 131, 135, 136, 138, 139, 140, 141, 142, 145, 164, 168, 172, 179, 181, 190, 193, 200, 201, 204, 207, 215, 218, 220, 229, 237, 238, 294, 306
Solutioning-Proactive, 223
Solutioning-scenarios, 179
Soma-Action, 9, 16, 95, 273, 286, 292
Soma-Catalogue, 244
Soma-Habitual, 10
Soma-Location-ID, 8, 36, 58, 59, 61, 62, 72
Soma-Response, 16, 38, 110, 187, 242, 280, 290
Soma-Self, 4, 5, 7, 8, 9, 10, 13, 14, 15, 16, 17, 19, 23, 28, 29, 33, 34, 36, 38, 39, 40, 41, 46, 49, 50, 51, 56, 57, 58, 59, 60, 61, 62, 65, 68, 69, 70, 71, 72, 73, 74, 75, 76, 94, 95, 99, 110, 111, 116, 117, 118, 119, 123, 124, 126, 129, 132, 134, 149, 150, 151, 157, 221, 241, 242, 245, 246, 254, 256, 260, 263, 272, 273, 274, 275, 277, 280, 284, 286, 288, 290, 292, 293, 294, 305, 306
Soma-Sense, 40
Soma-Sensor, 7, 8, 17, 19, 29, 39, 41, 70, 132, 133, 245, 272
Soma-Slotting, 7, 9, 16, 33, 35, 61
S-Pac, 251, 252, 254, 255, 256
Speed-of-Light, 41
SP-Harm, 257
sphere-of-influence, 70
SP-TC, 254, 255, 257
SP-Temp, 254, 255, 257
Standard-Response, 262
State-of-Affairs, 93, 94, 99, 100, 263, 278
Storage-centric, 200
Stream-Harmonic, 252
Stream-Package, 251
stronger-joins, 269, 282
Substantially-similar, 150, 152, 153, 156, 237
Substantial-similarity, 150
Sufficient-intensity, 195, 197, 201
Sufficiently-intense, 198, 200, 201, 202, 214, 270, 271, 283, 294
survival-critical, 6, 35, 61, 62, 265, 266, 288
Survival-Pattern, 35
Survival-Threat, 33, 35, 61, 263, 281

# T

Tag, 5, 6, 9, 33, 35, 36, 38, 57, 59, 60, 61, 62, 72, 91, 92, 94, 106, 107, 110, 116, 117, 118, 119, 120, 123, 125, 128, 129, 134, 135, 138, 140, 145, 150, 153, 154, 198, 211, 234, 247, 258, 263, 268, 281, 294, 301
Tag-Cluster, 60, 110, 118, 119, 120, 129, 134, 144, 248, 251, 255, 256, 257, 266, 268, 269, 279, 281, 282
Tag-Clusters, 5, 35, 38, 60, 62, 106, 107, 119, 128, 134, 145, 248, 250, 251, 254, 255, 257, 263, 265, 266, 271, 281, 283
Tags, 59, 60, 61, 92, 106, 108, 110, 134, 145, 178, 198, 211, 240, 263, 272, 279, 294
Targeted-Delving, 201, 202, 209, 213, 214, 215, 224, 261, 270, 276, 283, 291
TC-Stream, 245, 251
TEA-Dat, 111, 112, 139, 140, 142, 143, 144, 145, 149, 150, 152, 153, 156, 159, 160, 163, 167, 172, 175, 176, 178, 190, 195, 196, 197, 198, 204, 207, 208, 211, 212, 213, 215, 223, 225, 228, 235, 270, 273, 285
TEA-Dat // E-Har, 149
TEA-Dat // E-Hars, 207
Template, 7, 25, 26, 82, 94, 96, 98, 129, 138, 217, 234, 235, 240, 241, 242, 244, 250, 254, 260, 261, 272, 274, 280, 284, 290, 291
Template-Component, 138, 234, 242, 244, 246, 247, 258
Temporal-Clustering, 118, 119, 120
Temporal-juxtaposition, 179
Tepid, 7, 71, 97, 98, 100, 102, 124, 198, 224, 259, 262, 264, 268, 274, 280
Test-it, 82, 90, 98, 103, 124, 131, 142, 145, 160, 194, 195, 196, 197, 198, 200, 202, 204, 206, 207, 208, 209, 214, 234, 235, 244, 261, 265, 270, 271, 273, 274, 276, 280, 283, 284, 287, 291
Test-It, 7, 27, 28, 138, 181, 200, 201, 202, 203, 209, 210, 211, 212, 214, 215, 217, 223, 234, 236, 238, 242, 250, 254, 271, 272, 283, 284, 286, 289, 291, 292, 294, 305
**Test-IT**, 203, 210, 221, 222, 223, 224, 225, 226, 230, 231, 232, 273, 284, 285, 291
**TEST**-it, 203, 217, 218, 284, 291
**TEST-IT**, 219, 220, 221, 234
**Test-Its**, 19, 25, 28, 29, 135, 138, 199, 200, 210, 212, 213, 215, 223, 226, 234, 236, 239, 240, 242, 271, 272, 280, 284, 286, 289, 290, 291, 292
The Hot-Fat Scenario, 139
The-DO, 297
The-Flows, 240, 241, 244, 250, 252, 254, 256, 258, 272, 284
The-Ways, 7, 131, 135, 136, 138, 140, 141, 142, 163, 164, 177, 179, 181, 190, 193, 199, 200, 218, 220, 224, 271, 283, 284, 289, 291
The-Way-We-Cognitively-Work, 24
The-Way-We-Hide, 190
The-Way-We-Speak, 190
The-Way-We-Think, 190
The-Way-We-Work, 131
Threat-Check, 6, 9, 10, 17, 33, 34, 35, 38, 61, 99, 123, 263, 265, 279, 289, 290
Threshold-range, 129
Tier-Five, 191, 228
Tier-Four, 191
Tier-Three, 172
TI-Flow, 234, 240, 241, 242, 244, 245, 250, 251, 258, 272, 273, 284
TI-Flows, 272
TI-IN, 25, 81, 98, 129, 136, 138, 139, 212, 261, 270, 271, 276, 283, 287, 291
time-snippet, 5, 9

Time-Stamp, 108, 119, 146
TI-Notify, 212
TI-OUT, 25, 27, 98, 136, 138, 212, 261, 271, 272, 276, 283, 287
**TI-Outbound**, 136, 138, 142, 194, 197
TI-Package, 271, 283
TI-Parameter, 138, 197, 204, 234, 271
T-Patt, 96, 241, 242, 244, 245, 247, 250, 251, 252, 253, 254, 256, 257, 258, 259, 272, 273, 274, 284, 285, 286, 291, 292, 293
Transitional-Mode, 224, 225
Transitional-resource, 159, 161, 162
Transition-resource, 138
Trend-Analysis, 6, 35, 51, 69, 207, 214, 221, 265
Trigger-event, 149
Trio-member, 201, 202, 203
TS-Harm, 252
TS-Link, 252, 254, 258
TS-Pac, 251, 252
TS-Patt, 252, 258

## U

Universe-H, 151
UN-recognized, 9, 16, 38, 70
Up-link, 169, 173, 174, 177, 191, 301, 302, 303, 305

## V

Value-Senses, 180
V-FEP-Har, 170
Virtual-resource, 228, 230, 251
VisGridID, 50
Visual Currency, 34
Visual Works, 39
Visual-background, 262
**Visual-Currency**, 41
Visual-data, 39, 40
Visual-Location-ID, 72
visual-receptor, 19, 44
Visual-Scape, 81, 106, 114, 127, 128, 139, 216, 217, 220, 224, 267
Visual-Sensors, 39, 41, 42, 48, 66, 67, 70, 72, 73, 75, 122, 133, 260, 262, 265
Visual-System, 34, 40, 41, 46, 47, 48, 49, 63
**Visual-System Pillars**, 40
Visual-Works, 25, 26, 27, 39, 43, 48, 49, 55, 62, 63, 65, 66, 69, 70, 71, 72, 94, 98, 261, 262, 274, 276, 277, 286, 287
VLID, 50, 51, 52, 55, 65, 66, 69, 70, 71, 72, 73, 74, 75, 76, 94, 98, 135, 261
VLID-Traveler, 69, 262, 265, 267, 276, 281, 287, 288, 290, 291
VS, 267
VS-Facets, 106

## W

Warm, 7, 71, 198, 261, 262, 263, 264, 267, 268, 274, 277, 280, 281, 286, 290, 292
Waveform-Overlap, 152, 153

What is Cross-Sensory-Bundling, 55

## Y

Your Habits are Creating You, 189

## Z

Zeitgebers, 119

**Notes:**

**Notes:**

www.ingramcontent.com/pod-product-compliance
Lightning Source LLC
Chambersburg PA
CBHW080454110426
42742CB00017B/2889